'Tween Snow a

A Tale of the Last K

Bertram Mitford

Alpha Editions

This edition published in 2024

ISBN : 9789362516886

Design and Setting By
Alpha Editions
www.alphaedis.com
Email - info@alphaedis.com

As per information held with us this book is in Public Domain.
This book is a reproduction of an important historical work. Alpha Editions uses the best technology to reproduce historical work in the same manner it was first published to preserve its original nature. Any marks or number seen are left intentionally to preserve its true form.

Contents

Chapter One. .... - 1 -
Chapter Two. .... - 7 -
Chapter Three. .... - 11 -
Chapter Four. .... - 15 -
Chapter Five. .... - 21 -
Chapter Six. .... - 25 -
Chapter Seven. .... - 29 -
Chapter Eight. .... - 32 -
Chapter Nine. .... - 37 -
Chapter Ten. .... - 42 -
Chapter Eleven. .... - 47 -
Chapter Twelve. .... - 53 -
Chapter Thirteen. .... - 60 -
Chapter Fourteen. .... - 68 -
Chapter Fifteen. .... - 74 -
Chapter Sixteen. .... - 80 -
Chapter Seventeen. .... - 87 -
Chapter Eighteen. .... - 93 -
Chapter Nineteen. .... - 98 -
Chapter Twenty. .... - 104 -
Chapter Twenty One. .... - 108 -
Chapter Twenty Two. .... - 112 -
Chapter Twenty Three. .... - 117 -
Chapter Twenty Four. .... - 122 -
Chapter Twenty Five. .... - 128 -
Chapter Twenty Six. .... - 134 -

Chapter Twenty Seven. - 137 -
Chapter Twenty Eight. - 143 -
Chapter Twenty Nine. - 148 -
Chapter Thirty. - 154 -
Chapter Thirty One. - 160 -
Chapter Thirty Two. - 167 -
Chapter Thirty Three. - 177 -
Chapter Thirty Four. - 183 -
Chapter Thirty Five. - 192 -
Chapter Thirty Six. - 196 -
Chapter Thirty Seven. - 203 -
Chapter Thirty Eight. - 207 -
Chapter Thirty Nine. - 212 -
Chapter Forty. - 217 -
Chapter Forty One. - 220 -
Chapter Forty Two. - 226 -
Chapter Forty Three. - 229 -
Chapter Forty Four. - 234 -
Chapter Forty Five. - 240 -
Chapter Forty Six. - 247 -
Chapter Forty Seven. - 256 -
Chapter Forty Eight. - 262 -

Chapter One.

The Episode of the White Dog.

The buck is running for dear life.

The dog is some fifty yards behind the buck. The Kafir is about the same distance behind the dog, which distance he is striving right manfully to maintain; not so unsuccessfully, either, considering that he is pitting the speed of two legs against that of eight.

Down the long grass slope they course—buck, dog, and savage. The former, a game little antelope of the steinbok species, takes the ground in a series of long, flying leaps, his white tail whisking like a flag of defiance. The second, a tawny, black-muzzled grey-hound, stretching his snaky length in the wake of his quarry, utters no sound, as with arrow-like velocity he holds on his course, his cruel eyes gleaming, his jaws dripping saliva in pleasurable anticipation of the coming feast. The third, a fine, well-knit young Kafir, his naked body glistening from head to foot with red ochre, urges on his hound with an occasional shrill whoop of encouragement, as he covers the ground at a surprising pace in his free, bounding stride. He holds a knob-kerrie in his hand, ready for use as soon as the quarry shall be within hurling distance.

But of this there seems small chance at present. It takes a good dog indeed to run down an unwounded buck with the open *veldt* before him, and good as this one is, it seems probable that he will get left. Down the long grass slope they course, but the opposite acclivity is the quarry's opportunity. The pointed hoofs seem hardly to touch ground in the arrowy flight of their owner. The distance between the latter and the pursuing hound increases.

Along a high ridge overlooking this primitive chase grow, at regular intervals, several circular clumps of bush. One of these conceals a spectator. The latter is seated on horseback in the very midst of the scrub, his feet dangling loosely in the stirrups, his hand closed tightly and rather suggestively round the breech of a double gun—rifle and smooth bore—which rests across the pommel of his saddle. There is a frown upon his face, as, himself completely hidden, he watches intently the progress of the sport. It is evident that he is more interested than pleased.

For Tom Carhayes is the owner of this Kaffrarian stock run. In that part of Kaffraria, game is exceedingly scarce, owing to the presence of a redundant native population. Tom Carhayes is an ardent sportsman and spares no effort to protect and restore the game upon his farm. Yet here is a Kafir running down a buck under his very nose. Small wonder that he feels furious.

"That scoundrel Goníwe!" he mutters between his set teeth. "I'll put a bullet through his cur, and lick the nigger himself within an inch of his life!"

The offence is an aggravated one. Not only is the act of poaching a very capital crime in his eyes, but the perpetrator ought to be at that moment at least three miles away, herding about eleven hundred of his master's sheep. These he has left to take care of themselves while he indulges in an illicit buck-hunt. Small wonder indeed that his said master, at no time a good-tempered man, vows to make a condign example of him.

The buck has nearly gained the crest of the ridge. Once over it his chances are good. The pursuing hound, running more by sight than by scent, may easily be foiled, by a sudden turn to right or left, and a double or two. The dog is a long way behind now, and the spectator has to rise in his stirrups to command a view of the situation. Fifty yards more and the quarry will be over the ridge and in comparative safety.

But from just that distance above there suddenly darts forth another dog—a white one. It has sprung from a patch of bush similar to that which conceals the spectator. The buck, thoroughly demoralised by the advent of this new enemy, executes a rapid double, and thus pressed back into the very jaws of its first pursuer has no alternative but to head up the valley as fast as its legs can carry it.

But the new hound is fresh, and in fact a better dog than the first one. He presses the quarry very close and needs not the encouraging shouts of his master, who has leaped forth from his concealment immediately upon unleashing him. For a few moments the pace is even, *then it decreases.* The buck seemed doomed.

And, indeed, such is the case anyhow. For, held in waiting at a given point, ready to be let slip if necessary, is a third dog. Such is the Kafir method of hunting. The best dog ever whelped is not quite equal, either in speed or staying power, to running down a full-grown buck in the open *veldt*, but by adopting the above means of hunting in relays, the chance are equalised. To be more accurate, the quarry has no chance at all.

On speeds the chase; the new dog, a tall white grey-hound of surprising endurance and speed, gaining rapidly; the other, lashed into a final spurt by the spirit of emulation, not far behind. The two Kafirs, stimulating their hounds with yells of encouragement, are straining every nerve to be in at the death.

The buck—terror and demoralisation in its soft, lustrous eyes—is heading straight for the spectator's hiding place. The latter raises his piece, with the intention of sending a bullet through the first dog as soon as it shall come abreast of his position; the shot barrel will finish off the other.

But he does not fire. The fact is, the man is simply shaking with rage. Grinding his teeth, he recognises his utter inability to hit a haystack at that moment, let alone a swiftly coursing grey-hound.

The chase sweeps by within seventy yards of his position—buck, dog, and Kafirs. Then another diversion occurs.

Two more natives rise, apparently out of the ground itself. One of these, poising himself erect with a peculiar springy, quivering motion, holds his kerrie ready to hurl. The buck is barely thirty yards distant, and going like the wind.

"Whigge—woof!" The hard stick hurls through the air—aimed nearly as far ahead of the quarry as the latter is distant from the marksman. There is a splintering crash, and a shrill, horrid scream—then a reddish brown shape, writhing and rolling in agony upon the ground. The aim of the savage has been true. All four of the buck's legs are snapped and shattered like pipe-stems.

The two hounds hurl themselves upon the struggling carcase, their savage snarls mingling with the sickening, half-human yell emitted by the terrified and tortured steinbok. The four Kafirs gather round their prey.

"*Suka inja!*" ("Get out, dog!") cries one of them brutally, giving the white dog a dig in the ribs with the butt-end of his kerrie, and putting the wretched buck out of its agony by a blow on the head with the same. The hound, with a snarling yelp, springs away from the carcase, and lies down beside his fellow. Their flanks are heaving and panting after the run, and their lolling tongues and glaring eyes turn hungrily toward the expected prey. Their savage masters, squatted around, are resting after their exertions, chatting in a deep bass hum. To the concealed spectator the sight is simply maddening. He judges the time for swooping down upon the delinquents has arrived.

Were he wise he would elect to leave them alone entirely, and would withdraw quietly without betraying his presence. He might indeed derive some modicum of satisfaction by subsequently sjambokking the defaulting Goníwe for deserting his post, though the wisdom of that act of consolation may be doubted. But a thoroughly angry man is seldom wise, and Tom Carhayes forms no exception to the general rule. With a savage curse he breaks from his cover and rides furiously down upon the offending group.

But if he imagines his unlooked for arrival is going to strike terror to the hearts of those daring and impudent poachers, he soon becomes alive to his mistake. Two of them, including his own herd, are already standing. The others make no attempt to rise from their careless and squatting posture. All contemplate him with absolute unconcern, and the half-concealed and contemptuous grin spread across the broad countenance of his retainer in no wise tends to allay his fury.

"What the devil are you doing here, Goníwe?" he cries. "Get away back to your flock at once, or I'll tan your hide to ribbons. Here. Get out of the light you two—I'm going to shoot that dog—unless you want the charge through yourselves instead."

This speech, delivered half in Boer Dutch, half in the Xosa language, has a startling effect. The other two Kafirs spring suddenly to their feet, and all four close up in a line in front of the speaker, so as to stand between him and their dogs. Their demeanour is insolent and threatening to the last degree.

"*Whau 'mlúngu!*" ("Ho! white man!") cries the man whose successful throw has brought down the quarry—a barbarian of herculean stature and with an evil, sinister cast of countenance. "Shoot away, *'mlúngu!* But it will not be only a dog that will die."

The purport of this menace is unmistakable. The speaker even advances a step, shifting, as he does so, his assegais from his right hand to his left— leaving the former free to wield an ugly looking kerrie. His fellow-countrymen seem equally ready for action.

Carhayes is beside himself with fury. To be defied and bearded like this on his own land, and by four black scoundrels whom he has caught red-handed in the act of killing his own game! The position is intolerable. But through his well-nigh uncontrollable wrath there runs a vein of caution.

Were he to act upon his first impulse and shoot the offending hound, he would have but one charge left. The Kafirs would be upon him before he could draw trigger. They evidently mean mischief, and they are four to one. Two of them are armed with assegais and all four carry—in their hands the scarcely less formidable weapon—the ordinary hard-wood kerrie. Moreover, were he to come off victorious at the price of shooting one of them dead, the act would entail very ugly consequences, for although the frontier was practically in little short of a state of war, it was not actually so, which meant that the civil law still held sway and would certainly claim its vindication to the full.

For a moment or two the opposing parties stand confronting each other. The white man, seated on his horse, grips the breech of his gun convulsively, and the veins stand out in cords upon his flushed face as he realises his utter powerlessness. The Kafirs, their naked, muscular frames repulsive with red ochre, stand motionless, their savage countenances wreathed in a sneer of hate and defiance. There are scarcely ten yards between them.

The train is laid. It only needs the application of a spark to cause a magnificent flare-up. That spark is applied by the tall barbarian who has first spoken.

"*Au umlúngu!*" he cries in his great, sneering tones. "Go away. We have talked enough with you. Am I not Hlangani, a man of the House of Sarili, the Great Chief, and is not the white dog mine? Go away. *Suka!*" ("Get out." Usually only employed toward a dog.)

Now whether through pure accident—in other words, the "sheer cussedness" of Fate—or whether it imagines that its master's last word was a command to itself, the white dog at this juncture gets up, and leaving the protecting shadow of its master begins to slink away over the *veldt*. This and the swaggering insolence of the Kafir is too much for Carhayes. Up goes his piece: there is a flash and a report. The wretched hound sinks in his tracks without even a yelp, and lies feebly kicking his life away, with the blood welling from a great circular wound behind the shoulder. The poor beast has run down his last buck.

(Commonly known as Kreli—the paramount chief of all the Xosa tribes.)

The train is fired. Like the crouching leopard crawling nearer for a surer spring the great Kafir, with a sudden glide, advances to the horse's head, and makes a quick clutch at the bridle. Had he succeeded in seizing it, a rapidly followed up blow from the deadly kerrie would have stretched the rider senseless, if not dead, upon the *veldt*. But the latter is too quick for him. Jerking back his horse's head and driving in both spurs, he causes the animal to rear and plunge, thus defeating any attempt on the part of his enemies to drag him from the saddle, as well as widening the distance between himself and them.

"Stand back, you curs!" he roars, dropping his piece to a level with the chest of the foremost. "The first who moves another step shall be served the same as that brute of a dog!"

But the Kafirs only laugh derisively. They are shrewd enough to know that the civil law is still paramount, and imagine he dare not fire on them. A kerrie hurtles through the air with an ugly "whigge." Blind with fury, Carhayes discharges his remaining barrel full at the tall savage, who is still advancing towards him, and whose threatening demeanour and formidable aspect seems to warrant even that extreme step in self-defence. The Kafir falls.

Surprised, half cowed by this unlooked for contingency, the others pause irresolute. Before they can recover themselves a warning shout, close at hand, creates a diversion which seems likely to throw a new light on the face of affairs.

Chapter Two.

"You have Struck a Chief."

"*Baléka* (Run), you dogs!" cried Carhayes, who had taken the opportunity of slipping a couple of fresh cartridges into his gun. "*Baléka*, or I'll shoot the lot of you."

He looked as if he meant it, too. The Kafirs, deeming discretion the better part of valour, judged it expedient to temporise.

"Don't shoot again, *Baas*! (Master.) You have already killed one man!" they said significantly.

"And I'll kill four!" was the infuriated reply. "*Baléka*, do you hear—quick—sharp—at once, or you're dead men!"

"Don't do anything so foolish, Tom," said a voice at his side, and a hand was stretched out as though to arrest the aim of the threatening piece. "For God's sake, remember. We are not at war—yet."

"That be hanged!" came the rough rejoinder. "Anyway, we'll give these fellows a royal thrashing. We are two to three—that's good enough odds. Come along, Eustace, and we'll lick them within an inch of their lives."

"We'll do nothing of the sort," replied the other quietly and firmly. Then, with an anxiety in his face which he could not altogether conceal, he walked his horse over to the prostrate Kafir. But the latter suddenly staggered to his feet. His left shoulder was streaming with blood, and the concussion of the close discharge had stunned him. Even his would-be slayer looked somewhat relieved over this turn which affairs had taken, and for this he had to thank the plunging of his horse, for it is difficult to shoot straight, even point blank, with a restive steed beneath one, let alone the additional handicap of being in a white rage at the time.

Of his wound the Kafir took not the smallest notice. He stood contemplating the two white men with a scowl of bitter hatred deepening upon his ochre-besmeared visage. His three countrymen halted irresolute a little distance—a respectful distance, thought Carhayes with a sneer—in the background, as though waiting to see if their assistance should be required. Then he spoke:

"Now hear my words, you whom the people call Umlilwane. I know you, even though you do not know me—better for you if you did, for then you would not have wounded the sleeping lion, nor have aroused the anger of the hooded snake, who is swift to strike. Ha! I am Hlangani," he continued, raising his voice to a perfect roar of menace, and his eyes blazed like live coals as he pointed to the shot wounds in his shoulder, now black and hideous with clotted blood. "I am Hlangani, the son of Ngcesiba, a man of the House of Gcaléka. What man living am I afraid of? Behold me here as I stand. Shoot again, Umlilwane—shoot again, if you dare. *Hau*! Hear my 'word.' You have slain my dog—my white hunting dog, the last of his breed—who can outrun every other hunting dog in the land, even as the wind outstrippeth the crawling ox-wagon, and you have shed my blood, the blood of a chief. You had better first have cut off your right hand, *for it is better to lose a hand than one's mind*. This is my 'word,' Umlilwane—bear it in memory, *for you have struck a chief*—a man of the House of Gcaléka."

(Umlilwane: "Little Fire"—Kafirs are fond of bestowing nicknames. This one referred to its bearer's habitually short temper.)

"Damn the House of Gcaléka, anyway," said Carhayes, with a sneer as the savage, having vented his denunciation, stalked scowlingly away with his compatriots. "Look here, *isidenge*," (fool), he continued. "This is my word. Keep clear of me, for the next time you fall foul of me I'll shoot you dead. And now, Eustace," turning to his companion, "we had better load up this buck-meat and carry it home. What on earth is the good of my trying to preserve the game, with a whole location of these black scum not ten miles from my door?" he went on, as he placed the carcase of the unfortunate steinbok on the crupper of his horse.

"No good. No good, whatever, as I am always telling you," rejoined the other decisively, "Kafir locations and game can't exist side by side. Doesn't it ever strike you, Tom, that this game-preserving mania is costing you—costing us, excessively dear."

"Hang it. I suppose it is," growled Carhayes. "I'll clear out, *trek* to some other part of the country where a fellow isn't overrun by a lot of worthless, lazy, red Kafirs. I wish to Heaven they'd only start this precious war. I'd take it out of some of their hides. Have some better sport than buck-hunting then, eh?"

"Perhaps. But there may be no war after all. Meanwhile you have won the enmity of every Kafir in Nteya's and Ncanduku's locations. I wouldn't give ten pounds for our two hundred pound pair of breeding ostriches, if it meant leaving them here three days from now, that's all."

"Oh, shut up croaking, Eustace," snarled Carhayes, "And by the way, who the deuce is this sweep Hlangani, and what is he doing on this side of the river anyway?"

"He's a Gcaléka, as he said, and a petty chief under Kreli; and the Gaikas on this side are sure to take up his quarrel. I know them."

"H'm. It strikes me you know these black scoundrels rather well, Eustace. What a queer chap you are. Now, I wonder what on earth has made you take such an interest in them of late."

"So do I. I suppose, though, I find them interesting, especially since I have learned to talk with them pretty easily. And they are interesting. On the whole, I like them."

Carhayes made no reply, unless an inarticulate growl could be construed as such, and the two men rode on in silence. They were distant cousins, these two, and as regarded their farming operations, partners. Yet never were two men more utterly dissimilar. Carhayes, the older by a matter of ten years, was just on the wrong side of forty—but his powerfully built frame was as tough and vigorous as in the most energetic days of his youth. He was rather a good looking man, but the firm set of his lips beneath the thick, fair beard, and a certain shortness of the neck, set forth his choleric disposition at first glance. The other was slightly the taller of the two, and while lacking the broad, massive proportions of his cousin, was straight, and well set up. But Eustace Milne's face would have puzzled the keenest character reader. It was a blank. Not that there was aught of stupidity or woodenness stamped thereon. On the contrary, there were moments when it would light up with a rare attractiveness, but its normal expression was of that impassibility which you may see upon the countenance of a priest or a lawyer of intellect and wide experience, whose vocation involves an intimate and profoundly varied acquaintance with human nature in all its chequered lights and shades; rarely, however, upon that of one so young.

From the high ridge on which the two men were riding, the eye could wander at will over the rolling, grassy plains and mimosa-dotted dales of Kaffraria. The pure azure of the heavens was unflecked by a single cloud. The light, balmy air of this early spring day was as invigorating as wine. Far away to the southeast the sweep of undulating grass land melted into an indistinct blue haze—the Indian Ocean—while in the opposite direction the panorama was barred by the hump-like Kabousie Heights, their green slopes alternating with lines of dark forest in a straggling labyrinth of intersecting kloofs. Far away over the golden, sunlit plains, the white walls of a farmhouse or two were discernible, and here and there, rising in a line upon the still atmosphere, a column of grey smoke marked the locality of many a distant kraal lying along the spurs of the hills. So still, so transparent, indeed, was the air that even the voices of their savage inhabitants and the low of cattle floated faintly across the wide and intervening space. Beneath—against the opposite ridge, about half a mile distant, the red ochre on their clothing and persons showing in vivid and pleasing contrast against the green of the hillside, moved ten or a dozen Kafirs—men, women, and children. They stepped out in line at a brisk, elastic pace, and the lazy hum of their conversation drifted to the ears of the two white men so plainly that they could almost catch its burden.

To the younger of these two men the splendid vastness of this magnificent panorama, framing the picturesque figures of its barbarous inhabitants, made up a scene of which he never wearied, for though at present a Kaffrarian stock farmer, he had the mind of a thinker, a philosopher, and a poet. To the elder, however, there was nothing noteworthy or attractive about it. We fear he regarded the beautiful rolling plains as so much better or worse *veldt* for purposes of stock-feeding, and was apt to resent the continued and unbroken blue of the glorious vault above as likely to lead to an inconvenient scarcity of rain, if not to a positive drought. As for the dozen Kafirs in the foreground, so far from discerning anything poetical or picturesque about them, he looked upon them as just that number of black scoundrels making their way to the nearest canteen to get drunk on the proceeds of the barter of skins flayed from stolen sheep—his own sheep among those of others.

As if to emphasise this last idea, cresting the ridge at that moment, they came in sight of a large, straggling flock. Straggling indeed! In twos and threes, in clumps of a dozen, and in clumps of fifty, the animals, though numbering but eleven hundred, were spread over nearly two miles of *veldt*. It was the flock in charge of the defaulting and contumacious Goníwe, who, however, having caught a glimpse of the approach of his two masters, might be descried hurriedly collecting his scattered charges. Carhayes ground his teeth.

"I'll rip his black hide off him. I'll teach him to let the sheep go to the devil while he hunts our bucks." And gripping his reins he drove his spurs into his horse's flanks, with fell intent toward the offending Kafir.

"Wait—wait!" urged the more prudent Eustace. "For Heaven's sake, don't give yourself away again. If you must lick the boy, wait until you get him—and the sheep—safe home this evening. If you give him beans now, its more than likely he'll leave the whole flock in the *veldt* and won't come back at all—not forgetting, of course, to drive off a dozen or two to Nteya's location."

There was reason in this, and Carhayes acquiesced with a snarl. To collect the scattered sheep was to the two mounted men a labour of no great difficulty or time, and with a stern injunction to Goníwe not to be found playing the fool a second time, the pair turned their horses' heads and rode homeward.

Chapter Three.

Eanswyth.

Anta's Kloof—such was the name of Tom Carhayes' farm—was situated on the very edge of the Gaika location. This was unfortunate, because its owner got on but poorly with his barbarous neighbours. They, for their part, bore him no good will either.

The homestead comprised a comfortable stone dwelling in one story. A high *stoep* and veranda ran round three sides of it, commanding a wide and lovely view of rolling plains and mimosa sprinkled kloofs, for the house was built on rising ground. Behind, as a background, a few miles distant, rose the green spurs of the Kabousie Heights. A gradual ascent of a few hundred feet above the house afforded a splendid view of the rugged and table-topped Kei Hills. And beyond these, on the right, the plains of Gcalékaland, with the blue smoke rising from many a clustering kraal. Yet soft and peaceful as was the landscape, there was little of peace just then in the mind of its inhabitants, white or brown, for the savages were believed to be in active preparation for war, for a concerted and murderous outbreak on a large scale, involving a repetition of the massacres of isolated and unprepared settlers such as characterised similar risings on former occasions; the last, then, happily, a quarter of a century ago.

Nearer, nearer to his western bed, dipped the sinking sun, throwing out long slanting darts of golden rays ere bringing to a close, in a flood of effulgent glory, the sweet African spring day. They fell on the placid surface of the dam, lying below in the kloof, causing it to shine like a sea of quicksilver. They brought out the vivid green of the willows, whose feathery boughs drooped upon the cool water. They blended with the soft, restful cooing of ring doves, swaying upon many a mimosa spray, or winging their way swiftly from the mealie lands to their evening roost and they seemed to impart a blithe gladsomeness to the mellow shout of the hoopoe, echoing from the cool shade of yonder rugged and bush-clad kloof.

Round the house a dozen or so tiny ostrich chicks were picking at the ground, or disputing the possession of some unexpected dainty with a tribe of long-legged fowls. Quaint enough they looked, these little, fluffy balls, with their bright eyes, and tawny, spotted necks; frail enough, too, and apt to come off badly at the spur or beak of any truculent rooster who should resent their share of the plunder aforesaid. Nominally they are under the care of a small Kafir boy, but the little black rascal—his master being absent and his mistress soft hearted—prefers the congenial associations of yonder group of beehive huts away there behind the sheep kraals, and the fun of building miniature kraals with mud and three or four boon companions, so the ostrich chicks are left to herd themselves. But the volleying boom of their male parent, down there in the great enclosure, rolls out loudly enough on the evening air, and the huge bird may be described in all the glory of his jet and snowy plumage, with inflated throat, rearing himself to his full height, rolling his fiery eye in search of an adversary.

And now the flaming rays of the sinking sun have given place to a softer, mellower light, and the red afterglow is merging into the pearly grey of evening. The hillside is streaked with the dappled hides of cattle coming up the kloof, and many a responsive low greets the clamourous voices of the calves, shut up in the calf *hoek*, hungry and expectant. Then upon the ridge comes a white, moving mass of fleecy backs. It streams down the slope, raising a cloud of dust—guided, kept together, by an occasional kerrie deftly thrown to the right or left—and soon arrives at its nightly fold. But the herd is nonplussed, for there is no *Baas* there to count in. He pauses a moment, looks around, then drives the sheep into the kraal, and having secured the gate, throws his red kaross around him and stalks away to the huts.

Eanswyth Carhayes stood on the *stoep*, looking out for the return of her husband and cousin. She was very tall for a woman, her erect carriage causing her to appear even taller. And she was very beautiful. The face, with its straight, thoroughbred features, was one of those which, at first sight, conveyed an impression of more than ordinary attractiveness, and this impression further acquaintance never failed to develop into a realisation of its rare loveliness. Yet by no means a mere animal or flower-like beauty. There was character in the strongly marked, arching brows, and in the serene, straight glance of the large, grey eyes. Further, there was indication that their owner would not be lacking in tact or fixity of purpose; two qualities usually found hand in hand. Her hair, though dark, was many shades removed from black, and of it she possessed a more than bountiful supply.

She came of a good old Colonial family, but had been educated in England. Well educated, too; thanks to which salutary storing of a mind eagerly open to culture, many an otherwise dull and unoccupied hour of her four years of married life—frequently left, as she was, alone for a whole day at a time—was turned to brightness. Alone? Yes, for she was childless.

When she had married bluff, hot-tempered Tom Carhayes, who was nearly fifteen years her senior, and had gone to live on a Kaffrarian stock farm, her acquaintance unanimously declared she had "thrown herself away." But whether this was so or not, certain it is that Eanswyth herself evinced no sort of indication to that effect, and indeed more than one of the aforesaid acquaintance eventually came to envy her calm, cheerful contentment. To the expression of which sentiment she would reply with a quiet smile that she supposed she was cut out for a "blue-stocking," and that the restful seclusion, not to say monotony, of her life, afforded her ample time for indulging her studious tastes.

After three years her husband's cousin had come to live with them. Eustace Milne, who was possessed of moderate means, had devoted the few years subsequent on leaving college to "seeing the world," and it must be owned he had managed to see a good deal of it in the time. But tiring eventually of the process, he had made overtures to his cousin to enter into partnership with the latter in his stock-farming operations. Carhayes, who at that time had been somewhat unlucky, having been hard hit by a couple of very bad seasons, and thinking moreover that the presence in the house of his cousin, whom he knew and rather liked, would make life a little more cheerful for Eanswyth, agreed, and forthwith Eustace had sailed for the Cape. He had put a fair amount of capital into the concern and more than a fair amount of energy, and at this time the operations of the two men were flourishing exceedingly.

We fear that—human nature being the same all the world over, even in that sparsely inhabited locality—there were not wanting some—not many it is true, but still some—who saw in the above arrangement something to wag a scandalous tongue over. Carhayes was a prosaic and rather crusty personage, many years older than his wife. Eustace Milne was just the reverse of this, being imaginative, cultured, even tempered, and, when he chose, of very attractive manner; moreover, he was but three or four years her senior. Possibly the rumour evolved itself from the disappointment of its originators, as well as from the insatiable and universal love of scandal-mongering inherent in human nature, for Eustace Milne was eminently an eligible *parti*, and during nearly a year's residence at Anta's Kloof had shown no disposition to throw the handkerchief at any of the surrounding fair. But to Carhayes, whom thanks to his known proclivity towards punching heads this rumour never reached, no such nice idea occurred, for with all his faults or failings there was nothing mean or crooked-minded about the man, and as for Eanswyth herself, we should have been uncommonly sorry to have stood in the shoes of the individual who should undertake to enlighten her of the same, by word or hint.

As she stood there watching for the return of those who came not, Eanswyth began to feel vaguely uneasy, and there was a shade of anxiety in the large grey eyes, which were bent upon the surrounding *veldt* with a now growing intensity. The return of the flock, combined with the absence of its master to count in, was not a reassuring circumstance. She felt inclined to send for the herd and question him, but after all it was of no use being silly about it. She noted further the non-appearance of the other flock. This, in conjunction with the prolonged absence of her husband and cousin, made her fear that something had gone very wrong indeed.

Nor was her uneasiness altogether devoid of justification. We have said that Tom Carhayes was not on the best of terms with his barbarous neighbours. We have shown moreover that his choleric disposition was eminently calculated to keep him in chronic hot water. Such was indeed the case. Hardly a week passed that he did not come into collision with them, more or less violently, generally on the vexed question of trespass, and crossing his farm accompanied by their dogs. More than one of these dogs had been shot by him on such occasions, and when we say that a Kafir loves his dog a trifle more dearly than his children, it follows that the hatred which they cherished towards this imperious and high-handed settler will hardly bear exaggeration. But Carhayes was a powerful man and utterly fearless, and although these qualities had so far availed to save his life, the savages were merely biding their time. Meanwhile they solaced themselves with secret acts of revenge. A thoroughbred horse would be found dead in the stable, a valuable cow would be stabbed to death in the open *veldt*, or a fine, full-grown ostrich would be discovered with a shattered leg and all its wing-feathers plucked, sure sign, the latter, that the damage was due to no accident. These acts of retaliation had generally followed within a few days of one of the broils above alluded to, but so far from intimidating Carhayes, their only effect was to enrage him the more. He vowed fearful and summary vengeance against the perpetrators, should he ever succeed in detecting them. He even went boldly to the principal Gaika chiefs and laid claim to compensation. But those magnates were the last men in the world to side with, or to help him. Some were excessively civil, others indifferent, but all disclaimed any responsibility in the matter.

Bearing these facts in mind there was, we repeat, every excuse for Eanswyth's anxiety. But suddenly a sigh of relief escaped her. The tramp of hoofs reaching her ears caused her to turn, and there, approaching the house from a wholly unexpected direction, came the two familiar mounted figures.

Chapter Four.

"Love Settling Unawares."

"Well, old girl, and how have you been getting through the day," was Carhayes' unceremonious greeting as he slid from his horse. Eustace turned away his head, and the faintest shadow of contempt flitted across his impassive countenance. Had this glorious creature stood in the same relationship towards himself he could no more have dreamed of addressing her as "old girl" than he could have of carving his name across the front of the silver altar which is exhibited once a year in the "Battistero" at Florence.

"Pretty well, Tom," she answered smilingly. "And you? I hope you haven't been getting into any more mischief. Has he, Eustace?"

"Well, I have, then," rejoined Carhayes, grimly, for Eustace pretended not to hear. "What you'd call mischief, I suppose. Now what d'you think? I caught that *schelm* Goníwe having a buck-hunt—a buck-hunt, by Jove! right under my very nose; he and three other niggers. They'd got two dogs, good dogs too, and I couldn't help admiring the way the *schepsels* put them on by relays, nor yet the fine shot they made at the buck with a kerrie. Well, I rode up and told them to clear out of the light because I intended to shoot their dogs. Would you believe it? they didn't budge. Actually squared up to me."

"I hope you didn't shoot their dogs," said Eanswyth anxiously.

"Didn't I! one of 'em, that is. Do you think I'm the man to be bounced by Jack Kafir? Not much I'm not. I was bound to let daylight through the brute, and I did."

"Through the Kafir?" cried Eanswyth, in horror, turning pale.

"Through both," answered Carhayes, with a roar of laughter. "Through both, by Jove! Ask Eustace. He came up just in time to be in at the death. But, don't get scared, old girl. I only 'barked' the nigger, and sent the dog to hunt bucks in some other world. I had to do it. Those chaps were four to one, you see, and shied kerries at me. They had assegais, too."

"Oh, I don't know what will happen to us one of these days!" she cried, in real distress. "As it is, I am uneasy every time you are out in the *veldt*."

"You needn't be—no fear. Those chaps know me better than to attempt any tricks. They're all bark—but when it comes to biting they funk off. That *schelm* I plugged to-day threatened no end of things; said I'd better have cut off my right hand first, because it was better to lose one's hand than one's mind— or some such bosh. But do you think I attach any importance to that? I laughed in the fellow's face and told him the next time he fell foul of me he'd likely enough lose his life—and that would be worse still for him."

Eustace, listening to these remarks, frowned slightly. The selfish coarseness of his cousin in thus revealing the whole unfortunate episode, with the sure result of doubling this delicate woman's anxiety whenever she should be left—as she so often was—alone, revolted him. Had he been Carhayes he would have kept his own counsel in the matter.

"By the way, Tom," said Eanswyth, "Goníwe hasn't brought in his sheep yet, and it's nearly dark."

"Not, eh?" was the almost shouted reply, accompanied by a vehement and undisguised expletive at the expense of the defaulter. "He's playing Harry—not a doubt about it. I'll make an example of him this time. Rather! Hold on. Where's my thickest *sjambok*?"

(Sjambok: A whip, made out of a single piece of rhinoceros, or sea-cow hide, tapering at the point. It is generally in the shape of a riding-whip.)

He dived into the house, and, deaf to his wife's entreaties and expostulations, armed himself with the formidable rawhide whip in addition to his gun, and flinging the bridle once more across the horse's neck, sprang into the saddle.

"Coming, Eustace?" he cried.

"No. I think not. The sheep can't be far off, and you can easily bring them in, even if, as is not unlikely, Goníwe has sloped. Besides, I don't think we ought to leave Eanswyth all alone."

With a spluttered exclamation of impatience, Carhayes clapped spurs to his horse and cantered away down the kloof to recover his sheep and execute summary vengeance upon their defective herd.

"Do go after him, Eustace. Don't think about me. I don't in the least mind being left alone. Do go. You are the only one who can act as a check upon him, and I fear he will get himself—all of us—into some terrible scrape. I almost hope Goníwe has run away, for if Tom comes across him in his present humour he will half kill the boy."

"He won't come across him. On that point you may set your mind quite at ease. He will have no opportunity of getting into hot water, and I certainly shan't think of leaving you alone here to-night for the sake of salvaging a few sheep more or less. We must make up our minds to lose some, I'm afraid, but the bulk of them will be all right."

"Still, I wish you'd go," she pursued anxiously. "What if Tom should meet with any Kafirs in the *veldt* and quarrel with them, as he is sure to do?"

"He won't meet any. There isn't a chance of it. Look here, Eanswyth; Tom must take care of himself for once. I'm not going to leave you alone here now for the sake of fifty Toms."

"Why! Have you heard anything fresh?" she queried anxiously, detecting a veiled significance in his words.

"Certainly not. Nothing at all. Haven't been near Komgha for ten days, and haven't seen anyone since. Now, I'll just take my horse round to the stable and give him a feed—and be with you in a minute."

As a matter of fact, there was an *arrière-pensée* underlying his words. For Eustace had been pondering over Hlangani's strangely worded threat. And it was a strangely worded one. "*You had better have cut off your right hand... for it is better to lose a hand than one's mind.*" Carhayes had dismissed it contemptuously from his thoughts, but Eustace Milne, keen-witted, imaginative, had set to work to puzzle it out. Did the Gcaléka chief meditate some more subtle and hellish form of vengeance than the ordinary and commonplace one of mere blood for blood, and, if so, how did he purpose to carry it out? By striking at Carhayes through the one who was dearest to him? Surely. The words seemed to bear just this interpretation—and at the bare contemplation of a frightful danger hanging over Eanswyth, cool, even-minded Eustace Milne, felt the blood flow back to his heart. For he loved her.

Yes, he loved her. This keen-witted, philosophical man of the world was madly in love with the beautiful wife of his middle-aged cousin. He loved her with all the raging abandonment of a strong nature that does nothing by halves; yet during nearly a year spent beneath the same roof—nearly a year of easy, pleasant, social intercourse—never by word or sign had he betrayed his secret—at least, so he imagined.

But that no such blow should fall while he was alive, he resolved at all hazards. Why had he come there at all, was a question he had been asking himself for some time past? Why had he stayed, why did he stay? For the latter he hated and despised himself on account of his miserable weakness. But now it seemed that both were answered—that he had been brought there for a purpose—to protect *her* from the fearful consequences entailed by the blundering ferocity of him who should have been her first protector—to save her from some impending and terrible fate. Surely this was sufficient answer.

Then a wild thrill set his pulses tingling—a thrill of joy, of fierce expectation set on foot by a single thought, the intense expectation of the gambler who sees fortune brought within his reach by the potential turn of chances already strong in his favour. They were on the eve of war. What might the chances of war not entail? Blind, blundering Tom Carhayes running his head, like a bull, at every stone wall—were not the chances of war increased tenfold *against* such a man as this? And then—and then—?

No man could be more unfitted to hold possession of such a priceless treasure as this—argued the man who did not hold it.

"Confess, Eanswyth, that you are very glad I didn't take you at your word and go after Tom," said Eustace, as they were sitting cosily at table.

"Perhaps I am. I have been getting so dreadfully nervous and low spirited of late—so different to the strong-minded creature I used to be," she said with a rueful smile. "I am becoming quite frightened to be left alone."

"Are you? Well, I think I can undertake to promise that you shall not be left alone again. One of us must always make a point of being around the house while the other is away. But look here, Eanswyth; I really think you oughtn't to go on staying here at present. Why don't you go down to the Colony and stay in one or other of the towns, or even at that other farm of Tom's, until things are settled again?"

"I won't do that. And I'm really not in the least afraid for myself. I don't believe the Kafirs would harm me."

"Then why are you nervous at being left alone?" was the very pertinent rejoinder.

"Not on my own account. It is only that solitude gives me time to think. I am always imagining Tom coming to frightful grief in some form or other."

The other did not at once reply. He was balancing a knife meditatively on the edge of his plate, his fine features a perfect mask of impassibility. But in reality his thoughts ran black and bitter. It was all "Tom" and "Tom." What the deuce had Tom done to deserve all this solicitude—and how was it appreciated by its fortunate object? Not a hair's-breadth. Then, as she rose from the table and went out on the *stoep* to look out for any sign of the absent one's return, Eustace was conscious of another turn of the spear in the wound. Why had he arrived on the scene of the fray that morning just in time to intervene? suggested his evil angel. The delay of a few minutes, and...

"Would it do anything towards persuading you to adopt the more prudent course and leave here for a while, if I were to tell you that Josane was urging that very thing this morning?" said Eustace when she returned. The said Josane was a grizzled old Kafir who held the post of cattle-herd under the two cousins. He was a Gcaléka, and had fled from Kreli's country some years previously, thereby narrowly escaping one of the varied and horrible forms of death by torture habitually meted out to those accused of his hypothetical offence—for he had been "smelt out" by a witch-doctor. He was therefore not likely to throw in his lot with his own countrymen against his white protectors, by whom he was looked upon as an intelligent and thoroughly trustworthy man, which indeed he was.

"I don't think it would," she answered with a deprecatory smile. "I should be ten times more nervous if I were right away, and, as I said before, I don't believe the Kafirs would do me the slightest harm."

Eustace, though he had every reason to suppose the contrary, said nothing as he rose from the table and began to fill his pipe. He was conscious of a wild thrill of delight at her steadfast refusal. What would life be worth here without that presence? Well, come what might, no harm should fall upon her, of that he made mental oath.

Eanswyth, having superintended the clearing of the table by the two little Kafir girls who filled the *rôle* rather indifferent handmaidens, joined him on the *stoep*. It was a lovely night; warm and balmy. The dark vault above was so crowded with stars that they seemed to hang in golden patches.

"Shall we walk a little way down the kloof and see if we can meet Tom," she suggested.

"A good idea. Just half a minute though. I want to get another pipe."

He went into his room, slipped a "bull-dog" revolver of heavy calibre into his pocket, and quickly rejoined her.

Then as they walked side by side—they two, alone together in the darkness, alone in the sweet, soft beauty of the Southern night; alone, as it were, outside the very world; in a world apart where none might intrude; the rich shroud of darkness around them—Eustace began to wonder if he were really made of flesh and blood after all. The pent-up force of his self-contained and concentrated nature was in sore danger of breaking its barriers, of pouring forth the fires and molten lava raging within—and to do so would be ruin—utter, endless, irretrievable ruin to any hopes which he might have ventured to form.

He could see every feature of that sweet, patrician face in the starlight. The even, musical tones of that exquisitely modulated voice, within a yard of his ears, fairly maddened him. The rich, balmy zephyrs of the African night breathed around; the chirrup of the cricket, and now and again the deep-throated booming croak of a bull-frog from an adjacent *vlei* emphasising its stillness. Again those wild, raging fires surged up to the surface. "Eanswyth, I love you—love you—worship you—adore you! Apart from you, life is worse than a blank! Who, what, is the dull, sodden, senseless lout who now stands between us? Forget him, darling, and be all heaven and earth to me!" The words blazed through his brain in letters of flame. He could hardly feel sure he had not actually uttered them.

"What is the matter, Eustace? I have asked you a question three times, and you haven't answered me."

"I really beg your pardon. I—I—suppose I was thinking of something else. Do you mind asking it again?"

The strange harshness of his voice struck her. It was well for him—well for both of them—that the friendly darkness stood him in such good stead.

"I asked you, how far do you think Tom would have to ride before finding the sheep?"

"Tom" again! He fairly set his teeth. "Well into the Gaika location," was the savage reply that rose to his lips. But he checked it unuttered.

"Oh, not very far," he answered. "You see, sheep are slow-moving brutes and difficult to drive, especially in the dark. He'll turn up soon, never fear."

"What is that? Look! Listen!" she exclaimed suddenly, laying a hand upon his arm.

The loom of the mountains was blackly visible in the starlight. Away in the distance, apparently in the very heart of them, there suddenly shown forth a lurid glow. The V-shaped scarp of the slopes stood dully in relief against the glare, which was as that of a furnace. At the same time there floated forth upon the night a strange, weird chorus—a wild, long-drawn eerie melody, half chant, half howl, faint and distant, but yet distinct, though many miles away.

"What can they be up to at the location, Eustace? Can it be that they have risen already?" ejaculated Eanswyth, turning pale in the starlight.

The reddening glare intensified, the fierce, wild cadence shrilled forth, now in dirge-like wail, now in swelling notes of demon-like and merciless exultation. There was a faint, muffled roar as of distant thunder—a clamour as of fiends holding high revel—and still the wild chorus gathered in volume, hideous in its blood-chilling menace, as it cleft the dark stillness of the night.

"Oh, let us turn back!" cried Eanswyth. "There is something horrible going on to-night. I really am quite frightened now. That hideous noise! It terrifies me!"

Well it might. The deep-toned thunder note within the burning heart of the volcano is of terrible import, for it portends fire and ruin and widespread death. There were those who were then sitting on the verge of a volcano—a mere handful in the midst of a vast, teeming population of fierce and truculent savages. Well might that weird chorus strike dismay into the hearts of its hearers, for it was the preliminary rumble of the coming storm—the battle-song of the warlike and now hostile Gaika clans.

Chapter Five.

The War-Dance at Nteya's Kraal.

The sun has just touched the western horizon, bathing in a parting flood of red and gold the round spurs of the rolling hills and the straggling clusters of dome-shaped huts which lie dotted about the valley in irregular order for a couple of miles. There is a continuous hum of voices in the air, mingling with the low of cattle, and the whole place seems to be teeming with human life. Indeed, such is the case; for this kraal—or rather collection of kraals—is the head centre of Nteya's location and the residence of that chief himself.

Each group of huts owns its cattle inclosure, whose dark space, girdled with a strong thorn palisade, is now filled with the many-coloured forms of its horned denizens. It is milking time, and the metallic squirt of liquid into the zinc pails rises rhythmic above the deep hum of the monotonous chant of the milkers. Women step forth from the kraal gates balancing the full pails on their heads, their ochre-smeared bodies shining like new flower pots, while their lords, *reim* in hand, set to work to catch a fresh cow—for among Kafirs milking is essentially man's work. About the huts squat other groups of natives, men smoking their queer shaped, angular pipes, and exchanging *indaba* (Gossip or news); women also smoking, and busy with their household affairs, whether of the culinary or nursery order; round bellied, beady-eyed children tumbling over each other in their romps, and dogs ever on the prowl to pick up a stray bone, or to obtain a surreptitious lick at the interior of a cooking-pot; and over all the never-ending flow of voices, the deep bass of the men blending with the clearer feminine treble, but all rhythmic and pleasing, for the language and voices of the Bantu races are alike melodious. The blue reek of wood-smoke rising upon the evening air, mingles with that pungent odour of grease and kine inseparable from every Kafir kraal.

That something unwonted is impending here to-night is manifest. Men would start suddenly from beside their fellows and gaze expectantly out upon the approaches to the kraal, or now and again the heads of a whole group would turn in eager scrutiny of the surrounding *veldt*. For strung out upon the hillsides in twos and threes, or in parties of ten or a dozen, some mounted, some afoot, come a great number of Kafirs. On they come: those who are mounted kicking their shaggy little ponies into a headlong gallop; those who are not, starting into a run, leaping into the air, singing, or now and again venting a shrill and ear-splitting whistle. From far and near—from every direction converging upon the kraal, on they come. *And they are all armed.*

The excitement in the kraal itself intensifies. All rise to their feet to receive the newcomers, each group of whom is greeted with boisterous shouts of welcome. Snatches of war-songs rise upon the air, and the rattle of assegai hafts blends with the barbaric melody. Still, pouring in from all sides, come fresh arrivals, and by the time the sun has shot his last fading ray upon the stirring scene, the kraal cannot have contained far short of a thousand men.

Near the principal group of huts stands a circular inclosure about fifty yards in diameter. Above the thorn fence bristle the great branching horns of oxen. To this point all eyes are now turned, and the deafening clamour of voices is hushed in expectation of a new diversion.

A narrow opening is made in the fence and half a dozen Kafirs enter. An ox is turned out. No sooner is the poor beast clear of the fence than it is suddenly seen to plunge and fall forward in a heap, stabbed to the heart by a broad-bladed assegai. The slaughterer steps back to his lurking position and stands with arm upraised. Quickly another ox follows upon the first. The weapon, now dimmed and reddened with blood, flashes in the air. The second animal plunges forward dead. A third follows, with like result.

Then, scenting danger, and terrified moreover by the crowd which is gathering outside, the beasts stubbornly refuse to move. They huddle together with lowered heads, backing away from the opening and emitting the muffled, moaning noise evoked in cattle by the scent of blood. In vain their would-be drivers shout and goad them with assegais. Move they will not.

Another opening is made on the opposite side to that of the first. After some trouble two oxen are driven through. They rush out together, one falling by the hand of the lurking slaughterer, the other meeting a speedy death at the assegais of the spectators.

There still remain upwards of a dozen within the kraal, but of these not one can be induced to pass out. Panic-stricken they huddle together closer still, until at last, their terror giving way to a frenzy of rage, the maddened brutes turn and furiously charge their tormentors. The air is rent with savage bellowings and the clashing of horns. The dust flies in clouds from the rumbling earth as the frenzied creatures tear round and round the inclosure. Two of the Kafirs, less agile or less fortunate than their fellows, are flung high in the air, falling with a lifeless thud among the spectators outside; then, crashing through the fence in a body, the panic-stricken bullocks stream forth into the open, scattering the crowd right and left before the fury of their rush.

Then ensues a wild and stirring scene. Their great horns lowered, the infuriated animals course madly through the village, each beset by a crowd of armed savages whose dark, agile forms, avoiding the fierce impetus of their charge, may be seen to spring alongside, plying the deadly assegai. One turns suddenly and heads straight for its pursuers, bellowing hideously. Like magic the crowd parts, there is a whizz of assegais in the air, and the poor beast crashes earthward, bristling with quivering assegai hafts, as a pin cushion with pins. Yelling, whistling like fiends, in their uncontrollable excitement, the savages dart in and out among the fleeing beasts, and the red firelight gleams upon assegai points and rolling eyeballs, and the air rings with the frenzied bellowing of the pursued, and the wild shouts of the pursuers.

But it cannot last long. Soon the mad fury of the chase gives way to the nauseous accompaniments of a slaughter house on a large scale. In an incredibly short space of time, each of the bullocks is reduced to a disjointed heap of flesh and bones. Men, staggering beneath huge slabs of quivering meat, make their way to the fires, leaving the dogs to snarl and quarrel over an abundant repast of steaming offal.

The great joints frizzle and sputter over the red coals. Squatted around, a hungry gleam in their eyes, the Kafirs impatiently watch each roasting morsel. Then, hardly waiting until it is warmed through, they drag the meat from the fire. Assegais are plied, and soon the huge joints are reduced to strips of half-raw flesh, and the champing of hundreds of pairs of jaws around each red blaze takes the place of the deep bass hum of conversation, as the savages throw all their energies into the assimilation of their unwonted meal. It is like a cannibal feast—the smoky flare of the great fires—the mighty slabs of red flesh—the fierce, dark figures seated around—the gleam of weapons in the firelight.

(The unwonted meal. In former days, meat was very sparingly eaten among the Amaxosa races, milk and mealies being the staple articles of diet. When employed on such a scale as above described, it had a curiously stimulating effect upon a people habitually almost vegetarians. Hence it was looked upon as a preparation for war.)

At length even the very bones are picked clean, and thrown over the feasters' shoulders to the dogs. Then voices are raised and once more the kraal becomes a scene of wild and excited stir. Roused by a copious indulgence in an unwonted stimulant, the Kafirs leap to their feet. Weapons are brandished, and the firelight glows upon assegai points and rolling eyeballs. A wild war-song rises upon the air; then falling into circular formation, the whole gathering of excited warriors join in, beating time with their feet—clashing the hefts of their weapons together. The weird rhythm is led off in a high, wailing key by a kind of *choragus*, then taken up by the rest, rising louder and louder, and the thunder of hundreds of pairs of feet keeping regular time, make the very earth itself tremble, and the quivering rattle of assegai hafts is echoed back from the dark, brooding hills, and the volume of the fierce and threatening song, with its final chorus of "Ha—ha—ha!" becomes as the mad roaring of a legion of wild beasts, ravaging for blood. Worked up to a degree of incontrollable excitement, the savages foam at the lips and their eyeballs seem to start from the sockets, as turning to each other they go through the pantomime of encountering and slaying an imaginary foe; and even in the background a number of women have formed up behind the dancing warriors and with more than all the barbarity of the latter are playing at beating out the brains of the wounded with knob-kerries. The roar and rattle of the hideous performance goes up to the heavens, cleaving the solemn silence of the sweet African night. The leaping, bounding, perspiring shapes, look truly devilish in the red firelight. The excitement of the fierce savages seems to have reached a pitch little short of downright frenzy. Yet it shows no signs of abating. *For they have eaten meat.*

Chapter Six.

Hlangani, The Herald.

Suddenly, as if by magic, the wild war-dance ceased, and the fierce, murderous rhythm was reduced to silence. Sinking down in a half-sitting posture, quivering with suppressed excitement, their dark forms bent forward like those of so many crouching leopards, their eyeballs rolling in the lurid glow, the Kafirs rested eagerly, awaiting what was to follow.

A group of chiefs advanced within the circle of light. A little in front of these, prominent among them by reason of his towering stature and herculean build, was a warrior of savage and awe-inspiring aspect. His countenance bore an evil, scowling sneer, which looked habitual, and his eyes glowed like live coals. He wore a headdress of monkey skins, above which waved a tuft of plumes from the tail of the blue crane. His body was nearly naked, and his muscular limbs, red with ochre, were decorated with fringes of cows' tails and tufts of flowing hair. On his left arm, above the elbow, he wore a thick; square armlet of solid ivory, and in his hand he carried a large, broad-bladed assegai. One shoulder was swathed in a rude bandage, the latter nearly concealed by fantastic hair adornments.

A hum of suppressed eagerness went round the crowd of excited barbarians as this man stood forth in their midst. It subsided into a silence that might be felt as he spoke:

"I am Hlangani, the son of Ngcesiba, the Herald of the Great Chief Sarili (Or Kreli), the son of Hintza, of the House of Gcaléka. Hear my word, for it is the word of Sarili, the Great Chief—the chief paramount of all the children of Xosa.

"This is the word of the Great Chief to his children of the House of Ngqika (Or Gaika). Lo, the time has come when the Amanglézi (English) seek a quarrel with us. We can no longer live side by side, say they. There is no room for the Ama-Gcaléka in the land they have hitherto dwelt in. They must go.

"So they have located our dogs, the cowardly Amafengu (Fingoes), our slaves and our dogs, on the next land to ours, that we may have a continual plague to scourge us, that our sides may be wrung with the pest of these stinging flies, that our name may be spat upon and laughed at by those who were our own dogs. Thus would these English provoke us to quarrel.

"Who were these Amafengu? Were they not our dogs and our slaves? Who are they now? Still dogs—but not *our* dogs. Who will they be shortly? Not our dogs—not our slaves—but—our masters! Our masters!" roared the fierce savage, shaking the broad assegai which he held, until it quivered like a band of flame in the red firelight. "The sons of Gcaléka will be the slaves of their former slaves—the dogs of their former dogs. Not the sons of Gcaléka only, but all the children of Xosa. Not the House of Gcaléka only, but the House of Ngqika. Who is doing this? The Amanglezi! Who would tread upon the necks of our chiefs and place the fetters of their lying and hypocritical creeds upon the limbs of our young men till the latter are turned into slaves and drunkards? The Amanglezi! Who would stop the mouths of our *amapakati* (Councillors) and drown the collective wisdom of our nation in floods of fire-water? The Amanglezi. Are we men—I say? Are we men?"

A low suppressed roar ran through the circle of fierce and excitable barbarians as the orator paused. Again sounded the ominous rattle of assegai hafts. It needed all the self-control of their habitually self-contained race to restrain them from breaking forth anew into their frenzied war-dance. But a wave of the speaker's hand availed to quell the rising tumult and he continued:

"This is the 'word' of the rulers of the Amanglézi. The time has come when the Amaxosa races must be subdued. They are growing too numerous. They are waxing too strong. Their power must be broken. We must begin by breaking up the influence of the chiefs. We must put down chieftainship altogether. Hear ye this, ye sons of Ngqika? Hear you this, O Matanzima, warrior son of Saudili, the Great Chief of the House of Ngqika? Hear you this, O Nteya—*pakati* of the race of Ngqika? Hear you this, O Nxabahlana, of the House of the Great Chief, you who have led our bands to war before the very birth of many of the young men I see before me? Hear ye this, Maquades and Mpanhla and Sivuléle, and you, Panganisi and Untíwa, of the House of Seyolo of the House of Hlambi, golden mouthed in council—in the battle-field flames of consuming fire? Hear ye this, all ye gathered here before me this night—tried warriors, and young men who have never seen war. The children of Xosa are growing too strong. They must be subdued. The power of their chiefs must be broken. Such is the word of the rulers of the Amanglezi."

This time, as the orator paused, there was no restraining the fierce excitement of his hearers. Each warrior named, who had greeted the mention of himself with a low, but emphatic "*há*"—now sprang to his feet. No further example was needed. Again, the wild rhythm of the war-song rose upon the night; again the fierce thunder-roll of the tread of hundreds of feet shook the ground. Again the circle of firelight was alive with grim, threatening forms, swaying in measured time, to the unearthly chant, to the accompaniment of the shaking of fantastic adornments, to the quivering rattle of assegai hafts. For some minutes this continued—then when the excitement was almost at its height, a mysterious signal was given and the whole wild crowd dropped quickly into its listening attitude again.

"Such is the word of the Amanglezi," went on the speaker. "Now hear the word of Sarili, your father, the Paramount Chief, the father of all the children of Xosa. Hear the word of the Great Chief conveyed by the mouth of Hlangani, the herald—'Lo, the time has come when we must unite in the strength of brethren. The Amanglézi are urging our very dogs on to provoke us. The Amafengu are located on our borders, to taunt and jeer at our young men—to lure our young women over into their kraals that the very name of Gcaléka may be debased and defiled. Not a day passes that this does not happen. Why do we not revenge this? Why do we not execute a sudden and fearful vengeance upon these dogs who spit at our name and nation? We dare not. The Amanglézi say: "Your dogs are now our dogs. Touch them and we shall send armies of soldiers and you will be eaten up"—But, dare we not? Dare we not? Answer me, all ye children of the race of Xosa! I, Sarili, your father, call upon you—I, Sarili, your chief. Answer! Show that the war-fire of our free and warrior race is not dead. It has been smouldering for many years, but it is not dead. It is ready to break forth as the destroying lightning leaps from the black thunder-cloud. It is ready to blaze forth in its strength and to consume all within its reach.

"'Where is my father, Hintza? Where is he who was lured into the white man's camp by fair promises and then shot down? Do I not hear his spirit calling unto me day and night. I cannot sleep, for the spirit of my father is crying for vengeance. It is crying day and night from the depths. Yet, not to me only. Who was Hintza? My father, yet not my father only. The father of all the sons of Xosa!

"'Lo, the white Governor has summoned me, your chief, to meet him. He has invited me, your chief, with fair promises to visit him at his camp. Shall I go, that I, Sarili, may meet with the same dealing that laid low my father, Hintza? I will, indeed, go, but it will be with the whole array of the fighting men of the Amaxosa at my back.

"'Hear my "word," my children of the House of Nteya, *pakati* of the race of Ngqika. Hear my "word" as spoken through the mouth of Hlangani, my herald. Receive these oxen as a present from your father to his children. Eat them, and when you have eaten and your hearts are strong, stand prepared. Let the war-cry roll through the mountains and valleys of our fair land. Let the thunder of your war-dances shake the earth as the reeds by the water side quiver beneath the rushing of the storm wind. Let the trumpet tongues of your war-fires gleam from the mountain tops—tongue roaring to tongue—that the Amanglezi may hear it and tremble; for the spirit of Hintza, my father, which has slumbered for years, is awake again and is crying for vengeance—is crying and crying aloud that the time has come.'"

The speaker ceased. A dead silence fell upon his hearers—a weird silence upon that tumultuous crowd crouching in eager expectancy in the red firelight. Suddenly, upon the black gloom of the night, far away to the eastward, there gleamed forth a streak of flame. Then another and another. A subdued roar ran around the circle. Then, as by magic, a crimson glare fell upon the serried ranks of expectant listeners, lighting up their fantastic war panoply as with the light of day. From the hill top above the kraal there shot up a great tongue of red flame. It leaped high into the velvety blackness of the heavens. Splitting up into many a forking flash it roared in the air—the gleaming rays licking up into a cloud of lurid smoke which blotted out the stars in its reddening folds. The distant war signal of the Gcaléka chieftain was answered.

"Ha!" cried Hlangani, in a voice of thunder. "Ha! Now will the heart of your father, Sarili, be glad. Now have ye proved yourselves his children indeed, oh, sons of Ngqika! Now have you proved yourselves men, for the trumpet tongues of your war-flames are crying aloud—tongue roaring to tongue upon the wings of the night."

With the quickness of lightning the warriors had again thrown themselves into formation, and now worked up to a pitch of uncontrollable excitement, the unearthly cadence of the war-song rose into a fiendish roar, and the thunder of the demon dance rolled and reverberated among the hills, while lighting up the fierce array of grim, frenzied figures in its brooding glare, the huge beacon, high above on the hilltop, blazed forth sullenly upon the night in all its menacing and destructive significance.

Suddenly, as if by magic, the mad orgy of the savages was suspended. For advancing into their very midst—fearlessly, boldly, contemptuously, even—rode a solitary horseman—a white man, an Englishman.

Chapter Seven.

In the Lion's Den.

Every eye was bent upon the new arrival. With a quick, instinctive movement the savages closed around the foolhardy Englishman. There was a scowl of deadly import upon each grim face. Hundreds of assegais were poised with a quiver of suppressed eagerness. The man's life seemed not worth a moment's purchase.

"Out of my way, you *schepsels*!" he cried roughly, urging his horse through the sullen and threatening crowd, as though so many hundreds of armed and excited barbarians worked up to the highest pitch of blood-thirstiness were just that number of cowering and subservient slaves. "Out of my way, do you hear? Where is Nteya? I want Nteya, the chief. Where is he?"

"Here I am, *umlúngu* (White man). What do you want with me?" answered Nteya—making a rapid and peremptory signal to restrain the imminent resentment of his followers. "Am I not always here, that you should break in upon me in this violent manner? Do *I* go to *your* house, and ride up to the door and shout for you as though you were stricken with sudden deafness?"

The chief's rebuke, quiet and dignified, might have carried some tinge of humiliation to any man less overbearing and hot-headed than Tom Carhayes, even as the low growl of hardly contained exasperation which arose from the throng might have conveyed an ominous warning. But upon this man both were alike thrown away. Yet it may be that the very insanity of his foolhardiness constituted his safety. Had he quailed but a moment his doom was sealed.

"I didn't come here to hold an *indaba*," (Talk—palaver) he shouted. "I want my sheep. Look here, Nteya. You have put me off very cleverly time after time with one excuse or another. But this time you are *pagadi* (Cornered). I've run you to earth—or rather some of those *schepsels* of yours. That young villain Goníwe has driven off thirty-seven of my sheep, and two of your fellows have helped him. I've spoored them right into your location as straight as a line. Now?"

"When was this, Umlilwane?" said Nteya, imperturbably.

"When? When? To-night, man. This very night, do you hear?" roared the other.

"*Hau*! The white man has the eyes of twenty vultures that he can see to follow the spoor of thirty-seven sheep on a dark night," cried a mocking voice—and a great shout of derisive laughter went up from the whole savage crowd. The old chief, however, preserved his dignified and calm demeanour.

"You are excited, Umlilwane," he said—a faint smile lurking round the corners of his mouth. "Had you not better go home and return in the morning and talk things over quietly? Surely you would not forget yourself like a boy or a quarrelsome old woman."

If a soft answer turneth away wrath, assuredly an injunction to keep cool to an angry man conduceth to a precisely opposite result. If Carhayes had been enraged before, his fury now rose to white heat.

"You infernal old scoundrel!" he roared. "Don't I tell you I have spoored the sheep right bang into your kraal? They are here now, I tell you; here now. And you try to put me off with your usual Kafir lies and shuffling." And shaking with fury he darted forth his hand, which still held the heavy rhinoceros hide *sjambok*, as though he would have struck the chief then and there. But Nteya did not move.

"*Hau!*" cried Hlangani, who had been a silent but attentive witness to this scene. "*Hau!* Thus it is that the chiefs of the Amaxosa are trampled on by these *abelúngu* (whites). Are we men, I say? Are we men?" And the eyes of the savage flashed with terrible meaning as he waved his hand in the direction of the foolhardy Englishman.

Thus was the spark applied to the dry tinder. The crowd surged forward. A dozen sinewy hands gripped the bridle, and in a moment Carhayes was flung violently to the earth.

Stunned, half-senseless he lay. Assegais flashed in the firelight. It seemed that the unfortunate settler's hours were numbered. Another moment and a score of bright blades would be buried in his body.

But a stern and peremptory mandate from the chief arrested each impending stroke.

"Stop, my children!" cried Nteya, standing over the prostrate man and extending his arms as though to ward off the deadly blows. "Stop, my children! I, your chief; I, your father, command it. Would you play into the hands of your enemies? Be wise, I say. Be wise in time."

Sullenly the crowd fell back. With weapons still uplifted, with eyes hanging hungrily upon their chief's face, like tigers balked momentarily of their prey, the warriors paused. And the dull, brooding glare of the signal fire flashing aloft upon the hilltop fell redly upon that fierce and threatening sea of figures standing over the prostrate body of their hated and now helpless enemy. But the word of a Kafir chief is law to his followers. There was no disputing that decisive mandate.

"Rise, Umlilwane," went on Nteya. "Rise, and go in peace. In the evening, when the blood is heated, it is not well to provoke strife by angry words. In the morning, when heads are cool, return here and talk. If your sheep are here, they shall be restored to you. Now go, while it is yet safe."

Carhayes, still half-stunned by the violence of his fall, staggered to his feet.

"If they are here!" he repeated sullenly. "Damn it, they *are* here!" he blazed forth in a fresh access of wrath. Then catching the malevolent glance of Hlangani, and becoming alive to the very sinister and menacing expression on the countenances of the other Kafirs, even he began to realise that some degree of prudence was desirable, not to say essential. "Well, well, it's the old trick again, but I suppose our turn will come soon," he growled, as he proceeded to mount his horse.

The crowd parted to make way for him, and amid ominous mutterings and an unpleasantly suggestive shaking of weapons towards him, he rode away as he had come. None followed him. The chief's eye was upon his receding figure. The chief's "word" had been given. But even protected by that safe conduct, he would be wise to put as much space as possible between himself and that sullen and warlike gathering, and that, too, with the greatest despatch.

None followed him—at the moment. But Hlangani mixed unperceived among the crowd, whispering a word here and a word there. And soon, by twos and threes, a number of armed savages stole silently forth into the night, moving swiftly upon the retreating horseman's track.

Chapter Eight.

"On the Rock they Scorch, like a Drop of Fire."

"What are they really doing over there, do you suppose, Eustace?" said Eanswyth anxiously, as they regained the house. The thunder of the wild war-dance floated across the intervening miles of space, and the misty glare of many fires luridly outlined the distant mountain slopes. The position was sufficiently terrifying to any woman alone there save for one male protector, with hundreds of excited and now hostile savages performing their weird and clamourous war rites but a few miles away.

"I'm afraid there's no mistake about it; they are holding a big war-dance," was the reply. "But it's nothing new. This sort of fun has been going on at the different kraals for the last month. It's only because we are, so to say, next door to Nteya's location that we hear it to-night at all."

"But Nteya is such a good old man," said Eanswyth. "Surely he wouldn't harm us. Surely he wouldn't join in any rising."

"You are correct in your first idea, in the second, not. We are rapidly making such a hash of affairs *in re* Kreli and the Fingoes over in the Transkei, that we are simply laying the train for a war with the whole Amaxosa race. How can Nteya, or any other subordinate chief, refuse to join when called upon by Kreli, the Chief Paramount. The trouble ought to be settled before it goes any further, and my opinion is that it could be."

"You are quite a politician," said Eanswyth, with a smile. "You ought to put up for the Secretaryship for Native Affairs."

"Let us sit out here," he said, drawing up a couple of cane chairs which were always on the *stoep*. "Here is a very out-of-the-way phenomenon—one the like of which we might not witness again in a lifetime. We may as well see it out."

If Eanswyth had been rather alarmed heretofore, the other's perfect unconcern went far to reassure her. The wild, unearthly chorus echoing through the darkness—the glare of the fires, the distant, but thundrous clamour of the savage orgy, conveyed no terrors to this strong-nerved and philosophical companion of hers. He only saw in them a strange and deeply interesting experience. Seated there in the starlight, some of that unconcern communicated itself to her. A restful calm came upon her. This man beside her was as a very tower of strength. And then came over her a consciousness—not for the first time, but stronger than she had ever felt it—of how necessary his presence was to her. His calm, strong judgment had kept matters straight for a long time past. He had been the one to pour oil on the troubled waters; to allay or avert the evils which her husband's ungovernable temper and ill-judged violence had thickly gathered around them. Now, as he sat there beside her calmly contemplating the sufficiently appalling manifestations of that night—manifestations that would otherwise have driven her wild with terror—she was conscious of feeling hardly any fear.

And what of Eustace himself? Lucky, indeed, that his judgment was strong, his brain habitually clear and unclouded. For at that moment his mind could only be compared to the seething, misty rush of a whirlpool. He could see her face in the starlight—even the lustrous glow of the great eyes—could mark the clear outline or the delicate profile turned half away from him. He was alone with her in the sweet, soft African night—alone with her—her sole protector, amid the brooding peril that threatened. A silence had fallen between them. His love—his concealed and hopeless love for her overcame him. He could not command words—not even voice, for the molten, raging fires of passion which consumed him as he sat there. His hand clenched the arm of his cane chair—a jagged nail, which protruded, lacerating it nearly to the bone—still he felt nothing of physical pain—mind triumphed.

Yes, the anguish of his mind was so intense as to be akin to physical pain. Why could they not be thus together always? They could, but for one life. One life only, between him and such bliss that the whole world should be a bright and golden paradise! One life! A legion of fiends seemed to wrestle within the man's raging soul. "One life!" they echoed in jibbering, gnashing chorus. "One life!" they seemed to shriek aloud in his brain. "What more easily snapped than the cord of a life?"

The tumultuous thunder of the fierce war-dance sounded louder and louder upon the night—the glare of the distant fires reddened, and then glowed forth afresh. What if Tom Carhayes had come upon the spoor of his missing sheep—and in his blind rage had followed it right into Nteya's location? Might he not as well walk straight into a den of lions? The savage Gaikas, wound up to the highest pitch of bloodthirsty excitement, would at such a time be hardly less dangerous than so many beasts of prey. Even at that very moment the cord of that one life might be snapped.

Suddenly a great tongue of flame shot up into the night, then another and another. From a hilltop the red and threatening beacons flashed forth their message of hate and defiance. The distant tumult of the savage orgy had ceased. A weird and brooding silence lay upon the surrounding country.

"Oh, what does it mean? What does it all mean?" cried Eanswyth starting up from her chair. Her face was white with fear—her dilated eyes, gazing forth upon the gushing fires, were wild and horror-stricken. Eustace, standing there at her side, could hardly restrain himself from throwing his arms around her and pouring out a passionate storm of comforting, loving words. Yet she belonged to another man—was bound to him until death should them part. But what if death had already parted them? What if she were so bound no longer? he thought with a fierce, wild yearning that had in it something of the murderer's fell purpose, as he strained his gaze upon the wild signals of savage hostility.

"Don't be frightened, Eanswyth," he said reassuringly, but in a voice from which even he could not banish every trace of emotion. "You shall come to no harm to-night, dear, take my word for it. To-morrow, though, we must take you to some safer place than this is likely to prove for the next few days."

She made no answer. He had drawn his arm through hers and the strong, reassuring touch seemed to dispel her fears. It seemed to him that she leaned upon him, as though for physical support no less than for mental. Thus they stood, their figures silhouetted in the dull red glow. Thus they stood, the face of the one stormy with conflicting emotions—that of the other calm, restful, safe in that firm protecting companionship. Thus they stood, and to one of these two that isolated position in the midst of a brooding peril represented the sweetest, most ecstatic moment that life had ever afforded. And still upon the distant hilltops, gushing redly upward into the velvety darkness, the war-fires of the savages gleamed and burned.

"We had better go in now," said Eustace, after a while, when the flaming beacons had at length burnt low. "You must be tired to death by this time, and it won't do to sit out here all night. You must have some rest."

"I will try," she answered. "Do you know, Eustace, there is a something about you that seems to put everything right. I am not in the least frightened now."

There was a softness in her tone that bordered upon tenderness—a softness that was dangerous indeed to a man in his frame of mind.

"Ah! you find that, do you?" he answered, in a strained, harsh, unnatural voice. Then his utterance seemed choked. Their eyes met in the starlight—met in a long, clinging gaze—then their lips. Yet, she belonged to another man, and—a life stood between these two.

Thus to that extent Eustace Milne, the cool-headed, the philosophic, had allowed the impulse of his mad passion to overmaster him. But before he could pour forth the unrestrained torrent of words which should part them there and then forever, or bind them more closely for weal or for woe, Eanswyth suddenly wrenched herself from his close embrace. A clatter of rapidly approaching hoofs was borne upon the night.

"It's Tom!" she cried, at the same time fervently blessing the friendly darkness which concealed her burning face. "It must be Tom. What can he have been doing with himself all this time?"

"Rather! It's Tom, right enough, or what's left of him!" echoed the loud, well-known voice, as the horseman rode up to the *stoep* and flung himself from the saddle. "What's left of him," he repeated grimly. "Can't you strike a light, Eanswyth, instead of standing there staring at a man as if he had actually been cut into mince-meat by those infernal brutes, instead of having only had a very narrow escape from that same," he added testily, striding past her to enter the house, which up till now had been left in darkness for prudential reasons, lest by rendering it more conspicuous the sight might tempt their savage neighbours, in their present ugly humour, to some deed of violence and outrage.

A lamp was quickly lighted, and then a half-shriek escaped Eanswyth. For her husband presented a ghastly spectacle. He was hatless, and his thick brown beard was matted with blood, which had streamed down the side of his face from a wound in his head. One of his hands, too, was covered with blood, and his clothes were hacked and cut in several places.

"For Heaven's sake, Eanswyth, don't stand there screeching like an idiotic schoolgirl, but run and get out some grog, for I want an 'eye opener' badly, I can tell you," he burst forth with an angry stamp of the foot. "Then get some water and clean rag, and bandage me up a bit—for besides the crack on the head you see I've got at least half a dozen assegai stabs distributed about my carcase."

Pale and terrified, Eanswyth hurried away, and Carhayes, who had thrown himself on the sofa, proceeded growlingly to give an account of the rough usage he had been subjected to. He must have been stealthily followed, he said, for about half an hour after leaving Nteya's kraal he had been set upon in the darkness by a party of Kafirs. So sudden was the assault that they had succeeded in snatching his gun away from him before he could use it. A blow on the head with a kerrie—a whack which would have floored a weaker man—he parenthesised grimly and with ill-concealed pride—having failed to knock him off his horse, the savages endeavoured to stab him with their assegais—and in fact had wounded him in several places. Fortunately for him they had not succeeded in seizing his bridle, or at any rate in retaining hold of it, or his doom would have been sealed.

"The chap who tried it on dropped under my stirrup-iron," explained Carhayes. "I 'downed' him, by the living Jingo! He'll never kick again, I do believe. That scoundrel Nteya promised I shouldn't be molested, the living dog! There he was, the old *schelm*, he and our friend of to-day, Hlangani—and Matanzima, old Sandili's son, and Sivuléle, and a lot of them, haranguing the rest. They mean war. There couldn't have been less than six or seven hundred of them—all holding a big war-dance, got up in their feathers and fal-lals. What do you think of that, Eustace? And in I went bang into the very thick of them."

"I knew it would come to this one of these days, Tom," said Eanswyth, who now reappeared with the necessary refreshment, and water and towels for dressing his wounds.

"Of course you did," retorted her husband, with a savage snarl. "You wouldn't be a woman if you didn't, my dear. 'I told you so,' 'I *told* you so,'—isn't that a woman's invariable parrot cry. Instead of 'telling me so,' suppose you set to work and see what you can do for a fellow. Eh?"

Eustace turned away to conceal the white fury that was blasting him. Why had the Kafirs done things by halves? Why had they not completed their work and rid the earth of a coarse-minded brute who simply encumbered it. From that moment he hated his cousin with a secret and bitter hatred. And this was the life that stood between him and—Paradise.

Tom Carhayes was indeed in a vile humour—not on account of the wounds he had received, ugly as some of them were; for he was not lacking in brute courage or endurance. But his wrath burnt hot against the insolent daring of his assailants, who had presumed to attack him, who had, moreover, done so treacherously, had robbed him of his gun, as well as of a number of sheep, and had added insult to injury by laughing in his face when he asked for redress.

"I'll be even with them. I will, by the living Jingo!" he snarled as he sat sipping his brandy and water—while Eanswyth, still pale and agitated from the various and stirring events of the night, bathed his wounds with rather trembling fingers. "I'll ride into Komgha to-morrow and have the whole lot arrested—especially that lying dog, Nteya. I'll go with the police myself, if only to see the old scoundrel handcuffed and hauled off to the *tronk.*"

"What on earth induced you to run your head into such a hornet's nest for the sake of a few sheep?" said Eustace at last, thinking he ought to say something.

"Hang it, man!" was the impatient retort. "Do you suppose I was going to let these scoundrels have the laugh of me? I tell you I spoored the sheep slap into Nteya's kraal."

"Well, they seem to have the laugh of you now, anyhow—of *us,* rather," said Eustace drily, as he turned away.

Chapter Nine.

A Startling Surprise.

Nature is rarely sympathetic. The day dawned, fair and lovely, upon the night of terror and brooding peril. A few golden rays, darting horizontally upon the green, undulating slopes of the pleasant Kaffrarian landscape—then the sun shot up from the eastern skyline. Before him the white mist, which had settled down upon the land a couple of hours before dawn, now rolled back in ragged folds, leaving a sheeny carpet of silver dew—a glittering sparkle of diamond drops upon tree and shrub. Bird voices were twittering into life, in many a gladsome and varying note. Little meer-kats, startled by the tread of the horse, sat upon their haunches to listen, ere plunging, with a frisk and a scamper, into the safety of their burrows. A tortoise, his neck distended and motionless, his bright eye dilated with alarm, noiselessly shrank into the armour-plated safety of his shell, just in time to avoid probable decapitation from the falling hoof which sent his protective shell rolling half a dozen yards down the slope. But he now riding abroad thus early, had little attention to give to any such trivial sights and sounds. His mind was fully occupied.

No sleep had fallen to Eustace's lot that night. Late as it was when they retired to rest, fatiguing and exciting as the events of the day had been, there was no sleep for him. Carhayes, exasperated by the wrongs and rough treatment he had received at the hands of his barbarous neighbours, had withdrawn in a humour that was truly fearful, exacting unceasing attention from his wife and rudely repulsing his cousin's offer to take Eanswyth's place, in order that the latter might take some much-needed rest. A proceeding which lashed Eustace into a white heat of silent fury, and in his own mind it is to be feared he defined the other as a selfish, inconsiderate, and utterly irredeemable brute. Which, after all, is mere human nature. It is always the other fellow who is rather worse than a fiend. Were we in his shoes we should be something a little higher than an angel. That of course.

Unable to endure the feverish heat of restlessness that was upon him, with the first glimmer of dawn Eustace arose. One of his horses had been kept up in the stable, and having saddled the animal he issued forth. But the horse was a badly broken, vicious brute, and like the human heart was deceitful and desperately wicked, and when to the inherent villainy of his corrupt nature was superadded the tangible grievance of having to exchange a comfortable stable for the fresh, not to say raw, atmosphere of early dawn, he resolved to make himself as disagreeable as possible. He began by trying all he knew to buck the saddle off—but fruitlessly. He might, however, be more successful with the rider. So almost before the latter had deftly swung himself into his seat, down again went the perverse brute's head, and up went his back.

Plunging, rearing, kicking, squealing, the animal managed to waste five minutes and a great deal of superfluous energy, and to incur some roughish treatment into the bargain, for his rider was as firm in the saddle as a bullet in a cartridge, and moreover owned a stout crop and a pair of sharp spurs, and withal was little inclined to stand any nonsense that morning from man or beast.

But the tussle did Eustace good, in that it acted with bracing effect upon his nerves, and having reduced the refractory steed to order, he headed for the open *veldt*, not much caring where he went as long as he was moving. And now as the sun rose, flooding the air with a mellow warmth, a great elation came upon him. He still seemed to feel the pressure of those lips to his, the instinctive clinging to him in the hour of fear. He had yielded to the weird enchantment of the moment, when they two were alone in the hush of the soft, sensuous night—alone almost in the very world itself. His better judgment had failed him at the critical time—and for once his better judgment had been at fault all along—for once passion was truer than judgment. *She had returned his kiss.*

Then had come that horribly inopportune interruption. But was it inopportune? Thinking things over now he was inclined to decide that it was not. On the contrary, the ice must be broken gently at first, and this is just the result which that interruption had brought about. Again, the rough and bitter words which had followed upon it could only, to one of Eanswyth's temperament, throw out in more vivid contrast the nectar sweetness of that cup of which she had just tasted. He had not seen her since, but he soon would. He would play his cards with a master hand. By no bungling would he risk the game.

It was characteristic of the man that he could thus reason—could thus scheme and plot—that side by side with the strong whirl of his passion, he could calculate chances, map out a plan. And there was nothing sordid or gross in his thoughts of her. His love for Eanswyth was pure, even noble—elevating, perfect—but for the fact that she was bound by an indissoluble tie to another man.

Ah, but—there lay the gulf; there rose the great and invincible barrier. Yet, why invincible?

The serpent was abroad in Eden that morning. With the most sweet recollection of but a few hours back fresh in his heart, there rested within Eustace's mind a perfect glow of radiant peace. Many a word, many a tone, hardly understood at the time, came back to him now with startling clearness. For a year they had dwelt beneath the same roof, for nearly that period, for *quite* that period, as he was forced to own to himself, he had striven hard to conquer the hopeless, the unlawful love, which he plainly foresaw would sooner or later grow too strong for him. But now it had overwhelmed him, and—she had returned it. The scales had fallen from his eyes at last—from both their eyes. What a very paradise was opening out its golden glories before them. Ah, but—the barrier between them—and that barrier the life of another!

Yet what is held upon more desperately frail tenure than a life? What is more easily snapped than the cord of a life? It might have been done during the past night. By no more than a hair's-breadth had Carhayes escaped. The savages might on the next occasion strike more true. Yes, assuredly, the serpent was abroad in that Eden now—his trail a trail of blood. There was something of the murderer in Eustace Milne at that moment.

Mechanically still he rode on. He was skirting a high rounded spur. Rising from a bushy valley not many miles in front were several threads of blue smoke, and the faint sound of voices, with now and then the yelp of a dog, was borne upon the silent morning air. He had travelled some distance and now not far in front lay the outlying kraals of Nteya's location.

A set, ruthless look came over his fine face. Here were tools enough ready to his hand. Not a man among those clans of fierce and truculent barbarians but hated his cousin with a hatred begotten of years of friction. On the other hand he himself was on the best of terms with them and their rulers. A little finessing—a lavish reward, and—well, so far he shrank from deliberate and cold-blooded murder. And as though to cast off temptation before it should become too strong for him, he wrenched round his horse with a sudden jerk and rode down into a wild and bushy kloof which ran round the spur of the hill.

"Never mind!" he exclaimed half aloud. "Never mind! We shall have a big war on our hands directly. Hurrah for war, and its glorious chances!—Pincher, you fool, what the deuce is the matter with you?"

For the horse had suddenly stopped short. With his ears cocked forward he stood, snorting violently, trembling and backing. Then with a frantic plunge he endeavoured to turn and bolt. But his master's hand and his master's will were strong enough to defeat this effort. At the same time his master's eye became alive to the cause of alarm.

Issuing from the shade of the mimosa trees, seeming to rise out of the tangle of long, coarse herbage, were a number of red, sinuous forms. The ochre-smeared bodies, the gleaming assegai blades, the brawny, muscular limbs still bedecked with the barbarous and fantastic adornments of the night's martial orgy, the savage and threatening aspect of the grim, scowling countenances looked formidable enough, not merely to scare the horse, but to strike dismay into the heart of the rider, remembering the critical state of the times.

"Stop!" cried one of the Kafirs peremptorily. "Come no farther, white man!"

With a rapid movement two of them advanced as if to seize his bridle.

"Stop yourselves!" cried Eustace decisively, covering the pair with a revolver.

So determined was his mien, and withal so cool and commanding, that the savages paused irresolute. A quick ejaculation rose from the whole party. There was a flash and a glitter. A score of assegais were poised ready for a fling. Assailants and assailed were barely a dozen yards apart. It was a critical moment for Eustace Milne. His life hung upon a hair.

Suddenly every weapon was lowered—in obedience to a word spoken by a tall Kafir who at that moment emerged from the bush. Then Eustace knew the crisis was past. He, too, lowered his weapon.

"What does this mean, Ncandúku?" he said, addressing the new arrival. "Why do your people make war upon me? We are not at war."

"*Au*!" ejaculated several of the Kafirs, bringing their hands to their faces as if to hide the sarcastic grin evoked by this remark. He addressed shrugged his shoulders.

"Fear nothing, Ixeshane," (The Deliberate) he replied, with a half-amused smile. "No harm will be done *you*. Fear nothing."

The slight emphasis on the "you" did not escape Eustace's quick ear, coming as it did so close upon his recent train of thought.

"Why should I fear?" he said. "I see before me Ncandúku, the brother of Nteya, my friend—both my friends, both chiefs of the House of Gaika. I see before me, I say, Ncandúku, my friend, whom I know. I see before me also a number of men, fully armed, whom I do not know."

"*Hau*!" exclaimed the whole body of Kafirs, who, bending forwards, had been eagerly taking in every word of this address.

"These armed men," he continued, "have just threatened my life. Yet, I fear nothing. Look!"

He raised the revolver, which he now held by the barrel. In a twinkling he threw open the breech and emptied the cartridges into his hand. Another emphatic murmur rose from the Kafirs at this strange move.

"Look!" he went on, holding out the empty weapon towards them in one hand, and the half dozen cartridges in the other. "You are more than twenty men—armed. I am but one man—unarmed. Do I fear anything?"

Again a hum went round the party—this time of admiration—respect. Eustace had played a bold—a foolhardy stroke. But he knew his men.

"*Whau*, Ixeshane!" exclaimed Ncanduku. "You are a bold man. It is good that I have seen you this morning. Now, if you are going home, nobody will interfere with you."

"I am in no hurry, Ncandúku," replied Eustace, who, for purposes of his own, chose to ignore this hint. "It is a long while since I have seen you, and many things have happened in that time. We will sit down and hold a little *indaba*." (Talk.)

So saying, he dismounted, and flinging his bridle over a bush, he walked at least a dozen yards from the horse and deliberately seated himself in the shade, thus completely placing himself in the power of the savages. He was joined by Ncandúku and two or three more. The other Kafirs sank down into a squatting posture where they were.

"First we will smoke," he said, handing his pouch to the Gaika chief. "Though I fear the contents won't go very far among all our friends here."

Chapter Ten.

A Mutual Warning.

It may not here be out of place to offer a word of explanation as to the extraordinarily cordial relations existing between Eustace Milne and his barbarian neighbours. A student of nature all the world over, he had rejoiced in finding ready to his hand so promising a subject as this fine race of savages, dwelling in close proximity to, and indeed in and among, the abodes of the white colonists, and instead of learning to look upon the Kafirs as so many more or less troublesome and indifferent farm servants, actual stock-lifters and potential foemen, he had started by recognising their many good qualities and resolving to make a complete study of the race and its characteristics. And this he had effected, with the thoroughness which marked everything he undertook. A quick linguist, he soon mastered the rather difficult, but melodious and expressive Xosa tongue, in which long and frequent conversations with its speakers had by this time rendered him nearly perfect; a man of keen intellect, he could hold his own in argument with any of these people, who, on subjects within the scope of their acquaintance, are about the shrewdest debaters in the world. His cool deliberation of speech and soundness of judgment commanded their abundant respect, and the friendly and disinterested feeling which he invariably evinced towards them being once understood and appreciated, a very genuine liking sprang up on both sides.

Of course all this did not pass unnoticed by his white acquaintances and neighbours—who were wont to look upon him as an eccentricity in consequence, and to chaff him a good deal about his "blanket friends," or ask him when he expected to be in the Cabinet as Secretary for Native Affairs. A few of the more ill-natured would sneer occasionally, his cousin among the latter. But Eustace Milne could take chaff with perfect equanimity, and as for the approval or disapproval of anybody he regarded it not one whit.

Stay—of anybody? Yes—of one.

And that approval he had gained to the full. Eanswyth, watching her cousin during the year that he had been living with them, had felt her regard and respect for him deepen more and more. Many a time had his judgment and tact availed to settle matters of serious difficulty and, of late, actual peril, brought about by the hot-headed imperiousness of her husband in his dealings with the natives. Living a year beneath the same roof with anybody in ordinary work-a-day intercourse affords the best possible opportunity of studying the character of that person. Eanswyth, we say, had so studied the character of her husband's cousin and had pronounced it well-nigh flawless. But of this more elsewhere.

"Who are those people, Ncanduku?" said Eustace, after a few preliminary puffs in silence. "Except yourself and Sikuni here, they are all strangers to me. I do not seem to know one of their faces."

The chief shrugged his shoulders, emitting a thick puff of smoke from his bearded lips.

"They are strangers," he answered. "They are Ama-Gcaléka, and are returning to their own country across the Kei. They have been visiting some of their friends at Nteya's kraal."

"But why are they all so heavily armed? We are not at war."

"*Whau*, Ixeshane! You know there is trouble just now with the Amafengu (Fingoes). These men might be molested on their way back to their own country. They are afraid, so they go armed."

"Who are they afraid of? Not the Amafengu, their dogs? Why should they go armed and travel in such strength?"

The chief fixed his glance upon his interlocutor's face, and there was a merry twinkle in his eye as he turned away again.

"A man is not afraid of one dog, Ixeshane, nor yet of two," he replied. "But if a hundred set upon him, he must kill them or be killed himself."

Eustace uttered a murmur of assent. Then after a pause he said:

"To travel in a strong party like that in these times is not wise. What if these Gcalékas were to fall in with a Police patrol—would there not surely be a fight? That might bring on a war. I am a peaceable man. Everybody is not. What if they had met a less peaceable man than myself, and threatened him as they did me? There would have been a fight and the white man might have been killed—for what can one man do against twenty?"

"He need not have been killed—only frightened," struck in the other Kafir, Sikuni.

"Some men are easier killed than frightened," rejoined Eustace. "Last night some people from Nteya's kraal attacked my brother, (The term 'brother' is often colloquially used among Kafirs to designate other degrees of relationship) stole his gun, and tried to kill him. But they did not frighten him."

In spite of the conventional exclamation of astonishment which arose from his hearers, Eustace was perfectly well aware that this was no news to them.

"That is bad news," said Ncandúku, with well-feigned concern. "But it may not have been done by any of our people, Ixeshane. There may have been some Fingo dogs wandering about the land, who have done this thing in order that the English may blame us for it."

It was now Eustace's turn to smile.

"Does a dog wander to the mouth of a den of lions?" he said, keenly enjoying the notion of turning the tables. "Will a few Fingoes attack a guest of Nteya's within the very light of the fires of the Gaika location?"

"Your brother, Umlilwane, is too hot-headed," answered the chief, forced to shift his ground. "Yet he is not a young man. Our young men, too, are hot-headed at times and escape from under the controlling eye of the chiefs. But Nteya will surely punish those who have done this thing."

"Let your friends proceed on their way, Ncandúku," said Eustace suddenly, and in a low tone. "I would speak with you alone."

The chief assented, and at a word from him the Gcalékas rose to their feet and gathered up their weapons. With a respectful salute to the white man they filed off into the bush, and soon the faint rattle of assegai hafts and the deep bass hum of their voices faded into silence.

"Now we are alone," began Eustace after a pause. "We are friends, Ncandúku, and can talk freely. If there is trouble between the Gcalékas and the Fingoes, surely Kreli is able to take care of his own interests. Why, then, should the Gaikas have lighted the war-fires, have danced the war-dance? The quarrel is not theirs."

"The wrongs of the Paramount Chief are the wrongs of the whole Xosa race," answered the Kafir. "See now. We love not your brother, Umlilwane. Yet, tell him to collect his flocks and his herds and to leave, to depart into a quieter country, and that speedily; for the land will soon be dead." (Native idiom for war.)

"And what if he refuses?"

"Then he, too, will soon be dead."

For some minutes Eustace kept silence. The Kafir's remark had added fuel to the fire which was burning within his heart. It seemed a direct answer to lurid unspoken thoughts which had been surging through his mind at the time of his surprise by the at first hostile party.

"Umlilwane is an obstinate man," he said at length. "What if he laughs at the warning?"

"When a man sits inside his house and laughs while his house is burning, what happens to him, Ixeshane?"

"He stands a fair chance of being burnt too. But listen, Ncanduku. You have no quarrel against the *Inkosikazi*. (Literally Chieftainess. In this instance 'lady.') Surely not a man of the House of Gaika would harm her!"

The chief shook his head with a troubled expression.

"Let her go, too!" he said emphatically. "Let her go, too, and that as soon as possible. When the red wave of war is rolling over the land, there is no place where the delicate feet of white women may stand dry. We are friends, Ixeshane. For your sake, and for that of the *Inkosikazi*, tell Umlilwane to gather together his cattle and to go."

"We are friends, indeed, Ncanduku. But how long can we be so? If war breaks out between our people how can I sit still? I cannot. I must fight—must fight for my own race, and in defence of our property. How, then, can we remain friends?"

"In war-time every man must do his duty," answered the Gaika. "He must obey the word of his chief and fight for his race and colour."

"Truly spoken and well understood. And now a warning for a warning. If I had the ears of your chiefs and *amapakati* (Councillors) this is what I should say: Do not be drawn into this war. Let the Gcalékas fight out their own quarrel. They stand upon wholly different ground. If they are vanquished—as, of course, they will be in the long run—the Government will show them mercy, will treat them as a conquered people. But you, and the other tribes within the colonial border, are British subjects. Queen Victoria is your chief, not Kreli, not Sandili, not Seyolo, not Ndimba—no man of the House of Gaika or Hlambi, but the White Queen. If you make war upon the Colony the Government will treat you as criminals, not as a conquered people, but as rebels against the Queen, your chief. You will be shown no mercy. Your chiefs will very likely be hung and your fighting men will be sent to the convict prisons for many a long year. That when you are beaten. And how long can you carry on the war? Things are not as they were. The country is not as it was. Think of the number of soldiers that will be sent against you; of the police; of the settlers, who will turn out to a man—all armed with the best breechloaders, mind. And what sort of weapons have you? A few old muzzle loaders more dangerous to the shooter than to his mark. What can you do with these and your assegais against people armed with the best rifles in the world? I am indeed your friend, Ncanduku, and the friend of your race. Let my warning sink deep in your mind, and carry it to the chiefs. Let them be wise in time."

"The words of Ixeshane are always the words of wisdom," said the Kafir, rising in obedience to the other's example. "But the young men are turbulent. They will not listen to the counsels of their elders. The cloud grows darker every day. I see no light," he added, courteously holding the stirrup for Eustace to mount, "Go in peace, Ixeshane, and remember my warning."

And gathering up his assegais the chief disappeared among the trees, following the direction taken by the larger party.

Chapter Eleven.

"The Tail Wags the Dog."

Eustace had plenty to occupy his thoughts during his homeward ride. The emphatic warning of the Gaika chief was not to be set aside lightly. That Ncandúku knew more than he chose to say was evident. He had spoken out very plainly for one of his race, who dearly love veiled hints and beating around the bush. Still there was more behind.

Especially did the chief's perturbation when Eanswyth was referred to strike him as ominous to the last degree. Even in war-time there are few instances of Kafirs seriously maltreating white women, and Eanswyth was well liked by such of her dusky neighbours as she had come in contact with. Yet in the present case so thoroughly hated was her husband that it was conceivable they might even strike at him through her.

Why had Carhayes not fallen in with the armed party instead of himself, thought Eustace bitterly. That would have cut the knot of the difficulty in a trice. They would not have spared him so readily. They were Gcalékas, Hlangani's tribesmen. Hlangani's wound would have been avenged, and Eanswyth would by this time be free.

Very fair and peaceful was the aspect of the farm as the last rise brought it full into the horseman's view. The bleating of sheep, mellowed by distance, as the flocks streamed forth white upon the green of the *veldt*, and the lowing of cattle, floated upon the rich morning air—together with the sound of voices and laughter from the picturesque group of native huts where the farm servants dwelt. Doves cooed softly, flitting among the sprays of mimosa fringing the mealie lands; and upon the surface of the dam there was a shimmer of silver light. All seemed peaceful—happy—prosperous; yet over all brooded the red cloud of war.

Eustace felt his pulses quicken and his heart stir as he strained his eyes upon the house, to catch maybe the flutter of a light dress in the veranda. Many a morning had he thus returned from a ride without so much as a heartstirring. Yet now it was different. The ice had been broken. A new light had been let in—a sweet new light, glowing around his path like a ray of Paradise. They understood each other at last.

Yet did they? How would she receive him—how greet him after the disclosure of last night? Would she have thought better of it? For the first time in his life he felt his confidence fail him.

"Hallo, Eustace! Thought you had trekked off somewhere for the day," growled Carhayes, meeting him in the doorway. "Been looking up some of your blanket friends?"

"Where are you off to yourself, Tom?" was the reply. For the other was got up in riding boots and breeches, as if for a journey.

"To Komgha—I'm going over to lay an information against Nteya. I'll have the old *schelm* in the *tronk* by to-night."

"Not much to be taken by that, is there? Just come this way a minute, will you? I've heard something you may as well know."

With a mutter and a growl Carhayes joined him outside. In a few words Eustace conveyed to him Ncanduku's warning. It was received characteristically—with a shout of scornful laughter.

"Gammon, my dear chap. I never funked a nigger yet and I never will. And, I say. You'd better take a ride round presently and look after the sheep. I've been obliged to put on Josáne's small boy in Goníwe's place, and he may not be up to the mark. I daresay I'll be back before dark."

"Well, the sheep will have to take their chance, Tom. I'm not going out of call of the homestead while Eanswyth is left here alone."

"Bosh!" returned Carhayes. "She don't mind. Has she not been left alone here scores of times? However, do as you like. I must be off."

They had been walking towards the stable during this conversation. Carhayes led forth his horse, mounted, and rode away. Eustace put up his, and having cut up a couple of bundles of oat-hay—for they were short of hands—took his way to the house.

He had warned his cousin and his warning had been scouted. He had struggled with a temptation not to warn him, but now it came to the same thing, and at any rate his own hands were clean. The journey to Komgha was long, and in these times for a man so hated as Tom Carhayes, might not be altogether safe, especially towards dusk. Well, he had been warned.

Eustace had purposely taken time over attending to his horse. Even his strong nerves needed a little getting in hand before he should meet Eanswyth that morning; even his pulses beat quicker as he drew near the house. Most men would have been eager to get it over; would have blundered it over. Not so this one. Not without reason had the Kafirs nicknamed him "Ixeshane"— the Deliberate.

Eanswyth rose from the table as he entered. Breakfast was over, and Tom Carhayes, with characteristic impulsiveness, had started off upon his journey with a rush, as we have seen. Thus once more these two were alone together, not amid the romantic witchery of the southern night, but in the full broad light of day.

Well, and then? Had they not similarly been together alone countless times during the past year? Yes, but now it was different—widely different. The ice had been broken between them.

Still, one would hardly have suspected it. Eanswyth was perfectly calm and composed. There was a tired look upon the sweet face, and dark circles under the beautiful eyes as if their owner had slept but little. Otherwise both her tone and manner were free from any trace of confusion.

"I have put your breakfast to the kitchen fire to keep warm, Eustace," she said. "Well, what adventures have you met with in the *veldt* this morning?"

"First of all, how good of you. Secondly—leaving my adventures in abeyance for the present—did you succeed in getting any rest?"

He was looking straight at her. There was a latent caress in his glance—in his tone.

"Not much," she answered, leaving the room for a moment in order to fetch the hot dish above referred to. "It was a trying sort of a night for us all, wasn't it?" she resumed as she returned. "And now Tom must needs go rushing off again on a fool's errand."

"Never mind Tom. A little blood-letting seems good for him rather than otherwise," said Eustace, with a dash of bitterness. "About yourself. I don't believe you have closed your eyes this night through. If you won't take care of yourself, other people must do so for you. Presently I am going to sling the hammock under the trees and you shall have a right royal siesta."

His hand had prisoned hers as she stood over him arranging the plates and dishes. A faint colour came into her face, and she made a movement to withdraw it. The attempt, however, was a feeble one.

"I think we are a pair of very foolish people," she said, with a laugh whose sadness almost conveyed the idea of a sob.

"Perhaps so," he rejoined, pressing the hand he held to his cheek a moment, ere releasing it. "What would life be worth without its foolishness?"

For a few moments neither spoke. Eanswyth was busying herself arranging some of the things in the room, adjusting an ornament here, dusting one there. Eustace ate his breakfast in silence, tried to, rather, for it seemed to him at times as if he could not eat at all. The attempt seemed to choke him. His thoughts, his feelings, were in a whirl. Here were they two alone together, with the whole day before them, and yet there seemed to have arisen something in the nature of a barrier between them.

A barrier, however, which it would not be difficult to overthrow, his unerring judgment told him; yet he fought hard with himself not to lose his self-control. He noted the refined grace of every movement as she busied herself about the room—the thoroughbred poise of the stately head, the sheen of light upon the rich hair. All this ought to belong to him—did belong to him. Yet he fought hard with himself, for he read in that brave, beautiful face an appeal, mute but eloquent—an appeal to him to spare her.

A rap at the door startled him—startled them both. What if it was some neighbour who had ridden over to pay them a visit, thought Eustace with dismay—some confounded bore who would be likely to remain the best part of the day? But it was only old Josáne, the cattle-herd. His master had told him to look in presently and ask for some tobacco, which he had been promised.

"I'll go round to the storeroom and get it for him," said Eanswyth. "You go on with your breakfast, Eustace."

"No, I'll go. I've done anyhow. Besides, I want to speak to him."

Followed by the old Kafir, Eustace unlocked the storeroom—a dark, cool chamber forming part of an outbuilding. The carcase of a sheep, freshly killed that morning, dangled from a beam. Piles of *reims*, emitting a salt, rancid odour—kegs of sheep-dip, huge rolls of Boer tobacco, bundles of yoke-skeys, and a dozen other things requisite to the details of farm work were stowed around or disposed on shelves. On one side was a grindstone and a carpenter's bench. Eustace cut off a liberal length from one of the rolls of tobacco and gave it to the old Kafir. Then he filled his own pipe.

"Josane?"

"*Nkose!*"

"You are no fool, Josane. You have lived a good many years, and your head is nearly as snow-sprinkled as the summit of the Great Winterberg in the autumn. What do you thing of last night's performance over yonder?"

The old man's shrewd countenance melted into a slight smile and he shook his head.

"The Gaikas are fools," he replied. "They have no quarrel with the English, yet they are clamouring for war. Their country is fertile and well watered, yet they want to throw it away with both hands. They are mad."

"Will they fight, Josane?"

"*Au!* Who can say for certain," said the old man with an expressive shrug of the shoulders. "Yet, was ever such a thing seen? The dog wags his tail. But in this case it is the tail that wags the dog."

"How so, Josane?"

"The chiefs of the Gaikas do not wish for war. The old men do not wish for it. But the young men—the boys—are eager for it. The women taunt them, they say; tell them they have forgotten how to be warriors. So the boys and the women clamour for war, and the chiefs and the old men give way. Thus the tail wags the dog. *Hau*!"

"And what about the Gcalékas?"

"The Gcalékas? It is this way, *Nkose*. If you shut up two bulls alone in the same kraal, if you put two scorpions into a mealie stamp, how long will it be before they fight? So it is with the Gcalékas and the Fingoes. The land is not large enough for both. The Gcalékas are ready for war."

"And Kreli?"

"The Great Chief is in one of his red moods," answered Josane, in a different tone to that which he had employed when speaking of the Gaikas. "He has a powerful witch-doctress. I know her. Was I not 'smelt out' by her? Was I not 'eaten up' at her 'word'? The toad! The impostor! The jackal cat! The slimy fish! I know her. Ha!"

(Eaten up: Idiom for the total sequestration of a person's possessions.)

The old man's eyes glared and his tone rose to one of fierce excitement at the recollection of his wrongs. Eustace, accustomed to study his fellow-men, took careful note of the circumstance. Strange things happened. It might serve him in good stead one day.

"The Gcalékas will fight," went on Josane. "Perhaps they are fighting now. Perhaps the *Baas* will have some news to bring when he returns from Komgha. The telegraph is quick, but the voice of the bird in the air is quicker," he added with a meaning smile, which convinced his listener that he knew a great deal more than he chose to say.

"The fire stick is even now in the thatch," went on the Kafir, after a few more puffs at his pipe. "There is a herald from the Great Chief among the Gaika kraals."

"Hlangani?"

"Hlangani. The Gaikas are listening to his 'word,' and are lighting the war-fires. If he can obtain the ear of Sandili, his work is done. *Whau*, Ixeshane," he went on, slipping into the familiar name in his excitement. "You English are very weak people. You ought to arrest Matanzima, and several others, and send a strong Resident to Sandili, who should always keep his ear."

"We can't do that, Josane. There are wheels within wheels and a power behind the throne. Well, we shall see what happens," he went on, rising as a hint to the other to depart.

He did not choose, for reasons of his own, to ask Josane direct how imminent the danger might be. To do so would be ever so slightly to impair his own *prestige*. But in his own judgment he decided that the sooner they set their affairs in order against the coming storm the better.

Chapter Twelve.

"Ah, Love, but a Day!"

Pondering over what the old Kafir had said, Eustace busied himself over two or three odd jobs. Then, returning to the storeroom, he filled up a large measure of mealies and went to the house.

"I'm going down to the ostrich camp, Eanswyth. Do you feel inclined to stroll that far, or are you too tired?"

"Yes and no. I think it will do me good."

Flinging on a wide straw hat she joined him in the doorway. The ostrich camp was only a couple of hundred yards from the house, and at sight of them the great birds came shambling down to the fence, the truculent male having laid aside his aggressive ferocity for the occasion, as he condescended, with sullen and lordly air, to allow himself to be fed, though even then the quarrelsome disposition of the creature would find vent every now and again in a savage hiss, accompanied by a sudden and treacherous kick aimed at his timid consort whenever the latter ventured within the very outskirts of the mealies thrown down. But no sooner had the last grain disappeared than the worst instincts of the aggressive bully were all to the fore again, and the huge biped, rearing himself up to his full height, his jetty coat and snowy wing-feathers making a brave show, challenged his benefactors forthwith, rolling his fiery eyes as though longing to behold them in front of him with no protecting fence between.

"Of all the ungracious, not to say ungrateful, scoundrels disfiguring God's earth, I believe a cock ostrich is the very worst," remarked Eustace. "He is, if possible, worse in that line than the British loafer, for even the latter won't always open his Billingsgate upon you until he has fairly assimilated the gin with which your ill-judged dole 'to save him from starving' has warmed his gullet. But this brute would willingly kick you into smithereens, while you were in the very act of feeding him."

Eanswyth laughed.

"What strange ideas you have got, Eustace. Now I wonder to how many people any such notion as that would have occurred."

"Have I? I am often told so, so I suppose I must have. But the grand majority of people never think themselves, consequently when they happen upon anybody who does they gaze upon him with unmitigated astonishment as a strange and startling product of some unknown state of existence."

"Thank you," retorted Eanswyth with a laugh. "That's a little hard on me. As I made the remark, of course I am included in the grand majority which doesn't think."

"I have a very great mind to treat that observation with the silence it deserves. It is a ridiculous observation. Isn't it?"

"Perhaps it is," she acquiesced softly, in a tone that was half a sigh, not so much on account of the actual burden of the conversation, as an involuntary outburst of the dangerous, because too tender, undercurrent of her thoughts. And of those two walking there side by side in the radiant sunshine—outwardly so tranquilly, so peacefully, inwardly so blissfully—it was hard to say which was the most fully alive to the peril of the situation. Each was conscious of the mass of molten fires raging within the thin eggshell crust; each was rigidly on guard; the one with the feminine instinct of self-preservation superadded to the sense of rectitude of a strong character; the other striving to rely upon the necessity of caution and patience enjoined by a far-seeing and habitually self-contained nature. So far, both forces were evenly matched—so far both could play into each other's hands, for mutual aid, mutual support against each other. Had there been aught of selfishness—of the mere unholy desire of possession—in this man's love, things would have been otherwise. His cool brain and consummate judgment would have given him immeasurably the advantage—in fact, the key of the whole situation. But it was not so. As we have said, that love was chivalrously pure—even noble—would have been rather elevating but for the circumstance that its indulgence meant the discounting of another man's life.

Thus they walked, side by side, in the soft and sensuous sunshine. A shimmer of heat rose from the ground. Far away over the rolling plains a few cattle and horses, dotted here and there grazing, constituted the only sign of life, and the range of wooded hills against the sky line loomed purple and misty in the golden summer haze. If ever a land seemed to enjoy the blessings of peace assuredly it was this fair land here spread out around them.

They had reached another of the ostrich camps, wherein were domiciled some eight or ten pairs of eighteen-month-old birds, which not having yet learned the extent of their power, were as tame and docile as the four-year-old male was savage and combative. Eustace had scattered the contents of his colander among them, and now the two were leaning over the gate, listlessly watching the birds feed.

"Talking of people never thinking," continued Eustace, "I don't so much wonder at that. They haven't time, I suppose, and so lose the faculty. They have enough to do to steer ahead in their own narrow little groves. But what does astonish me is that if you state an obvious fact—so obvious as to amount to a platitude—it seems to burst upon them as a kind of wild surprise, as a kind of practical joke on wheels, ready to start away down-hill and drag them with it to utter crash unless they edge away from it as far as possible. You see them turn and stare at each other, and open an amazed and gaping mouth into which you might insert a pumpkin without them being in the least aware of it."

"As for instance?" queried Eanswyth, with a smile.

"Well—as for instance. I wonder what the effect would be upon an ordinary dozen of sane people were I suddenly to propound the perfectly obvious truism that life is full of surprises. I don't wonder, at least, for I ought to know by this time. They would start by scouting the idea; ten to one they would deny the premise, and retort that life was just what we chose to make it; which is a fallacy, in that it assumes that any one atom in the human scheme is absolutely independent—firstly, of the rest of the crowd; secondly, of circumstances—in fact, is competent to boss the former and direct the latter. Which, in the words of the immortal Euclid, is absurd."

"Yet if any man is thus competent, it is yourself, Eustace."

"No," he said, shaking his head meditatively. "You are mistaken. I am certainly not independent of the action of anyone who may elect to do me a good or an ill turn. He, she, or it, has me at a disadvantage all round, for I possess the gift of foresight in a degree so limited as to be practically *nil*. As for circumstances—so far from pretending to direct them I am the mere creature of them. So are we all."

"What has started you upon this train of thought?" she asked suddenly.

"Several things. But I'll give you an instance of what I was saying just now. This morning I was surprised and surrounded by a gang of Kafirs, all armed to the teeth. Nearly all of them were on the very verge of shying their assegais bang through me, and if Ncanduku—you know him—Nteya's brother—hadn't appeared on the scene just in the very nick of time, I should have been a dead man. As it was, we sat down, had an *indaba* and a friendly smoke, and parted on the best of terms. Now, wasn't I helplessly, abjectly, the creature of circumstances—first in being molested at all—second in Ncandúku's lucky arrival?"

"Eustace! And you never told me this!"

"I told Tom—just as he was starting—and he laughed. He didn't seem to think much of it. To tell the truth, neither did I. Why—what's the matter, Eanswyth?"

Her face was deathly white. Her eyes, wide open, were dilated with horror; then they filled with tears. The next moment she was sobbing wildly—locked in his close embrace.

"Eanswyth, darling—my darling. What is it? Do not give way so! There is nothing to be alarmed about now—nothing."

His tones had sunk to a murmur of thrilling tenderness. He was showering kisses upon her lips, her brow, her eyes—upon stray tresses of soft hair which escaped beneath her hat. What had become of their attitude of guarded self-control now? Broken down, swept away at one stroke as the swollen mountain stream sweeps away the frail barricade of timber and stones which thought to dam its course—broken down before the passionate outburst of a strong nature awakened to the knowledge of itself—startled into life by the magic touch, by the full force and fury of a consciousness of real love.

"You are right," she said at last. "We must go away from here. I cannot bear that you should be exposed to such frightful peril. O Eustace! Why did we ever meet!"

Why, indeed! he thought. And the fierce, wild thrill of exultation which ran through him at the consciousness that her love was his—that for good or for ill she belonged to him—belonged to him absolutely—was dashed by the thought: How was it going to end? His clear-sighted, disciplined nature could not altogether get rid of that consideration. But clear-sighted, disciplined as it was, he could not forego that which constituted the whole joy and sweetness of living. "Sufficient for the day" must be his motto. Let the morrow take care of itself.

"Why did we ever meet?" he echoed. "Ah, does not that precisely exemplify what I was saying just now? Life is full of surprises. Surprise Number 1, when I first found *you* here at all. Number 2, when I awoke to the fact that you were stealing away my very self. And I soon did awake to that consciousness."

"You did?"

"I did. And I have been battling hard against it—against myself—against you—and your insidiously enthralling influence ever since."

His tone had become indescribably sweet and winning. If the power of the man invariably made itself felt by all with whom he was brought into contact in the affairs of everyday life, how much more was it manifested now as he poured the revelation of his long pent-up love—the love of a strong, self-contained nature which had broken bounds at last—into the ears of this woman whom he had subjugated—yes, subjugated, utterly, completely.

And what of her?

It was as though all heaven had opened before her eyes. She stood there tightly clasped in that embrace, drinking in the entrancing tenderness of those tones—hungrily devouring the straight glance of those magnetic eyes, glowing into hers. She had yielded—utterly, completely, for she was not one to do things by halves. Ah, the rapture of it!

But every medal has its obverse side. Like the stab of a sword it came home to Eanswyth. This wonderful, enthralling, beautiful love which had thrown a mystic glamour as of a radiant Paradise upon her life, had come just a trifle too late.

"O Eustace," she cried, tearing herself away from him, and yet keeping his hands clenched tightly in hers as though she would hold him at arm's length but could not. "O Eustace! my darling! How is it going to end? How?"

The very thought which had passed unspoken through his own mind.

"Dearest, think only of the present. For the future—who knows! Did we not agree just now—life is full of surprises?"

"*Au!*"

Both started. Eanswyth could not repress a little scream, while even Eustace realised that he was taken at a disadvantage, as he turned to confront the owner of the deep bass voice which had fired off the above ejaculation.

It proceeded from a tall, athletic Kafir, who, barely ten yards off, stood calmly surveying the pair. His grim and massive countenance was wreathed into an amused smile. His nearly naked body was anointed with the usual red ochre, and round the upper part of his left arm he wore a splendid ivory ring. He carried a heavy knob-kerrie and several assegais, one of which he was twisting about in easy, listless fashion in his right hand.

At sight of this extremely unwelcome, not to say formidable, apparition, Eustace's hand instinctively and with a quick movement sought the back of his hip—a movement which a Western man would thoroughly have understood. But he withdrew it—empty. For his eye, familiar with every change of the native countenance, noted that the expression of this man's face was good-humoured rather than aggressive. And withal it seemed partly familiar to him.

"Who are you—and what do you want?" he said shortly. Then as his glance fell upon a bandage wrapped round the barbarian's shoulder: "Ah. I know you—Hlangani."

"Keep your 'little gun' in your pocket, Ixeshane," said the Kafir, speaking in a tone of good-humoured banter. "I am not the man to be shot at twice. Besides, I am not *your* enemy. If I were, I could have killed you many times over already, before you saw me; could have killed you both, you and the *Inkosikazi*."

This was self-evident. Eustace, recognising it, felt rather small. He to be taken thus at a disadvantage, he, who had constituted himself Eanswyth's special protector against this very man! Yes. He felt decidedly small, but he was not going to show it.

"You speak the truth, Hlangani," he answered calmly. "You are not my enemy. No man of the race of Xosa is. But why do you come here? There is bad blood between you and the owner of this place. Surely the land is wide enough for both. Why should your pathways cross?"

"Ha! *You* say truly, Ixeshane. There *is* blood between me and the man of whom you speak. Blood—the blood of a chief of the House of Gcaléka. Ha!"

The eyes of the savage glared, and his countenance underwent a transformation almost magical in its suddenness. The smiling, good-humoured expression gave way to one of deadly hate, of a ruthless ferocity that was almost appalling to contemplate. So effective was it upon Eustace that carelessly, and as if by accident, he interposed his body between Eanswyth and the speaker, and though he made no movement, his every sense was on the alert. He was ready to draw his revolver with lightning-like rapidity at the first aggressive indication. But no such indication was manifested.

"No. You have no enemies among our people—neither you nor the *Inkosikazi*"—went on Hlangani as his countenance resumed its normal calm. "You have always been friends to us. Why are *you* not living here together as our friends and neighbours—you two, without the poison of our deadly enemy to cause ill-blood between us and you—you alone together? I would speak with you apart, Ixeshane."

Now, Eanswyth, though living side by side with the natives, was, like most colonial people, but poorly versed in the Xosa tongue. She knew a smattering of it, just sufficient for kitchen purposes, and that was all; consequently, but for a word here and there, the above dialogue was unintelligible to her. But it was otherwise with her companion. His familiarity with the language was all but complete, and not only with the language, but with all its tricks. He knew that the other was "talking dark," and his quick perception readily grasped the meaning which was intended to be conveyed. With the lurid thoughts indulged in that morning as regarded his cousin still fresh in his mind, it could hardly have been otherwise.

He hated the man: he loved the man's wife. "How is it going to end?" had been his unuttered cry just now. "How is it going to end!" she had re-echoed. Well, here was a short and easy solution ready to hand. A flush of blood surged to his face, and his heart beat fiercely under the terrible temptation thus thrown in his way. Yet so fleeting was it as scarcely to constitute a temptation at all. Now that it was put nakedly to him he could not do this thing. He could not consent to a murder—a cold-blooded, treacherous murder.

"I cannot talk with you apart, Hlangani," he answered. "I cannot leave the *Inkosikazi* standing here alone even for a few minutes."

The piercing glance of the shrewd savage had been scrutinising his face—had been reading it like a book. Upon him the terrible struggle within had not been lost.

"Consider, Ixeshane," he pursued. "What is the gift of a few dozen cows, of *two hundred cows*, when compared with the happiness of a man's lifetime? Nothing. *Is it to be? Say the word. Is it to be?*"

The barbarian's fiery eyes were fixed upon his with deep and terrible meaning. To Eustace it seemed as if the blasting glare of the Arch fiend himself shone forth from their cruel depths.

"It is *not* to be. The 'word' is No! Unmistakably and distinctly No. You understand, Hlangani?"

"*Au*! As you will, Ixeshane," replied the Kafir, with an expressive shrug of his shoulders. "See. You wear a 'charm'," referring to a curious coin which Eustace wore hanging from his watch-chain. "If you change your mind send over the 'charm' to me at Nteya's kraal this night—it shall be returned. But after to-night it may be too late. Farewell."

And flinging his blanket over his shoulder the savage turned and strode away into the *veldt*—Eustace purposely omitting to offer him a little tobacco, lest this ordinary token of good will should be construed into a sort of earnest of the dark and terrible bargain which Hlangani had proposed to him—by mere hints it is true—but still had none the less surely proposed.

Chapter Thirteen.

"...And the World is Changed."

They stood for some moments watching the receding figure of the Kafir in silence. Eanswyth was the first to break it.

"What have you been talking about all this time, Eustace? Is it any new danger that threatens us?"

"N-no. Rather the reverse if anything," and his features cleared up as if to bear out the truth of his words. "I don't see, though, why you shouldn't know it. That's the man we fell foul of in the *veldt* yesterday—you remember the affair of the white dog?"

"Oh!" and Eanswyth turned very pale.

"Now don't be alarmed, dearest. I believe he only loafed round here to try and collect some compensation."

"Is that really all, Eustace?" she went on anxiously. "You seemed very much disturbed, dear. I don't think I ever saw you look so thoroughly disturbed."

There was no perturbation left in his glance now. He took her face lovingly between his hands and kissed it again and again.

"Did you not, my sweet? Well, perhaps there has never existed such ground for it. Perhaps I have never met with so inopportune an interruption. But now, cheer up. We must make the most of this day, for a sort of instinct tells me that it is the last we shall have to ourselves, at any rate for some time to come. And now what shall we do with ourselves? Shall we go back to the house or sit here a little while and talk?"

Eanswyth was in favour of the latter plan. And, seated there in the shade of a great acacia, the rich summer morning sped by in a golden dream. The fair panorama of distant hills and wooded kloofs; the radiant sunlight upon the wide sweep of mimosa-dotted plains, shimmering into many a fantastic mirage in the glowing heat; the call of bird voices in the adjacent brake, and the continuous chirrup of crickets; the full, warm glow of the sensuous air, rich, permeating, life-giving; here indeed was a very Eden. Thus the golden morning sped swiftly by.

But how was it all to end? That was the black drop clouding the sparkling cup—that was the trail of the serpent across that sunny Eden. And yet not, for it may be that this very rift but served only to enhance the intoxicating, thrilling delights of the present—that this idyl of happiness, unlawful alike in the sight of God or man, was a hundredfold sweetened by the sad vein of undercurrent running through it—even the consciousness that it was not to last. For do we not, in the weak contrariety of our mortal natures, value a thing in exact proportion to the precariousness of our tenure!

Come good, come ill, never would either of them forget that day: short, golden, idyllic.

"Guess how long we have been sitting here!" said Eanswyth at last, with a rapid glance at her watch. "No—don't look," she added hurriedly, "I want you to *guess*."

"About half an hour, it seems. But I suppose it must be more than that."

"Exactly two hours and ten minutes."

"Two hours and ten minutes of our last peaceful day together—gone. Of our first and our last day together."

"Why do you say our last, dear?" she murmured, toying with his hair. His head lay on her lap, his blue eyes gazing up into her large grey ones.

"Because, as I told you, I have a strong inkling that way—at any rate, for some time to come. It is wholly lamentable, but, I'm afraid, inevitable."

She bent her head—her beautiful stately head—drooped her lips to his and kissed them passionately.

"Eustace, Eustace, my darling—my very life! Why do I love you like this!"

"Because you can't help it, my sweet one!" he answered, returning her kisses with an ardour equalling her own.

"Why did I give way so soon? Why did I give way at all? As you say, because I couldn't help it—because—in short, because it was *you*. You drew me out of myself—you forced me to love you, forced me to. Ah-h! and how I love you!"

The quiver in her tones would not be entirely suppressed. Even he had hardly suspected the full force of passion latent within this woman, only awaiting the magic touch to blaze forth into bright flame. And his had been the touch which had enkindled it.

"You have brought more than a Paradise into my life," he replied, his glance holding hers as he looked up into her radiant eyes. "Tell me, did you never suspect, all these months, that I only *lived* when in the halo-influence of your presence?"

"I knew it."

"You knew it?"

"Of course I did," she answered with a joyous laugh, taking his face between her hands and kissing it again. "I should have been no woman if I had not. But, I have kept my secret better than you. Yes, my secret. I have been battling against your influence far harder than you have against mine, and you have conquered." He started, and a look of something like dismay came into his face.

"If that is so, you witching enchantress, why did you not lift me out of my torment long ago," he said. "But the worst is this. Just think what opportunities we have missed, what a long time we have wasted which might have been—Heaven."

"Yet, even then, it may be better as things have turned out. My love—my star—I could die with happiness at this moment. But," and then to the quiver of joy in her voice succeeded an intonation of sadness, "but—I suppose this world does not contain a more wicked woman than myself. Tell me, Eustace," she went on, checking whatever remark he might have been about to make, "tell me what you think. Shall we not one day be called upon to suffer in tears and bitterness for this entrancingly happy flood of sunshine upon our lives now?"

"That is an odd question, and a thoroughly characteristic one," he replied slowly. "Unfortunately all the events of life, as well as the laws of Nature, go to bear out the opinions of the theologians. Everything must be paid for, and from this rule there is no escape. Everything, therefore, resolves itself into a mere question of price—e.g., Is the debt incurred worth the huge compound interest likely to be exacted upon it in the far or near future? Now apply this to the present case. Do you follow me?"

"Perfectly. If our love is wrong—wicked—we shall be called upon to suffer for it sooner or later?"

"That is precisely my meaning. I will go further. The term 'poetic justice' is, I firmly believe, more than a mere idiom. If we are doing wrong through love for each other we shall have to expiate it at some future time. We shall be made to suffer *through* each other. Now, Eanswyth, what do you say to that?"

"I say, amen. I say that the future can take care of itself, that I defy it—no—wait!—not that. But I say that if this delirious, entrancing happiness is wrong, I would rather brave torments a thousand-fold, than yield up one iota of it," she answered, her eyes beaming into his, and with a sort of proud, defiant ring in her voice, as if throwing down the gage to all power, human or divine, to come between them.

"I say the same—my life!" was his reply.

Thus the bargain was sealed—ratified. Thus was the glove hurled down for Fate to take up, if it would. The time was coming when she—when both—would remember those defiant, those deliberate words.

Not to-day, however, should any forebodings of the Future be suffered to cloud the Present. They fled, all too quickly, those short, golden hours. They melted one by one, merged into the dim glories of the past. Would the time come when those blissful hours should be conjured forth by the strong yearnings of a breaking heart, conjured forth to be lived through again and again, in the day of black and hopeless despair, when to the radiant enchantment of the Present should have succeeded the woe of a never-ending and rayless night?

But the day was with them now—idyllic, blissful—never to be forgotten as long as they two should live. Alas, that it fled!

Tom Carhayes returned that evening in high good humour. He was accompanied by another man, a neighbouring settler of the name of Hoste, a pleasant, cheery fellow, who was a frequent visitor at Anta's Kloof.

"Well, Mrs Carhayes," cried the latter, flinging his right leg over his horse's neck and sliding to the ground side-saddle fashion, "your husband has been pretty well selling up the establishment to-day. What do you think of that? Hallo, Milne. How 'do?"

"I've made a good shot this time," assented Carhayes, "I've sold off nearly three thousand of the sheep to Reid, the contractor, at a pound a head all round. What do you think of that, Eustace? And a hundred and thirty cattle, too, heifers and slaughter stock."

"H'm! Well, you know best," said Eustace. "But why this wholesale clearance, Tom?"

"Why? Why, man, haven't you heard? No, of course he hasn't. War! That's why. War, by the living Jingo! It's begun. Our fellows are over the Kei already, peppering the niggers like two o'clock."

"Or being peppered by them—which so far seems to be the more likely side of the question," struck in Hoste. "A report came into Komgha to-day that there had been a fight, and the Police had been licked. Anyhow, a lot more have been moved across the river."

"Wait till *we* get among them," chuckled Carhayes. "Eh, Hoste? We'll pay off some old scores on Jack Kafir's hide. By the Lord, won't we?"

"*Ja.* That's so. By-the-by, Mrs Carhayes, I mustn't forget my errand. The wife has picked up a cottage in Komgha, and particularly wants you to join her.

She was lucky in getting it, for by now every hole or shanty in the village is full up. There are more waggons than houses as it is, and a lot of fellows are in tents. They are going to make a big *laager* of the place."

Eanswyth looked startled. "Are things as bad as all that?" she said.

"They just are," answered Hoste. "You can't go on staying here. It isn't safe—is it, Carhayes? Everyone round here is trekking, or have already trekked. I met George Payne in Komgha to-day. Even he had cleared out from Fountains Gap, and there's no fellow laughs at the scare like he does."

"Hoste is right, Eanswyth," said Carhayes. "So you'd better roll up your traps and go back with him to-morrow. I can't go with you, because Reid is coming over to take delivery of the stock. Eustace might drive you over, if he don't mind."

Eustace did *not* mind—of that we may be sure. But although no glance passed between Eanswyth and himself, both were thinking the same thing. To the mind of each came back the words of that morning: "*A sort of instinct tells me it is the last day we shall have to ourselves for some time to come!*" And it would be.

They sat down to supper. Tom Carhayes was in tremendous spirits that evening. He breathed threatenings and slaughter against the whole of the Xosa race, chuckling gleefully over the old scores he was going to pay off upon it in the persons of its fighting men. In fact, he was as delighted over the certainty of an outbreak as if he held half a dozen fat contracts for the supply of the troops and levies.

"I'll keep a tally-stick, by Jove; and every nigger I pot I'll cut a nick," he said. "There'll be a good few notches at the end of the war! It was a first-class stroke of luck doing that deal with Reid, wasn't it, Eustace? We shall have our hands entirely free for whatever fun turns up."

Eustace agreed. He had reasons of his own for wanting to keep his hands free during the next few months—possibly, however, they were of a different nature to those entertained by his cousin.

"We can move the rest of the stock to Swaanepoel's Hoek," went on Carhayes. "Bentley will be only too glad to look after it for a consideration. Then for some real sport! Eustace, pass the grog to Hoste."

"That your Somerset East farm?" said the latter, filling his glass.

"Yes. Not a bad place, either; only too stony."

"You're a jolly lucky fellow to have a Somerset East farm to send your stock to," rejoined Hoste. "I wish I had, I know. The few sheep I have left are hardly worth looking after. There are safe to be a lot of Dutchmen in *laager* with *brandt-zick* flocks, and ours will be covered with it by the time it's all over. Same thing with cattle. Red water and lung sickness will clear them all out too."

"Well, we'll lift a lot from old Kreli to make up for it," said Carhayes. "By the way, Eustace. Talking of Kreli—he's been summoned to meet the Governor and won't go."

"H'm. Small wonder if he won't. What was the upshot of his father, Hintza, being summoned to meet the Governor?"

"Oh, you're always harping on that old string," said Carhayes impatiently. "Hang it all—as if a lot of red-blanket niggers are to be treated like civilised beings! It's ridiculous, man. They've got to do as they are told, or they must be made to."

"That's all very pretty, Tom. But the 'making' hasn't begun yet. By the time it's ended, we shall have a longish bill to pay—and a good many vacant chairs at various household tables. Fair play *is* fair play—even between our exalted selves and 'a lot of red-blanket niggers.'"

"Milne is right, Carhayes," struck in Hoste. "Milne is right so far. Kafirs have got long memories, and I, for one, don't blame old Kreli for snapping his fingers at the Governor. But I don't agree with him that we haven't treated him fairly on the whole. Hang it, what have they got to complain of?"

"I don't say they have anything in that line," said Eustace. "My remark about treating them fairly was only in answer to what Tom suggested. Still, I think it a mistake to have located the Fingoes and Gcalékas next door to each other, with a mere artificial boundary between. It was safe to produce a shindy sooner or later."

Thus the ball of conversation rolled on. Carhayes, excited over the prospect of hostilities, took a glass or two of grog more than was good for him, and waxed extremely argumentative as they adjourned to the *stoep* for an *al fresco* smoke. So he and his guest began, continued, and ended the campaign according to a great diversity of plans, each highly satisfactory to its originators and proportionately disastrous to the dark-skinned enemy.

In this conversation Eanswyth did not join. The sweet and soothing influences of the day just passed filled her mind—and all this noisy talk jarred upon her. To her also the prospect of the coming campaign was a welcome one. After the events of the last twenty-four hours to go on living as heretofore would be a terrible strain. Her newly awakened love for the one man was so overwhelming as to engender in her a proportionate feeling of aversion towards the other. It was a fearful position. The temporary separation involved by the campaign would be more than welcome. But separation from the one meant separation from the other. That was not welcome.

And that other—what if he were to fall? He was so fearless—so foolhardy and confident. What if he undertook some insane mission and was treacherously murdered?—O Heaven—what would life be without him now? And a rush of tears brimmed to her eyes at the mere thought.

Eustace, who had remained behind for a moment, to light his pipe, looked up and caught her glance.

"I suppose I had better arrange to drive you over to Komgha to-morrow?" he said, aloud and in an ordinary voice. Outside the other two were talking and arguing at a great rate.

"Yes, I would not forego that for anything," she whispered. "But—leave me now, or I shall break down. Quick! I wish it."

One glance, straight into her eyes, and he obeyed. But that glance had said enough—had said more than many words could have done.

"By the way, Tom," said Eustace, joining the pair of wranglers outside. "What about Nteya? You were going to have him run in, you know."

"So! Well, you see, it's this way: I got on that deal with Reid, first thing, and that drove the other out of my head. I had a job to find Reid, in the first place, but when you hear of a man willing to give a lumping big price for what you want to sell, that man's worth some hunting for, I can tell you. So I let Nteya slide—until we reach the Gaika location. Then I'll take it out of him, and a good many more of them too."

Next morning, shortly after sunrise, the contractor arrived to take delivery of the stock. So he and Carhayes were extremely busy, the latter too much so to be able to afford more than an off-hand and hurried farewell to his wife.

But the same held not good of his cousin and partner. Indeed one would think that Eustace had no concern whatever in the sale for all the interest he took in it. Far more concerned was he to ensure that Eanswyth had every conceivable thing that might conduce to her comfort and convenience during her journeying to and sojourn in the settlement, than to satisfy himself that Contractor Reid, a canny Scot and a knowing file at a deal, should be allowed no loop-hole for climbing down from or getting behind his bargain.

"I say, Milne," cried Hoste, while the horses were being inspanned. "It's rather slow work riding by one's self. Let's span in my horse as a leader, and drive unicorn. There's room for my saddle if we tie it on behind—and I can get in the cart with you. More sociable like. See?"

But Eustace didn't see, or rather didn't want to see. This was clearly a case of "two's company, three's a crowd."

Equally clearly was it a case wherein the third might be excused for omitting to apply the maxim.

"There's a goodish weight in the trap already," he replied dubiously. But Eanswyth struck in:

"We can make room for you, Mr Hoste. Certainly. And if we have the additional pull of your horse it will neutralise the additional weight."

Eustace said nothing. If Eanswyth's mood had undergone something of a change since last night, that was only natural, he allowed. The arrangement was not to his liking. But then, of most arrangements in this tiresome world the same held good. With which reflection, being a philosopher, he consoled himself.

There was not much sign of the disturbed state of the country during the first part of the drive. But later, as they drew nearer the settlement, an abandoned homestead—standing silent and deserted, its kraals empty and the place devoid of life, or a trek of sheep and cattle raising a cloud of dust in the distance, together with a waggon or two loaded with the families and household goods of those, like themselves, hastening from their more or less isolated positions to seek safety in numbers, spoke eloquently and with meaning. Now and again a small group of Kafirs would pass them on the road, and although unarmed, save for their ordinary kerries, there seemed a world of grim meaning in each dark face, a menace in the bold stare which did duty for the ordinarily civil, good-humoured greeting, as if the savages knew that their time was coming now.

It was a splendid day, sunny and radiant. But there was an oppressiveness in the atmosphere which portended a change, and ever and anon came a low boom of thunder. An inky cloud was rising behind the Kabousie Heights, spreading wider and wider over the plains of Kafirland. A lurid haze subdued the sunshine, as the rumble of the approaching storm drew nearer and nearer, and the blue electric flashes played around the misty hilltops where the ill-omened war-fires had gleamed two nights before. Even so, in like fashion, the brooding cloud of war swept down upon the land, darker and darker.

Chapter Fourteen.

A Curtain Secret.

The settlement of Komgha—called after an infinitesimal stream of that name—was, like most frontier townships, an utterly insignificant place. It consisted of a few straggling blocks of houses plumped down apparently without rhyme or reason in the middle of the *veldt*, which here was open and undulating. It boasted a few stores and canteens, a couple of institutions termed by courtesy "hotels," an exceedingly ugly church, and a well-kept cricket ground. To the eastward rose the Kei Hills, the only picturesque element about the place, prominent among these the flat, table-topped summit of Moordenaar's Kop, (Dutch, "Murderer's Peak") a tragical spot so named on account of the surprise and massacre of a party of officers who had incautiously ventured up there in small force during one of the previous wars. The village was virtually the headquarters of the Frontier Armed and Mounted Police, the substantial square barracks, which harboured the artillery troop of that useful force, crowning the hill nearly a mile away, and there was generally another troop or two quartered around the place. The main road from King Williamstown to the Transkeian territories ran through the village.

At the period of our story, however, there was no lack of life or stir about the normally sleepy little place, for it was in process of transformation into a huge *laager* or armed camp. Waggons were coming in from several directions—laden mostly with the families and household goods of fleeing settlers, and the sharp crack of whips and the harsh yells of their drivers rose high above the general turmoil. Men were bustling to and fro, bent upon nothing in particular and looking as though each and all carried the fate of a nation in his pockets, or standing, in knots at street corners, discussing the situation, each perchance with a little less knowledge than his neighbour. All sorts of wild rumours were in the air, the least of which was that every white in the Transkei had been massacred, and that Kreli was marching upon Komgha at the head of the whole Gcaléka army.

Mrs Hoste, with her two young daughters, were at the door as the party drove up. They received Eanswyth very cordially.

"At last—at last! Why, we have been looking out for you for the last hour. I declare, I began to think you had stayed too long at Anta's Kloof, and the Kafirs had taken you prisoner or something. How do you do, Mr Milne? But—come in. We are going to have a dreadful storm in a minute. Mercy on us! What a flash!"

The blue, steely gleam was followed by a roll of thunder, long, loud, reverberating. There was a patter upon the zinc roof. A few raindrops, nearly as large as saucers, splashed around, and then, almost before the two men could get into their waterproof coats, the rain descended with a roar and a rush, in such a deluge that they could hardly see to outspan the trap.

"*Allamaghtaag*! but that's a fine rain," cried Hoste, with a farmer's appreciation, as he swung himself free of his dripping mackintosh in the little veranda.

"Especially for those who are under canvas," said Eustace with a significant glance at a group of tents pitched upon the plain just outside the village. For the surrounding *veldt* had been turned into something like a sea, and a miniature torrent roared down every depression in the ground.

"Well, Mr Milne," cried Mrs Hoste, from the head of the table, as the two men entered. "Its past three o'clock and dinner has been ready since half-past one. We quite expected you then."

"Which, being interpreted, means that I must prepare for the worst," was the rejoinder. "Never mind. I dare say we shan't starve. Well, and what's the latest absurdity in the way of news?"

"Just what I was going to ask you. You're hand-in-glove with all the Kafir chiefs. You ought to be able to give *us* all the news."

Eustace smiled to himself. He could tell them a few things that would astonish them considerably, if he chose. But he did not choose.

"We'll loaf round the village presently," said Hoste. "Likely enough we'll hear something then."

"Likely enough it'll be about as reliable as usual," said Eustace. "What was the last report? Kreli and the Gcaléka army encamped at the Kei Drift—be here in two hours?"

"It's all very well to laugh," said Mrs Hoste. "But what if we were attacked some fine night?"

"There isn't the ghost of a chance of it. Especially with all these wondrous fortifications about."

"I wish I thought you were serious. It would be a relief to me if I could think so."

"Pray do think so, Mrs Hoste. There is no sort of chance of this place being attacked; so make your mind easy."

"What do you think of our crib, Milne?" struck in Hoste.

"It seems snug enough. Not palatial, but good enough for all purposes. You were lucky to light upon it."

"Rather. There isn't so much as the corner of a rat hole to be had in the whole place now. But, it's knocked off raining," as a bright gleam of sunlight shot into the room. "Only a thunder-shower. We seem to have done dinner. Let's go out and pick up the latest lie. By the way, you don't want to go home again to-night, Milne? We can give you a shake-down on the sofa."

"The fact is I don't. To-morrow will do just as well, and then I suppose I'll have to trek with the stock down to Swaanepoel's Hoek, while Tom, thirsting for death or glory, fills up that tally slick he was telling us about last night."

"But don't you intend to volunteer for the front, like the rest?" asked Mrs Hoste in astonishment.

"No. Not at present, anyway. *I've* no quarrel with Jack Kafir; rather the reverse. I own I should like to *see* the campaign, but I couldn't do that without drawing trigger, and that's just what I'd rather avoid, except in a case of absolute necessity."

It might have been imagination, but Eustace fancied he could detect a look of intense relief pass over Eanswyth's features as he announced his desire to avoid the scene of hostilities. Yet with so many eyes upon him—upon them both—he would not look directly at her. Such is the effect of an *arrière-pensée*. Two days ago he would not have been careful to study appearances. But a good deal can happen in two days, notably the establishment of a thorough understanding between two persons.

"We'll go round to Pagel's first," said Hoste, as the two men strolled forth. "If rumour has taken shape at all, likely as not it's there we shall pick it up."

They soon reached the hotel. The bar and smoking-room were crammed with men—and smoke; men mostly of the farming class; men with large, sinewy hands, and habited partially or entirely in corduroy. There was a very Babel of tongues, for pretty nearly every man was talking at once, mostly on the all-absorbing topic. Some were indulging in chaff and loud laughter, and a few, we regret to say, were exceedingly unsteady on their pins.

Rumour, our two friends found, had taken shape, and the great item of news which everybody was discussing had received the *imprimatur* of official announcement. There had been a fight between the Gcalékas and the Fingoes, and a body of Mounted Police, interfering on behalf of the latter, had been defeated and forced to retire with the loss of a sub-inspector and half a dozen men. This had happened in the Idutywa Reserve two days previously.

Grave news, was the unanimous verdict. Grave news that the enemy should have triumphed in the very first engagement. Another such success, and every native from Natal to the Great Fish River would be up in arms. The news would flash from tribe to tribe, from kraal to kraal, quicker than a telegraphic message.

"That you, Payne?" cried Hoste.

The man addressed, who formed one of an arguing knot, turned.

"Thought it was," went on the first speaker, shaking hands. "Here's Milne, on the scare like the rest of us. Carhayes is still on his farm, standing out longer than even you, eh Payne? We brought in his wife to-day, Milne and I."

"Then he's all right. If it wasn't for our women-kind we could all stick to our farms right through," answered Payne. "Just think what sort of effect it has on Jack Kafir to see every fellow cutting away from him like mad."

"Why don't you practise what you preach then, old chap?" put in another man, while three or four more laughed significantly, for Payne's opinions were decidedly in disfavour among that gathering. "Why do you *trek* away and leave your own place?"

"Oh, blazes take you all! Ain't I jolly well hung round with women-kind?" was the reply, in a rueful, comic tone which raised a roar of laughter. "How can I?"

"What has become of that Britisher who was staying with you?" asked Hoste.

A very quaint expression came into the other's face. "He's thinking more of love than of war," he answered, lowering his voice for Hoste's benefit. "Expect he'll take one of the said women-kind off my hands mighty sharp. Won't be his fault if he doesn't."

"Britishers ain't no damn good!" said a burly fellow in corduroy, with a lurch up against Eustace.

Some of the men looked awkward; others interested. The remark was enough to provoke half a dozen fights, especially in that room, frequented as it often was by Police troopers, many of whom were young Englishmen of recent importation and thus likely to resent such a slur upon the home-grown article. But it took a good deal more than this to embark Eustace in active hostilities. The expression of his immobile features was as if the remark had passed unheard. Besides, he saw at a glance that the fellow was drunk.

"I say, you fellows—Hoste, Milne. Lets go and have a wet!" said Payne, making a move towards the bar, partly with a view to avoiding any further chance of a row. "Put a name to your pet poison and we'll drink confusion to old Kreli. Hang it. This atmosphere is enough to float a line-of-battle ship. Let's get out of it—when we've had our moistener, not before."

"It's rather rough on me, this shindy," he continued as they found themselves outside again. "What's the good of a fellow laying himself out to improve his place? Here I've got a lot of splendid lands under cultivation. Fountains Gap is a perfect jewel in that line, and now I must sacrifice the whole lot. Well, we're all in the same boat, that's one thing," he added philosophically. "So long, you fellows. I must go home. Hallo! Wonder if those chaps have brought any news."

Three Police troopers rode quickly by, heading for the quarters of their commanding officer. They had evidently ridden express direct from the Transkei, and had not spared their horses either, for both the latter and themselves looked jaded and travel-worn, besides being splashed from head to foot with mud.

The evening passed pleasantly enough. Eustace declined his friend's invitation to accompany him again into the village to try and learn some more news. After that night Eanswyth and he would be parted—for how long, Heaven only knew. But in that rather crowded circle there was no such thing as even a minute's *tête-à-tête*, and this he well knew. The conversation was all general, still he could delight his eyes with the mere sight of her—could let his ears revel in the music of her voice. Yet was there a something underlying the tone, the glance, of one or both of them, which conveyed a more than ordinary meaning?

For, that night, long after the bugle calls from the Police camps and the carolling of jolly souls wending somewhat unsteadily homeward from the convivial bar, had sunk into silence, Mrs Hoste made unto her lord and master a strange remark.

"What a pity Eanswyth didn't marry her husband's cousin instead of her husband."

"Great Scott! What the very deuce do you mean?"

"Well, I mean it is a pity. Look how well they seem to suit each other. Look at them here to-day. Anyone, any stranger coming in hap-hazard, would at once have jumped to the conclusion that they belonged to each other. And it's a pity they don't. Tom Carhayes isn't at all the man for that dear Eanswyth. I should be uncommonly sorry to be his wife myself, I know that much."

"I daresay you would. But Providence has been much kinder to you in that line than you deserve. But oh, good Heavens, Ada, do be mighty careful what you say. If you had propounded that idea of yours to anyone else, for instance, there's no knowing what amount of mischief it might open up."

"So? All right. There's no fear of my being such a fool. If you've preached enough—have you? Well, go to sleep."

Chapter Fifteen.

"But I am thy Love."

Three days later Carhayes arrived. He was in high spirits. The remainder of his stock was under way, and, in charge of Eustace, was trekking steadily down to his other farm in the Colony, which was sufficiently remote from the seat of hostilities to ensure its safety. He had ridden with them a day and a half to help start the *trek*, and had then returned with all haste to enrol himself in the Kaffrarian Rangers—a mounted corps, raised among the stock-farmers of the district, of whom it consisted almost entirely.

"Wish I was you, Tom," Hoste had said ruefully. "Wouldn't I just like to be going bang off to the front to have a slap at old Kreli instead of humbugging around here looking after stock. This *laager* business is all fustian. I believe the things would be just as safe on the farm."

"Well, shunt them back there and come along," was Carhayes' reply.

"We are not all so fortunate as you, Mr Carhayes," retorted Mrs Hoste with a trifle of asperity, for this advice was to her by no means palatable. "What would you have done yourself, I should like to know, but for that accommodating cousin, who has taken all the trouble off your hands and left you free to go and get shot if you like?"

"Oh, Eustace? Yes, he's a useful chap," said Carhayes complacently, beginning to cram his pipe. "What do you think the beggar has gone and done? Why, he has inspanned four or five boys from Nteya's location to help him with the *trek*! The very fellows we are trekking away from, by Jove! And they will help him, too. An extraordinary fellow, Eustace—I never saw such a chap for managing Kafirs. He can make 'em do anything."

"Well, its a good thing he can. But doesn't he want to go and see some of the fun himself?"

"Not he. Or, if he does, he can leave Bentley in charge and come back as soon as he has put things straight. Bentley's my man down there. I let him live at Swaanepoel's Hoek and run a little stock of his own on consideration of keeping the place in order and looking after it generally. He'll be glad enough to look after our stock now for a consideration—if Eustace gets sick of it and really does elect to come and have a shot at his 'blanket friends'—Ho-ho!"

The Kaffrarian Rangers were, as we have said, a corps raised in the district. The farmers composing it mounted and equipped themselves, and elected their own leaders. There was little discipline, in the military sense of the word, but the men knew each other and had thorough confidence in their leaders.

They understood the natives, and were as much at home on the *veldt* or in the bush as the Kafirs themselves. They affected no uniforms, but all were clad in a serviceable attire which should not be too conspicuous in cover—an important consideration—and all were well equipped in the way of arms and other necessaries. They asked for no pay—only stipulating that they should be entitled to keep whatever stock they might succeed in capturing from the enemy—which in many cases would be merely retaking their own. The Government, now as anxious as it had been sceptical and indifferent a month previously, gladly accepted the services of so useful a corps. The latter numbered between sixty and seventy men.

This, then, was the corps to which Carhayes had attached himself, and among the ranks of which, after two or three days of enforced delay while waiting for orders—and after a characteristically off-hand farewell to the Hostes and his wife—he proceeded to take his place.

They were to march at sundown and camp for the night at the Kei Drift. All Komgha—and its wife—turned out to witness their departure. Farmers and storekeepers, transport-riders and Mounted Police, craftsmen and natives of every shade and colour, lined the roadway in serried ranks. There was a band, too, blowing off "God Save the Queen," with all the power of its leathern lungs. Cheer after cheer went up as the men rode by, in double file, looking exceedingly workman-like with their well filled cartridge belts and their guns and revolvers. Hearty good-byes and a little parting chaff from friends and intimates were shouted after them through the deafening cheers and the brazen strains of the band, and, their numbers augmented by a contingent of mounted friends, who were to ride a part of the way with them, "just to see them squarely off," the extremely neat and serviceable corps moved away into a cloud of dust.

There was another side to all this enthusiasm, however. A good many feminine handkerchiefs waved farewell to that martial band. A good many feminine handkerchiefs were, pressed openly or furtively to tearful eyes. For of those threescore and odd men going forth that evening in all the pride of their strength and martial ardour, it would be strange, indeed, if some, at any rate, were not destined to leave their bones in a far-away grave—victims to the bullet and assegai of the savage.

The days went by and grew into weeks, but there was no want of life and stir in the little settlement. As Carhayes had remarked grimly during his brief sojourn therein—life appeared to be made up of bugle calls and lies. Hardly a half-hour that the bugle was not sounding—either at the Police camps, or at those of the regular troops now being rapidly moved to the front, and scarcely a day went by but a corps of mounted burghers or volunteers passed through, *en route* for the seat of war. The store keepers and Government contractors laughed and waxed fat.

All sorts of rumours were in the air, and as usual wildly contradictory. The white forces in the Transkei were in imminent peril of annihilation. The Gcaléka country had been swept clear from end to end. Kreli was sueing for peace. Kreli had declared himself strong enough to whip all the whites sent against him, and then with the help of the Gaikas and Hlambis to invade and ravage the Eastern Province of the Colony. The Gaikas were on the eve of rising, and making common cause with their Gcaléka brethren. The Gaikas had not the slightest wish for war. The Gaikas were never more insolent and threatening. The Gaikas were thoroughly cowed and lived in mortal dread of being attacked themselves. Thus Rumour many tongued.

The while events had taken place at the seat of war. The Kafirs had attacked the Ibeka, a hastily fortified trading post in the Transkei, in great force, and after many hours of determined fighting had been repulsed with great loss, repulsed by a mere handful of the Mounted Police, who, with a Fingo levy, garrisoned the place. Kreli's principal kraal on the Xora River had been carried by assault and burnt to the ground,—the Gcaléka chieftain, with his sons and councillors, narrowly escaping falling into the hands of the Colonial forces—and several other minor engagements had been fought. But the powerful Gaika and Hlambi tribes located throughout British Kaffraria, though believed to be restless and plotting, continued to "sit still," as if watching the turn of events, and night after night upon the distant hills the signal fires of the savages gleamed beneath the midnight sky in flashing, lurid tongues, speaking their mysterious, awesome messages from the Amatola to the Bashi.

Hoste—who, with other of his neighbours, was occupied with the armed tending of his stock in *laager*—was growing daily more restless and discontented. It was cruelly rough on him, he declared, to be pinned down like that. He wanted to go and have his share of the fun. The war might be brought to an end any day, and he would have seen nothing of it. He would try and make some satisfactory arrangement and then get away to the front at once, he vowed. In which resolution he met with but lukewarm encouragement from his wife.

"You should just see the yarn that friend of Payne's wrote him about the fight at Kreli's kraal, Ada," he remarked one day, having just ridden in. "He says it was the greatest sport he ever had. Eh, Payne?"

That worthy, who had accompanied him, nodded oracularly—a nod which might mean anything. Taught wisdom by the possession of a partner of his own joys and sorrows, he was not going to put himself in active opposition to what he termed the Feminine Controller-General's Department. But he and Hoste had hatched out between them a little plan which should leave them free, in a day or two, to start off in search of the death or glory coveted by their martial souls.

The cottage which Hoste had taken for his family was a tiny pill-box of a place on the outer fringe of the settlement, fronting upon the *veldt*, which situation rendered the ladies a little nervous at night, notwithstanding an elaborate system of outposts and pickets by which the village was supposed to be protected. At such a time the presence of Eanswyth, of whom they were very fond, was a perfect godsend to Mrs Hoste and her daughters. The latter were nice, bright children of fifteen and thirteen, respectively, and there were also two boys—then away at a boarding school in Grahamstown. If Eanswyth ever had reason to complain of the dullness or loneliness of her life on the farm, here it was quite the reverse. Not only was the house so small that four persons were sufficient to crowd it, but somebody or other, situated like themselves, was always dropping in, sitting half the day chatting, or gossiping about the progress of the war and the many rumours and reports which were flying around. In fact, there was seldom a respite from the "strife of tongues," for no sooner had one batch of visitors departed than another would arrive, always in the most informal manner. Now, of all this excess of sociability, Eanswyth was becoming a trifle weary.

To begin with, she could obtain little or no privacy. Accustomed to full measure of it in her daily life, she sorely missed it now. She even began to realise that what she had taken as a matter of course—what, indeed, some of her neighbours had half commiserated her for—was a luxury, and, like other articles falling under that category, a thing to be dispensed with now that they were living, so to say, in a state of siege.

She was fond of the two girls, as we have said; yet there were times when she would have preferred their room to their company—would have preferred a long, solitary walk. She was fond of her friend and entertainer; yet that cheery person's voluble tongue was apt to be sometimes a trifle oppressive. She liked her neighbours and they liked her; yet the constant and generally harmless gossip of the other settlers' wives and daughters, who were ever visiting or being visited by them, regarding work, native servants, babies, engagements, the war, and so forth, would strike her as boring and wearisome to the last degree. There were times when she would have given much to be alone—absolutely and entirely alone—and think.

For she had enough to think about now, enough to occupy every moment of her thoughts, day and night. But was it good that it should be so—was it good?

"I am a wicked woman!" she would say to herself, half bitterly, half sadly, but never regretfully—"a fearfully wicked woman. That is why I feel so restless, so discontented."

Never regretfully? No; for the sudden rush of the new dawn which had swept in upon her life had spread over it an enchanted glamour that was all-powerful in its surpassing sweetness. That first kiss—alone in the darkness of that peril-haunted midnight—had kindled the Fire of the Live Coal; that one long, golden day, they two alone together, had riveted the burning link. There was no room for regret.

Yet there were times when she was a prey to the most poignant anguish—a woman of Eanswyth's natural and moral fibre could never escape that—could never throw herself callously, unthinkingly, into the perilous gulf. A mixture of sensuousness and spirituality, the spirit would ever be warring against the mind—which two are *not* convertible terms by any means—and often in the dark, silent hours of night a sense of the black horror of her position would come upon her in full force. "Heaven help me!" she would cry half aloud in the fervour of her agony. "Heaven help me!" And then would be added the mental reservation, "But *not* through the means of loss—not through the loss of this new and enthralling influence which renders the keenest of mental anguish, engrossingly, indescribably sweet!"

"Save me from the effect, but, oh, remove not the cause!" A strange, a paradoxical prayer, but a genuine one; a terribly natural one. Thus poor humanity, from—and before—the days of Augustine of Hippo until now—until the consummation of the world.

As the days grew into weeks, the strain upon such a nature as Eanswyth's began to tell—as it was bound to do. She began to look pale and worn, and in such close companionship the change could not escape the eyes of her friends.

"Don't you let yourself be anxious, my dear," said a motherly settler's wife one day, bursting with a desire to administer comfort. "The Rangers will soon be back now. And they're all right so far—have had some rough work and haven't lost a man. Your husband knows how to take care of himself; never fear. Yes, they'll soon be back now."

This was the sort of consolation she had to acquiesce in—to receive with a glad smile at the time, and for hours after to torture herself with the miserable guilty consciousness that the fate of the Kaffrarian Rangers was to her a matter of infinitesimal account. There was one, however, whom appearances were beginning no longer to deceive, who, in pursuance of the strange and subtle woman's instinct, which had moved her to make that remark to her husband *in camera*, as recorded in a former chapter, began to feel certain that the real object of Eanswyth's solicitude was to be found west, not east—back in the peaceful Colony instead of in the Transkei braving peril at the hands of the savage enemy. That one was Mrs Hoste. She was not a clever woman by any means—not even a sharp woman, yet her mind had leaped straight to the root of the matter. And the discovery made her feel exceedingly uncomfortable.

That farewell, made in outwardly easy social fashion, under several pairs of eyes, had been a final one. Eustace had not ridden over on another visit, not even a flying one, as Eanswyth had hoped he would. Still, bitterly disappointed as she was, she had appreciated the wisdom of his motives—at first. If there was one quality more than another she had admired in him in times past, it was his thorough and resolute way of doing a thing. If anything had to be done, he did it thoroughly. The undertaking upon which he was then engaged certainly demanded all his time and attention, and he had given both, as was his wont. Still she had hoped he would have found or made some opportunity for seeing her once more.

She had heard from him two or three times, but they were letters that all the world might have seen, for Eustace was far too prudent to send anything more meaning into a house full of other people, and a small and crowded house at that. The mere glance of an eye—purely accidental, but still a mere glance—on the part of a third person, no matter who, would be more than sufficient to tumble down his fair house of cards in great and irreparable ruin. He was not a man to take any such risks.

She had appreciated his caution—at first. But, as time went by, the black drop of a terrible suspicion distilled within her heart. What if he had begun to think differently! What if he had suffered himself to be carried away by a mere moment of passing passion! What if time and absence had opened his eyes! Oh, it was too terrible! It could not be. Yet such things had happened—were happening every day.

An awful sense of desolation was upon her. She hungered for his presence— for the sound of his voice—for even a scrap of paper containing one loving word which his hand had written. To this had the serene, proud, strong-natured woman come. Her love had humbled her to the dust. Thus do we suffer through those for whom we transgress—thus does the delight of an hour become the scourge of a year.

Chapter Sixteen.

"A Madness of Farewells."

One afternoon Eanswyth managed to steal away for a solitary ramble unperceived. In the joy of having actually succeeded, she had wandered some little distance from the settlement. She felt not the slightest fear. No Kafirs would be in the least likely to molest her so near a strongly garrisoned post, even if the tribes in the immediate neighbourhood had been in a state of open hostility, which was not at present the case. As for solitude, it was not complete enough, for the country was open and sweeping and there were always horsemen in sight, coming and going in the distance, along the main road.

Half unconsciously she walked in the direction of her deserted home. It was a lovely, cloudless afternoon and the sun was already beginning to slant towards his western bed, darting long rays of gleaming gold upon the wide, rolling plains, throwing out with photographic clearness the blue outlines of the distant hills. Crickets chirruped gleefully in the grass, and away down in the hollow a pair of blue cranes were stalking mincingly along, uttering their metallic, but not unmelodious, cry.

Suddenly the clink of a horse's hoof smote upon her ear. It was advancing along the roadway in front. A flush of vexation spread over her face. It might be somebody she knew—and who would insist upon accompanying her back on the score of the disturbed state of the country, if not upon that of politeness. She had not stolen away, to rejoice like a schoolgirl in her sense of freedom, for that. It was very annoying.

The horseman topped the rise. She gave a little cry, and stood rooted to the ground as though her limbs were turned to stone. Could it be—? Yes—it was!

In a moment he had sprung to the ground beside her. She could not move now if she had desired to, for she was held fast in a strong embrace. A rain of warm kisses was falling upon her lips—her face.

"Eanswyth—my darling—my love! Did you come to meet me?"

"O Eustace! I had begun to think you were never coming back to me! Ah, you little know what I have gone through. Dear one, I never knew till now how my very life was wrapped up in you!" she gasped, her voice thrilling with a very volcano of tenderness and passion as she clung to him, returning his kisses again and again, as if she could never let him go.

She did not look unhappy and worn now. Her eyes shone with the light of love—the beautiful lips wreathed into smiles—her whole face was transfigured with her great happiness.

"Dear love, you have grown more beautiful than ever; and all for me," he murmured in that peculiar tone of his which bound her to him with a magnetic force that was almost intoxicating. "It is all for me—isn't it?"

"Yes," she answered without hesitation; looking him straightly, fearlessly in the eyes. Heaven help her!

"And yet you doubted me!"

"Eustace, darling, why did you never write to me? At least, why did you only write in that ordinary, formal and matter-of-fact way?"

"Because it would have been the height of insanity, under existing circumstances, to have done otherwise. And so you doubted me? You thought that I had only been playing with you? Or that even otherwise I had only to be away from you two or three weeks and I could forget?"

His tone, low and quiet, was just tinged with reproach. But it contained a subtle consciousness of power. And to her ears it sounded inexpressibly sweet, for it was this very sense of power that constituted the magnetism which drew her to him.

"Yes, I will confess. I did think that," she answered. "I can hide nothing from you. You have read my thoughts exactly. Ah, my own—my own! What have I not gone through! But you are with me again. Life seems too good altogether."

"It was our first parting, and a longish one," he said musingly as he walked beside her towards the settlement—his horse, with the bridle over its neck, following behind with the docility of a dog. "It was good for both of us, Eanswyth, my life. Now, do you think it was exactly delightful to me."

"N-no," she replied plaintively, pressing to her side the arm which he had passed through hers as they walked. "Though, of late, I haven't known what to think."

"They will know what to think if you go on looking so ridiculously happy," he said meaningly. "The gossip-loving soul of mother Hoste will be mighty quick at putting two and two together. And then?"

"And then? And then—I don't care—I've got *you* again," she answered with a gleeful laugh. "You—do you hear? You—you—*you*."

He looked rather grave. A struggle seemed to be going on within him.

"But you won't have me very long, my dear one. I am on my way to the front. In fact, I start this very night. I, and Hoste, and Payne."

No fear of her too happy look betraying her now. It faded from her eyes like the sunlight from the surface of a pool when the black thunder-cloud sweeps over it. It gave place to a stricken, despairing expression, which went to his heart.

"You have come back to me only to leave me again? O Eustace—Eustace! I am a very wicked woman, and this is my punishment. But how can I bear it!"

Then he calmed her. Strong as he was, his voice shook a little as he reasoned with her, pointing out how this course was in every way the best. He could not remain away down in the Colony, he said, and he had absolutely no pretext for staying on at Komgha. Besides, in a small, crowded and gossipy place, it would be downright madness to attempt it. Their secret would be common property in a day. He was too restless and unhappy away from her, and at present it was impossible to remain near her. The chances and excitement of the campaign offered the only way out of it. After that, brighter times were in store—brighter times, perhaps, than they dared dream of.

He calmed her—by the force of his reasoning—by the very magnetism of his influence; most of all, perhaps, by the power and certainty of his love. Never again could she doubt this—never—come what might. And she was to that extent happy amid her grief.

Though they were at all times the best of friends, the welcome Eustace met with at the hands of Mrs Hoste on this occasion was of doubtful cordiality. And the reason for this was twofold. First, the fact of his arrival in company with Eanswyth went to confirm her rapidly developing suspicions. Of course, it was a preconcerted arrangement. Narrowly, she scrutinised the pair, and failed not to discern traces of agitation and anxiety in the demeanour and appearance of, at any rate, one of them. Then, again, she had just learned, to her dismay, the intention of her husband to proceed to the front in a few hours. With this defection she did not hesitate to connect Eustace, and she was right. Wherefore, she regarded him as a treacherous friend at best and scrupled not to tell him as much.

"It's all very well for you, Mr Milne," she said. "You have only got yourself to please. But others haven't, and you ought to have more sense than to aid and abet a couple of responsible fathers of families like Mr Payne there and my stupid husband in any such folly."

"Ought he?" guffawed the stupid husband aforesaid, from another room where he was cleaning a gun. "But I say, Ada? How is he to get to the front by himself? It wouldn't be altogether safe. So, you see, he's absolutely dependent on our escort. Eh, Payne?"

"*Ja*," replied that worthy, laconically.

"You should be more patriotic, Mrs Hoste," murmured Eustace. "You see, you give us precious poor encouragement to die for our country—which process is defined by the poet as a sweet and decorous one."

"Die for your fiddlestick!" was the half-laughing, half-angry reply. "But, as I said before, it's all very well for you. Nobody is dependent on you. Nobody cares what becomes of you."

Did they not? There was one in that room to whom his safety was dearer than a hundred lives, whose heart was well-nigh bursting with unspoken agony at the prospect of the parting which was drawing so near—that parting which should send him forth for weeks, for months perhaps, with peril and privation for daily companions. Yet she must keep up appearances—must maintain a smooth and untroubled aspect. Nobody cared for him!

The three men were to start an hour before midnight, and with two more whom they were to meet just outside the settlement, reckoned themselves strong enough to cross the hostile ground in comparative safety—reckoning rather on evading the enemy than on meeting him in battle with such small numbers. And this would be easier, for the Gcaléka country had been swept from end to end and its inhabitants driven beyond the Bashi—for a time. In which process the Kaffrarian Rangers had gallantly borne their part.

As the hour for starting drew near, prodigious was the fussiness displayed by Hoste over the preparations. He couldn't find this, and he couldn't find that—he wanted this done and that done—in short made himself a signal nuisance. Now all this was done in accordance with a crafty idea of Payne's. "The women will be bound to turn on the waterworks. Therefore, give them plenty to do. Fuss them out of their very lives so that they won't have time so much as to think of snivelling—until we're gone, and then it won't matter," had enjoined that unprincipled philosopher—who had sent his own family down to King Williamstown some days previously.

"Do you mind taking a quarter of an hour's stroll, Eanswyth?" said Eustace in his most matter-of-fact way, shortly before they were due to start. "You see, neither Tom nor I can tell how long we may be away, and there are two or three things in connection with our joint possessions which I should like to discuss with you."

Eanswyth's heart gave a bound. The time of parting was drawing very near, and it seemed as if no opportunity would be offered them of seeing each other alone; that their farewell must be made, even as that other farewell, in the presence of half a dozen people. But his readiness of resource had hit upon a way, while she, all unnerved as she was, could think of nothing.

It was a lovely night. The thin sickle of a new moon hung in the heavens, and the zenith was ablaze with stars. Behind, the lights of the village, the sound of voices and laughter; in front, the darkness of the silent *veldt*. Far away against the blackness of the hills glowed forth a red fire.

Thus they stood—alone—and the time seemed all too short. Thus they stood—alone beneath the stars, and heart was opened to heart in the terrible poignancy of that parting hour.

"Oh, my darling, what if I were never to see you again! What if you were never to come back to me!" burst forth Eanswyth in a wail of anguish. "You are going into all kinds of danger, but oh, my loved one, think of me through it all—think of me if you are tempted to do anything foolhardy. My heart is almost broken at parting with you like this. Anything—anything more, would break it quite."

"I wish to Heaven mere danger was the only thing we had to trouble about," he said, rather bitterly. "But let this cheer you, my sweet—cheer us both. You doubted me before—you cannot again. We are both so strong in each other's love that beside such a possession the whole world is a trifle. And better and brighter times may be—must be, before us—"

"Hallo, Milne," shouted the voice of Hoste in the distance. "Where are you, man? Time's up!"

Both started—in each other's embrace—at this horribly jarring and unwelcome reminder. "The fellow needn't bawl like all the bulls of Bashan, confound him!" muttered Eustace with a frown.

"Eustace—dearest—must we really part now?" she murmured in a broken sob, clinging to him more closely. "First of all, take this," slipping a small, flat, oblong packet into his hand. "Open it—read it—when you are on your way. I got it ready, thinking we should have no opportunity of being alone together again. And now, love—dear, dear love—good-bye. Heaven bless you—no, I must not say that, I am too wicked. It would be of no avail coming from me—"

"I say, Milne! Are you coming along with us or are you not?" roared Hoste again from his front door. "Because if not, just kindly say so."

"You are under no precise necessity to cause the dead to rise, are you, Hoste?" said Eustace tranquilly, a couple of minutes later, as they stepped within the light of the windows. "Because, if you had whispered I should have heard you just as well. As it is, you have about woke up the whole of British Kaffraria, and we shall have the sentries opening fire upon the *veldt* at large in a minute. There—there goes the Police bugle already."

"Don't care a hang. We are waiting to start. Here come the horses. Now—Good-bye, everyone, and hurrah for old Kreli!"

A couple of native stable-hands appeared, leading three horses, saddled and bridled. Then there was a good deal of tumultuous leave-taking between Hoste and his family circle, mingled with sniffling and handkerchiefs, and of quieter farewells as concerned the rest of the party. But the torn heart of one in that group suffered in silence. Eanswyth's sweet, proud face was marvellously self-possessed.

"Extraordinary creatures, women," said Payne, as the three men rode out of the settlement. "I believe they positively enjoy the fun of a good snivel. It's just the same with my own crowd. When I left home I was obliged to send a note by a boy to say 'ta-ta' to escape it all, don't you know."

Hoste guffawed. It was just the sort of thing that George Payne, philosopher and cynic, would do.

"Some few of them are sensible, though," went on the latter, flaring up a vesuvian to light his pipe. "Mrs Carhayes, for instance. She don't make any fuss, or turn on the hose. Takes things as they come—as a rational person should."

Hoste guffawed again.

"Now, George, who the very deuce should she make a fuss over or turn on the hose for?" he said. "You or me, for instance. Eh?"

"N-no, I suppose not. Milne, perhaps. He's a sort of brother or cousin or something, isn't he?"

If Eustace had felt disposed to resent this kind of free-and-easiness he forebore, and that for two reasons. He liked the speaker, who, withal, was something of an original, and therefore a privileged person, and again the very carelessness of the remark of either man showed that no suspicion as to his secret had found place in their minds—a matter as to which he had not been without a misgiving a few minutes back.

On opening the packet which Eanswyth had put into his hand at parting, Eustace found it to consist of a little antique silver tobacco-box, beautifully chased. This contained a photograph of herself, and a letter; the last a short, hurriedly penned note, which, perused there alone, with all the desolation of the recent parting fresh upon him, was effectual to thrill his heart to the very core.

"And now," it ended—"And now, oh, my precious one, good-bye—I dare not say 'God bless you.' Coming from me it would entail a curse rather than a blessing. I am too wicked. Yet, is our love so wicked? Could it be so divinely, so beautifully sweet if it were? Ah, I neither know nor care. I only know that were anything to befall you—were you never to come back to me—my heart would be broken. Yes, broken. And yet, it would be only just that I should suffer through you. Good-bye, my dearest one—my only love. We may not meet again alone before you start, but I want you, in all your dangers and hardships, to have always with you these poor little lines, coming, as they do, warm from my hand and heart—"

The writing broke off abruptly and there were signs that more than one tear had fallen upon the silent, but oh, so eloquent paper.

Chapter Seventeen.

In the Enemy's Country.

"Hi, Hoste, Eustace! Tumble up! We are to start in half an hour."

It is dark as Erebus—dark as it can only be an hour or so before daybreak. The camp-fires have long since gone out and it is raining heavily. The speaker, stooping down, puts his head into a patrol tent wherein two sleepers lie, packed like sardines.

A responsive grunt or two and Hoste replies without moving.

"Bosh! None of your larks, Tom. Why, it's pitch dark, and raining as if some fellow were bombarding the tent with a battery of garden hoses."

"Tom can't sleep himself, so he won't let us. Mean of him—to put it mildly," remarks the other occupant of the tent, with a cavernous yawn.

"But it isn't bosh," retorts Carhayes testily. "I tell you we are to start in half an hour, so now you know," and he withdraws, growling something about not standing there jawing to them all day.

Orders were orders, and duty was duty. So arousing themselves from their warm lair the two sleepers rubbed their eyes and promptly began to look to their preparations.

"By Jove!" remarked Eustace as a big, cold drop hit him on the crown of the head, while two more fell on the blanket he had just cast off. "Now one can solve the riddle as to what becomes of all the played out sieves. They are bought up by Government Contractors for the manufacture of canvas for patrol tents."

"The *riddle*! Yes. That's about the appropriate term, as witness the state of the canvas."

"Oh! A dismal jest and worthy the day and the hour," rejoined the other, lifting a corner of the sail to peer out. It was still pitch dark and raining as heavily as ever. "We can't make a fire at any price—that means no coffee. Is there any grog left, Hoste?"

"Not a drop."

"H'm! That's bad. What is there in the way of provender?"

"Nothing."

"That's worse. Gcalékaland, even, is of considerable account in the world's economy. It is a prime corner of the said orb wherein to learn the art of 'doing without.'"

The two, meanwhile, had been preparing vigorously for their expedition, which was a three days patrol. By the light of a tiny travelling lamp, which Eustace always had with him when possible, guns were carefully examined and rubbed over with an oil-rag; cartridges were unearthed from cunning waterproof wrappers and stowed away in belts and pockets where they would be all-ready for use; and a few more simple preparations—simple because everything was kept in a state of readiness—were made. Then our two friends emerged from the narrow, kennel-like and withal leaky structure which had sheltered them the night through.

Except those who were to constitute the patrol, scarcely anybody was astir in the camp of the Kaffrarian Rangers that dark, rainy morning. All who could were enjoying a comfortable sleep warmly rolled up in their blankets, as men who are uncertain of their next night's rest will do—and the prospect looked cheerless enough as the dawn lightened. A faint streak in the eastern sky was slowly widening, but elsewhere not a break in the clouds, and the continual drip, drip, of the rain, mingled with the subdued tones of the men's voices, as they adjusted bit and stirrup and strapped their supplies in blanket and holster. Three days' rations were issued, and with plenty of ammunition, and in high spirits the prevailing wetness notwithstanding, the men were ready to set forth.

"This won't last. By ten o'clock there won't be a cloud in the sky," said the commander of the corps, a grizzled veteran, elected to that post by the unanimous vote of his men. In keeping with his habitual and untiring energy, which caused his followers often to wonder when he ever did sleep, he had been up and astir long before any of them. And now he bade them good-bye, and, the patrol having mounted, they filed out of camp, the rain running in streams down the men's waterproofs.

More than three weeks have elapsed since the sacking of Kreli's principal kraal, and during this time reinforcements, both of colonial levies and Imperial troops, have been pouring into the Transkei. Several conflicts of greater or less importance have taken place, and the Gcaléka country has been effectually cleared, its warlike inhabitants having either betaken themselves to the dense forest country along the coast, or fled for refuge across the Bashi to their more peaceful neighbours, the Bomvanas, who dare not refuse them shelter, even if desirous to do so. On the whole, the progress of the war has been anything but satisfactory. A number of the Gcalékas have been killed, certainly, but the tribe is unsubdued. The Great Chief, Kreli, is still at large, as are also his sons and principal councillors; and although the land has been swept, yet its refugee inhabitants are only awaiting the departure of the colonial forces to swarm back into their old locations. Meanwhile, a large force is kept in the field, at heavy expense to the Colony, and in no wise to the advantage of the burghers and volunteers themselves, whose farms or businesses are likely to suffer through their prolonged absence. Of late, however, operations have been mainly confined to hunting down stray groups of the enemy by a system of patrols—with poor results—perhaps killing a Kafir or two by a long and lucky shot, for the savages have learnt caution and invariably show the invaders a clean pair of heels.

But no one imagines the war at an end, and that notwithstanding a proclamation issuing from the office of the Commissioner of Crown Lands offering free grants of land in the Gcaléka country conditional upon the residence of the grantee on his exceedingly perilous holding. This proclamation, however, is regarded as a little practical joke on the part of the Honourable the Commissioner. Few, if any, make application, and certainly none comply with the conditions of the grant. The while patrolling goes on as vigorously as ever.

Eustace and his travelling companions had reached the camp of the Kaffrarian Rangers in due course. Hoste, indeed, would have been elected to a subordinate command in the troop had he taken the field at first, but now his place was filled up and he must perforce join in a private capacity; which position he accepted with complete equanimity. He could have all the fun, he said, and none of the responsibility, whereas in a post of command he would have been let in for no end of bother. So he and Eustace chum up together, and share tent and supplies and danger and duty, like a pair of regulation foster-brothers.

Our patrol rode steadily on, keeping a sharp look out on all sides. Its instructions were to ascertain the whereabouts of the enemy and his cattle, rather than to engage him in actual conflict. Should he, however, appear in such moderate force as to render an engagement feasible with a fair chance of success, then by all means let them teach him a lesson—and ardently did the men hope for such an opportunity. They numbered but forty all told, all more or less experienced frontiersmen, who knew how to use their rifles—all well versed in the ways of bush fighting, and thoroughly understanding how to meet the savage on his own ground and in his own way. In short, they reckoned themselves well able to render account of at least six times that number of the enemy, their only misgiving being lest the wily sons of Xosa should not afford them the chance.

In spite of his predilection for the dark-skinned barbarians aforesaid and his preference for the ways of peace, there was something wonderfully entrancing to Eustace Milne in this adventurous ride through the hostile country, as they held on over hill and valley, keeping a careful watch upon the long reaches of dark bush extending from the forest land which they were skirting, and which might conceal hundreds—nay thousands—of the savage foe lying in wait in his lurking place for this mere handful of whites—a something which sent a thrill through his veins and caused his eye to brighten as he rode along in the fresh morning air; for the clouds had dispersed now, and the sun, mounting into his sphere of unbroken blue, caused the wet earth to glisten like silver as the raindrops hung about the grass and bushes in clusters of flashing gems.

"So! That's better!" said one of the men, throwing open his waterproof coat. "More cheerful like!"

"It is," assented another. "We ought to have a brush with Jack Kafir to-day. It's Sunday."

"Sunday is it?" said a third. "There ain't no Sundays in the Transkei."

"But there are though, and its generally the day on which we have a fight."

"That's so," said the first speaker, a tall, wiry young fellow from the Chalumna district. "I suppose the niggers think we're such a bloomin' pious lot that we shan't hurt 'em on Sunday, so they always hit upon it to go in at us."

"Or p'r'aps they, think we're having Sunday school, or holdin' a prayer meeting. Eh, Bill?"

"*Ja.* Most likely."

They were riding along a high grassy ridge falling away steep and sudden upon one side. Below, on the slope, were a few woebegone looking mealie fields and a deserted kraal, and beyond, about half a mile distant, was the dark forest line. Suddenly the leader of the party, who, with three or four others, was riding a little way ahead, was seen to halt, and earnestly to scrutinise the slope beneath. Quickly the rest spurred up to him.

"What is it?"—"What's up, Shelton?" were some of the eager inquiries.

"There's something moving down there in that mealie field, just where the sod-wall makes a bend—there, about four hundred yards off," replied Shelton, still looking through his field glasses. "Stay—it's a Kafir. I saw him half put up his head and bob down again."

Every eye was bent upon the spot, eager and expectant. But nothing moved. Then the leader took a careful aim and fired. The clods flew from the sod-wall, heavy and sticky with the recent rain, as the bullet knocked a great hole in it. Simultaneously two naked Kafirs sprang up and made for the bush as hard as they could run.

Bang—bang! Bang—bang—bang! A rattling volley greeted their appearance. But still unscathed they ran like bucks; bounding and leaping to render themselves more difficult as marks.

Bang—bang! Ping—ping! The bullets showered around the fleeing savages, throwing up the earth in clods. Each carried a gun and had a powder horn and ammunition pouch slung round him, besides a bundle of assegais, and one, as he ran, turned his head to look at his enemies. Full three hundred yards had they to cover under the fire of a score of good marksmen. But these were excited.

"Steady, men! No good throwing away ammunition!" cried Shelton, the leader. "Better let 'em go."

But he might as well have spoken to the wind. As long as those naked, bounding forms were in sight so long would the more eager spirits of the party empty their rifles at them. Not all, however. Eustace Milne had made no attempt to fire a shot. He was not there, as he said afterwards, to practise at a couple of poor devils running away. Others, somewhat of the same opinion, confined themselves to looking on. But to a large section there present no such fastidious notions commended themselves. The secret of war, they held, was to inflict as much damage upon the enemy as possible, and under whatever circumstances. So they tried all they knew to act upon their logic.

"Whoop! Hurrah! They're down!" shouted some one, as the fugitives suddenly disappeared.

"Nay what!" said a tall Dutchman, shaking his head. "They are only sneaking," and as he spoke the Kafirs reappeared some fifty yards further, but were out of sight again in a second. They were taking advantage of a *sluit* or furrow—crawling like serpents along in this precarious shelter.

"Stay where you are—stay where you are," cried Shelton in a tone of authority, as some of the men made a movement to mount their horses and dash forward in pursuit. "Just as like as not to be a trap. How many more do we know are not 'voer-ly-ing' (Dutch: 'Lying in wait') in the bush yonder. The whole thing may be a plant."

The sound wisdom of this order availed to check the more eager spirits. They still held their pieces in readiness for the next opportunity.

"Hoste—Eustace—watch that point where the pumpkin patch ends. They'll have a clear run of at least a hundred yards there," said Carhayes, who was sitting on an ant-heap a little apart from the rest, every now and then taking a shot as he saw his chance.

"It's a devil of a distance," growled Hoste. "Six hundred yards if it's an inch—Ah!"

For the Kafirs sprang up just where Carhayes had foretold, and again, with a crash, many rifles were emptied at them. Fifty—thirty—twenty yards more and they will be safe. Suddenly one of them falls.

"He's down—fairly down!" yelled someone. "A long shot, too. Oh-h-h! He's only winged! Look! He's up again?"

It was so. The fallen man was literally hopping on one leg, with the other tucked up under him. In a moment both Kafirs had reached the cover and disappeared.

"Well, I never!" cried Hoste; "Heaven knows how many shots we've thrown away upon those devils and now they've given us the slip after all."

"Anyone would take us for a pack of bloomin' sojers. Can't hit a nigger in a dozen shots apiece. Pooh!" growled a burly frontiersman, in tones of ineffable disgust, as he blew into the still smoking breech of his rifle. "Eh, what's that?" he continued as all eyes were bent on the spot where the fugitives had disappeared.

For a tall savage had emerged from the bush, and with a howl of derision began to execute a *pas seul* in the open. Then with a very contemptuous gesture, and shaking his assegai at his white enemies, he sprang into the forest again, laughing loudly. They recognised him as the man who had escaped unhurt.

"Well, I'm somethinged!" cried Carhayes. "That nigger has got the laugh of us now."

"He's a plucky dog," said another. "If any fellow deserved to escape he did. Four hundred yards and a score of us blazing away at him at once! Well, well!"

"I've known that sort of thing happen more than once," said Shelton, the leader of the party, an experienced frontiersman who had served in two previous wars. "Same thing in buck shooting. You'll see a score of fellows all blazing at the same buck, cutting up the dust all round him till you can hardly see the poor beast, and yet not touching him. That's because they're excited, and shooting jealous. Now with one or two cool shots lying up and taking their time, the buck wouldn't have a ghost of a show—any more than would those two Kafirs have had. But we'd better get on, boys. We'll off-saddle further ahead, and then our horses will be fresh for whatever may turn up. It's my opinion there are more of those chaps hanging about."

Chapter Eighteen.

The Tables Turned.

Eager at the prospect of a brush, their appetites for which had been whetted by what had just occurred, they resumed their way in the best of spirits, and at length fixing upon a suitable spot the party off-saddled for breakfast.

"We ought to fall in with a patrol of Brathwaite's Horse lower down," remarked a man, stirring the contents of a three-legged cooking-pot with a wooden spoon. "Then we should be strong enough to take the bush for it and pepper Jack Kafir handsomely."

"If we can find him," rejoined another with a loud guffaw. "Hallo! Who's this?"

A dark form appeared in the hollow beneath. Immediately every man had seized his rifle, and the moment was a perilous one for the new arrival.

"Hold hard! Don't fire!" cried Shelton. "It's only a single Kafir. Let's see what the fellow wants." And lowering their weapons they awaited the approach of a rather sulky looking native, who drew near with a suspicious and apprehensive expression of countenance.

"Who are you and where do you come from?" asked Shelton.

"From down there, *Baas*," replied the fellow, in fair English, jerking his thumb in the direction of a labyrinth of bushy kloofs stretching away beneath. "They have taken all my cattle—the Gcalékas have. I can show you where to find theirs."

The men looked at each other and several shook their heads incredulously.

"What are you? Are you a Gcaléka?" asked Shelton.

"No, *Baas*. Bomvana. I'm Jonas. I'm a loyal Mission-station boy."

"Oh, the devil you are! Now, then, Jonas, what about these cattle?"

Then the native unfolded his tale—how that in the forest land immediately beneath them was concealed a large number of the Gcaléka cattle—a thousand of them at least. There were some men in charge, about sixty, he said, but still the whites might be strong enough to take the lot; only they would have to fight, perhaps.

Carefully they questioned him, but from the main details of his story he never swerved. His object, he said, was to be revenged on the Gcalékas, who had billeted themselves in the Bomvana country and were carrying things with a high hand. But Shelton was not quite satisfied.

"Look here, Jonas," he said impressively. "Supposing I were to tell you that this yarn of yours is all a cock-and-bull lie, and that you've come here to lead us into a trap? And supposing I were to tell half a dozen men here to shoot you when I count twenty? What then?"

All eyes were fixed upon the native's face, as the leader left off speaking. But not a muscle therein quailed. For a minute he did not reply. Then he shook his head, with a wholly incredulous laugh.

"Nay, *Baas*," he said. "*Baas* is joking."

"Well, you must be telling the truth or else you must be the pluckiest nigger in all Kafirland to come here and play the fool with us," said Shelton. "What do you say, boys? Shall we trust to what this fellow tells us and make a dash for the spoil?"

An acclamation of universal assent hailed this proposal. In an incredibly short space of time the horses were saddled, and with the native in their midst the whole party moved down in the direction of the bush.

"In here, *Baas*," said the guide, piloting them down a narrow path where they were obliged to maintain single file. On either side was a dark, dense jungle, the plumed euphorbia rising high overhead above the bush. The path, rough and widening, seemed to lead down and down—no one knew whither. The guide was not suffered to lead the way, but was kept near the head of the party, those immediately around him being prepared to shoot him dead at the first sign of treachery.

"Damned fools we must be to come into a place like this on the bare word of a black fellow," grunted Carhayes. "I think the cuss means square and above board—but going down here in this picnicking way—it doesn't seem right somehow."

But they were in for it now, and soon the path opened, and before and beneath them lay a network of kloofs covered with a thick, jungly scrub, here and there a rugged *krantz* shooting up from the waves of foliage. Not a sound was heard as they filed on in the cloudless stillness of the sunny forenoon. Even the birds were silent in that great lonely valley.

"There," whispered the Bomvana, when they had gone some distance further. "There is the cattle."

He pointed to a long, winding kloof whose entrance was commanded by cliffs on either side. Looking cautiously around, they entered this. Soon they could hear the sound of voices.

"By George! We are on them now," said Shelton in a low tone. "But, keep cool, men—only keep cool!"

They passed a large kraal which was quite deserted, but only just, for the smoke still rose from more than one fire, and a couple of dogs were yet skulking around the huts. Eagerly and in silence they pressed forward, and lo—turning an angle of the cliff—there burst upon their view a sight which amply repaid the risk of the enterprise they had embarked upon. For the narrow defile was full of cattle—an immense herd—which were being driven forward as rapidly and as quietly as the two score armed savages in their rear could drive them. Clearly the latter had got wind of their approach.

"*Allamaghtaag!*" exclaimed one of the men, catching sight of the mass of animals, which, plunging and crowding over each other, threaded their way through the bush in a dozen separate, but closely packed, columns. "What a take! A thousand at least!"

"Ping—ping! Whigge!" The bullets began to sing about their ears, and from the bush around there issued puffs of smoke. The Kafirs who were driving the cattle, seeing that the invaders were so few, dropped down into cover and opened a brisk fire, but too late. Quickly the foremost half of the patrol, reining in, had poured a couple of effective volleys into them, and at least a dozen of their number lay stretched upon the ground, stone dead or writhing in the throes of death; while several more might be seen limping off as well as they could, their only thought now being to save their own lives. The rest melted away into the bush, whence they kept up a tolerably brisk fire, and the bullets and bits of pot-leg began to whistle uncomfortably close.

"Now, boys!" cried Shelton. "Half of you come with me—and Carhayes, you take the other half and collect the cattle, but don't separate more than to that extent." And in furtherance of this injunction the now divided force rode off as hard as it could go, to head the animals back—stumbling among stones, crashing through bushes or flying over the same—on they dashed, helter-skelter, hardly knowing at times how they kept their saddles.

Amid much shouting and whistling the terrified creatures were at last turned. Down the defile they rushed—eyes rolling and horns clashing, trampling to pulp the dead or helpless bodies of some of their former drivers, who had been shot in the earlier stages of the conflict. It was an indescribable scene—the dappled, many-coloured hides flashing in the sun as the immense herd surged furiously down that wild pass. And mingling with the shouting and confusion, and the terrified lowing of the cattle half-frenzied with the sight and smell of blood—the overhanging cliffs echoed back in sharper tones the "crack-crack" of the rifles of the Kaffirs, who, well under cover themselves, kept up a continuous, but luckily ineffective, fire upon the patrol.

Suddenly a dark form rose up in front of the horsemen. Springing like a cat the savage made a swift stab at the breast of his intended victim, who swerved quickly, but not quickly enough, and the blade of the assegai descended, inflicting an ugly wound in the man's side. Dropping to the ground again, the daring assailant ducked in time to avoid the revolver bullet aimed at him, and gliding in among the fleeing cattle, escaped before the infuriated frontiersman could get in another shot. So quickly did it all take place that, except the wounded man himself, hardly anybody knew what had happened.

"Hurt, Thompson?" sung out Hoste, seeing that the man looked rather pale.

"No. Nothin' to speak of, at least. Time enough to see to it by and by."

As he spoke the horse of another man plunged and then fell heavily forward. The poor beast had been mortally stricken by one of the enemy's missiles, and would never rise again. The dismounted man ran alongside of a comrade, holding on by the stirrup of the latter.

"Why, what's become of the Bomvana?" suddenly inquired someone.

They looked around. There was no sign of their guide. Could he have been playing them false and slipped away in the confusion? Even now the enemy might be lying in wait somewhere in overwhelming force, ready to cut off their retreat.

"By Jove! There he is!" cried another man presently. "And—the beggar's dead!"

He was. In the confusion of the attack they had forgotten their guide, who must have fallen into the hands of the enemy, and have been sacrificed to the vengeance of the latter. The body of the unfortunate Bomvana, propped up in a sitting posture against a tree by his slayers in savage mockery, presented a hideous sight. The throat was cut from ear to ear, and the trunk was nearly divided by a terrible gash right across it just below the ribs, while from several assegai stabs the dark arterial blood was still oozing forth.

"Faugh!" exclaimed Hoste with a grimace of disgust, while two or three of the younger men of the party turned rather pale as they shudderingly gazed upon the sickening sight. "Poor devil! They've made short work of him, anyhow."

"H'm! I don't wonder at it," said Shelton. "It must be deuced rough to be sold by one of your own men. Still, if that chap's story was true he was the aggrieved party. However, let's get on. We've got our work all before us still."

They had. It was no easy matter to drive such an enormous herd through the thick bush. Many of the animals were very wild, besides being thoroughly scared with all the hustling to and fro they had had—and began to branch off from the main body, drawing a goodly number after them. These had to be out-manoeuvred, yet it would never do for the men to straggle, for the Kafirs would hardly let such a prize go without straining every effort to retain it. Certain it was that the savages were following them in the thick bush as near as they dared, keenly watching an opportunity to retrieve—or partially retrieve—the disaster of the day.

Cautiously, then, the party retreated with their spoil, seeking a favourable outlet by which they could drive their unwieldy capture into the open country; for on all sides the way out of the valley was steep, broken, and bushy. Suddenly a shout of warning and of consternation went up from a man on the left of the advance. All eyes were turned on him—and from him upon the point to which he signalled.

What they saw there was enough to send the blood back to every heart.

Chapter Nineteen.

The Last Cartridge.

This is what they saw.

Over the brow of the high ridge, about a mile in their rear, a dark mass was advancing. It was like a disturbed ants' nest—on they came, those dark forms, swarming over the hill—and the sun glinted on assegai blades and gun-barrels as the savage host poured down the steep slope, glancing from bush to bush, rapidly and in silence.

"I'm afraid we shall have to give up the cattle, lads, and fight our way out," said Shelton, as he took in the full strength of the advancing Kafirs. "Those chaps mean business, and there are too many of them and too few of us."

"We'll make it hot for 'em, all the same," said Carhayes, with a scowl. "I have just put two more nicks on my gun-stock—not sure I oughtn't to have had four or five, but am only certain of two—Hallo! That's near."

It was. A bullet had swept his hat off, whirling it away a dozen yards. At the same time puffs of smoke began to issue from the hillside, and the twigs of the bushes beyond were sadly cut about as the enemy's missiles hummed overhead—but always overhead—pretty thickly. At first, the said enemy was rather chary of showing himself, although they could see groups of red figures flitting from bush to bush, and the whigge of bullets and potlegs became more and more unpleasantly near, while from the slope above jets of smoke and flame kept bursting forth at all points.

The plan of the whites was to make a running fight of it. While one-half of the patrol drove on the cattle, the other half was to fight on foot, covering their comrades' retreat, but always keeping near enough to close up, if necessary.

"Now, boys—let 'em have it!" cried Shelton, as a strong body of the enemy made a sudden rush upon their left flank to draw their attention, while another party, with a chorus of shouts and deafening whistles, and waving their assegais and karosses, darted in between the cattle and their captors, with the object of separating and driving off the former.

A volley was discharged—with deadly effect, as testified by the number who fell, wounded, maimed, or stone dead. The rest rushed on, gliding in among the fleeing cattle—whistling and yelling in a frenzy of excitement.

"Keep cool, boys, and fire low," cried Carhayes—who was in command of the dismounted party—as a crowd of Kafirs suddenly started up on their rear, and, with assegais uplifted, threatened a determined charge. "Now!"

Again there was a roar, as the whole fire was poured into the advancing mass. Even the horses, steady, trained steeds as they were, began to show restiveness, terrified by the continuous crash of firing and the fierce yells of the savages. Then, without pausing to reload, every man discharged his revolver into the very thick of the leaping, ochre-smeared warriors. It was too much. The latter wavered, then dropped into cover.

But the respite was only a temporary one. Changing his tactics, the fierce foe no longer attempted an open *coup de main*, but taking advantage of the bush he pressed the handful of whites who formed the rear guard so hotly as to force them to close up on their comrades, in order to avoid being entirely surrounded and cut off from the latter. But however bad had been their marksmanship earlier in the day, while excited and practising at the two fleeing Kafirs at long range, our frontiersmen were now in a different vein. There was nothing wild about their shooting now. Steady of eye, and cool of brain, they were keenly alive to every opportunity. Directly a Kafir showed his head he was morally certain to receive a ball through it, or so uncomfortably close as to make him feel as if he had escaped by a miracle, and think twice about exposing himself a second time.

Meanwhile the cattle were being driven off by the enemy, and indeed matters had become so serious as to render this a mere secondary consideration. From the bush on three sides a continuous fire was kept up, and had the Kafirs been even moderately decent shots not a man of that patrol would have lived to tell the tale; but partly through fear of exposing themselves, partly through fear of their own fire-arms, to the use of which they were completely unaccustomed, the savages made such wild shooting that their missiles flew high overhead. Now and then, however, a shot would take effect. One man received a bullet in the shoulder, another had his bridle hand shattered. Several of the horses were badly wounded, but, as yet, there were no fatalities. The enemy, confident in the strength of his overwhelming numbers, waxed bolder—crowding in closer and closer. Every bush was alive with Kafir warriors, who kept starting up when and where least expected in a manner that would have been highly disconcerting to any but cool and determined men.

But this is just what these were. All hope of saving the spoil had been abandoned. The frontiersmen, dismounted now, were fighting the savages in their own way, from bush to bush.

"This is getting rather too hot," muttered Shelton, with an ominous shake of the head. "We shall be hemmed in directly. Our best chance would be for someone to break through and ride to the camp for help." Yet he hesitated to despatch anyone upon so dangerous a service.

Just then several assegais came whizzing in among them. Two horses were transfixed, and Hoste received a slight wound in the leg.

"Damn!" he cried furiously, stamping with pain, while a roar of laughter went up from his fellows, "Let me catch a squint at John Kafir's sooty mug! Ah!"

His piece flew to his shoulder—then it cracked. He had just glimpsed a woolly head, decked with a strip of jackal's skin, peering from behind a bush not twenty yards away, and whose owner, doubtless, attracted by the laughter of those devil-may-care whites, had put it forward to see what the fun was about. A kicking, struggling sound, mingled with stifled groans, seemed to show that the shot had been effective.

"Downed him! Hooray!" yelled Hoste, still squirming under the smart of the assegai prick in his calf. "Charge of *loepers* that time—must have knocked daylight through him!"

Taking advantage of this diversion, a tall, gaunt Kafir, rising noiselessly amid a mass of tangled creepers, was deliberately aiming at somebody. So silent had been his movements, so occupied were the other whites, that he was entirely unperceived. His eye went down to the breech. He seemed to require a long and careful aim.

But just then he was perceived by one, and instinctively Eustace brought his piece to bear. But he did not fire. For like a flash he noted that the savage was aiming *full at Carhayes' back.*

The latter, sublimely unconscious of his deadly peril, was keenly alert on the look out for an enemy in the other direction. Eustace felt his heart going like a hammer, and he turned white and cold. There in the wild bush, surrounded by ruthless enemies, the sweet face of Eanswyth passed before him, amid the smoke of powder and the crash of volleys. She was his now—his at last. The life which had stood between them now stood no more.

With a frightful fascination, he crouched motionless. Carhayes was still unconscious of his imminent peril—his broad back turned full to the deadly tube of the savage. The distance was barely fifteen yards. The latter could not miss.

It all passed like lightning—the awful, the scathing temptation. He could not do it. And with the thought, his finger pressed ever so lightly on the trigger, and the Kafir crashed heavily backward, shot through the brain—while the ball from his gun, which, with a supreme effort he had discharged in his death throes, hummed perilously near his intended victim's head.

"Hallo, Milne! You got in that shot just right," cried one of the men, who had turned in time to take in the situation—not the whole of it, luckily.

Eustace said nothing. His better nature had triumphed. Still, as he slipped a fresh cartridge into his smoking piece, there was a feeling of desolation upon him, as though the intoxicating sense of possessing the whole world had been within his grasp, and as suddenly reft from it again. The extremely critical position in which he—in which the whole party—stood, passed unheeded. "Fool!" whispered the tempting, gibing fiend. "You had your opportunity and you threw it away. You will never have it again. She is lost to you forever now. Never can you hope to possess her!"

And now the firing opened from an unexpected quarter—and behold, the bushy slope in front was alive with Kafir warriors. The patrol was entirely surrounded, and now the savages began to shout exultantly to each other.

"We have got the white men in a hole," they cried. "Ha! They cannot get out. Look, the sun is shining very bright, but it will be dark for the white men long before it touches the hill. They are caught like wolves in a trap. *Hau*!"

"Ho-ho! Are they!" sung out Carhayes, in reply to this taunt. "When a wolf is caught in a trap, the dogs cannot kill him without feeling his teeth. The Amaxosa dogs have caught not a wolf, but a lion. Here is one of his bites." And quick as lightning he brought up his rifle and picked off a tall Gcaléka, who was flitting from one bush to another a couple of hundred yards above. The Kafir lurched heavily forward, convulsively clutching the earth with both hands. A yell of rage arose from the savages and a perfect hail of bullets and assegais came whistling around the whites—fortunately still overhead.

"Aha!" roared Carhayes with a shout of reckless laughter. "Now does any other dog want to feel the lion's bite? Ha, ha! I am he whom the people call Umlilwane. 'The Little Fire' can burn. He it was who helped to burn the kraal of Sarili, the Great Chief of the House of Gcaléka. He it is who has 'burned' the life out of many dogs of the race of Xosa. He will burn out the lives of many more! Ha, ha—dogs—black scum! Come forth! Try who can stand before The Little Fire and not be burned up—utterly consumed away! Come forth, dogs, come forth!"

Catching their comrade's dare-devil spirit, the men laughed and cheered wildly. But the Kafirs, full of hate and rage, forgot their prudence. A great mass of them leaped from their cover, and shrilling their wild war-whistles, snapped their assegais off short, and bore down upon the handful of whites in full impetuous charge.

Critical as the moment was, the latter were prepared never more dangerously cool than now when it was almost a case of selling their lives dearly. They instantly gave way, melting into cover with the serpent-like celerity of the savages themselves, and before these could so much as swerve, they poured such a deadly cross-fire upon the compact onrushing mass that in a second the ground was strewn with a groaning, writhing heap of humanity.

With a roar like a wild beast, Carhayes sprang from his cover and, wrenching a heavy knob-kerrie from the hand of a dead Kafir, dashed among the fallen and struggling foe, striking to right and left, braining all those who showed the slightest sign of resistance or even of life. A Berserk ferocity seemed to have seized the man. His hair and beard fairly bristled, his eyes glared, as he stood erect, whirling the heavy club, spattered and shiny with blood and brains. He roared again:

"Ho, dogs! Come and stand before the lion! Come, feel his bite—who dares? Ha, ha!" he laughed, bringing the kerrie down with a sickening crash upon the head of a prostrate warrior whom he had detected in the act of making a last desperate stab at him with an assegai—shattering the skull to atoms. "Come, stand before me, cowards. Come, and be ground to atoms."

But to this challenge no answer was returned. There was a strange silence among the enemy. What did it portend? That he was about to throw up the game and withdraw? No such luck. His strength was too great, and he was burning with vengeful rage at the loss of so many men. It could only mean that he was planning some new and desperate move.

"I say, Milne, lend us a few cartridges; I've shot away all mine."

Eustace, without a word, handed half a dozen to the speaker. The latter, a fine young fellow of twenty-one, was enjoying his first experience in the noble game of war. He had been blazing away throughout the day as though conscious of the presence of a waggon-load of ammunition in the patrol.

"Thanks awfully—Ah-h!"

The last ejaculation escaped him in a kind of shuddering sigh. His features grew livid, and the cartridges which he had just grasped dropped from his grasp as he sank to the ground with scarcely a struggle. A Kafir had crawled up behind him, and had stabbed him between the shoulders with a broad-bladed assegai—right through to the heart. A deep vengeful curse went up from his comrades, and they looked wildly around for an object on which to exact retribution. In vain. The wily foe was not going to show himself.

But the incident threw a new light upon the state of affairs, and a very lurid one it was. Several had run out of ammunition, but had refrained from saying so lest the fact, becoming known, should discourage the others. Now it was of no use disguising matters further. There were barely fifty rounds left among the whole patrol—that is to say, something less than a round and a half per man. And they were still hemmed in by hundreds of the enemy, closely hemmed in, too, as the recent fatality proved, and it still wanted a good many hours till dark. Small wonder that a very gloomy expression rested upon almost every countenance. The position was almost as bad as it could possibly be.

Chapter Twenty.

The Tables Turned Again.

Suddenly a tremendous volley crashed forth from the hillside on their left front, followed immediately by another on the right. For a moment the men looked at each other in silence, and the expression of gloomy determination hitherto depicted on their countenances gave way to one of animated and half-incredulous relief.

For no sound of hostile volley was that. No. Help was at hand. Already they could see the Kafirs gliding from bush to bush in groups, hastening to make good their retreat, thoroughly disconcerted by this new and disastrous surprise.

"Whoop!—Hooray! Yoicks forward!" shouted the beleaguered combatants, each man giving his particular form of cheer, varying from savage war-cry to view halloo. They were wild with excitement, not only by reason of their unlooked for deliverance from almost certain massacre, but also on account of being in a position to turn the tables upon their skulking foe.

Then came the crack—crack—crack—of the rifles of the new arrivals, who advanced rapidly, yet not entirely without caution, through the bush, picking off the retreating Kafirs as these showed themselves in fleeing from cover to cover. And above the crackle of the dropping shots rang out the wild notes of a bugle, villainously played. A roar of laughter went up from our friends.

"Brathwaite's Horse for a fiver!" cried Hoste. "That's Jack Armitage's post-horn. I know its infamous old bray—And—there's Brathwaite himself."

"Any of you fellows hurt?" sung out the latter, a fine, stalwart frontiersman, who, with several of his men, rode down upon the group. The remainder were spread out in skirmishing line on either side, the irregular rattle of their fire showing that they were still busy peppering the enemy in sight.

"One man killed," answered Shelton. "It's Parr, poor chap."

"So? Well, fall in with us and come on. We haven't done with Jack Kafir yet."

"Can't. We're all but cleaned out of ammunition."

"So?" said Brathwaite again. "We've turned up none too soon then. Fortunately we've got plenty."

A hurried levy was made upon the cartridge belts of the new arrivals, and thus reinforced in every sense of the word, the Kaffrarian men, keen to avenge their comrade and retrieve their position, fell in with their rescuers, and the whole force moved rapidly forward in pursuit of the enemy.

But the latter had hastened to make himself scarce. With characteristic celerity, the wily savages seemed to have melted into earth or air. If thirty-five whites—a mere handful—had given them about as much fighting as they could stomach, they were not going to stand against that handful multiplied by three.

"There they go!" suddenly shouted someone, pointing to the almost bare brow of a hill about half a mile away, over which a number of Kafirs were swarming in full retreat. A tremendous fusillade was opened upon this point, but with slight effect. The distance was too great.

"We must get the cattle," cried Brathwaite, Shelton having hurriedly given him the particulars. "And we must race for them, too, for they'll have got a good start. They are sure to take them right away to that big bit of forest which runs down to the coast. Once there they are safe as far as we are concerned. I know this strip of country."

Armitage, the man who owned the bugle, and who was known to most there present either personally or by name, as a licenced wag and an incorrigible practical joker, was instructed to blow a call of assembly. This he did, in hideous and discordant fashion, and the men collected. Briefly Brathwaite explained the situation.

"Beyond this first rise there's another," he said. "Beyond, that there's five miles of open *veldt*; then the strip of forest I was mentioning. If we don't get the cattle in the open we shan't get them at all. Forward!"

No second command was needed. The whole force pressed eagerly forward. At length, after a toilsome ride, during which not an enemy was seen, except here and there the body of a dead one lying in a pool of blood, they crested the brow of the second ridge. A great shout arose.

"There they are! Now then, boys—cut 'em out!"

Away in front, about five miles distant, lay a long, dark line of forest. Half-way between this and themselves an immense herd of cattle was streaming across the *veldt*. The drivers, about two score in number, were at first seen to redouble their efforts to urge on the animals. Then, at sight of the white horsemen bearing down upon them with a wild cheer, they incontinently abandoned their charge and fled for dear life.

"Never mind the niggers," sang out Brathwaite, as one or two of his men tried to rein in for a snap shot at the flying Kafirs. "Never mind them. Head the cattle round for all you know. If once they get into the bush we may lose any number of them." And spurring into a gallop he circled round before the excited herd, followed by his whole troop. The foremost beasts stopped short, throwing up their heads with many a snort and bellow of bewilderment and terror, while the bulk of the herd pressed on. For some minutes the clashing of horns and frenzied bellowing, the clouds of dust, and the excited shouts of the horsemen made up an indescribable scene of din and confusion. Many of the animals, rolled on the ground by the plunging, swaying mass, were trampled or gored to death by their bewildered companions. At last the tumultuous excitement began to subside, and the animals, with heaving flanks and rolling eyes, stood huddled together as if awaiting the pleasure of their new drivers.

"Steady! Don't rush them," shouted Brathwaite. "Head them away quietly for the open for all you know, and don't let them break through."

More than one comical scene was enacted as the line of horsemen, extended so as to gradually work the herd away from the bush, drove their charge forward. Now and then a cow, with a calf at her side, or haply missing her progeny, would turn and furiously charge the line of horsemen, causing an abrupt scatter, and in one or two instances the utter and ignominious flight of the doughty warrior singled out, who perchance was only too thankful to lay her out with a revolver shot in the nick of time to save himself and his steed, or both, from being ripped up or impaled by those vicious horns. But the best fun of all was afforded by a huge old black-and-white bull.

Jack Armitage, we have said, was bursting with animal spirits; consequently when the aforesaid quadruped took it into his massive cranium to suddenly break away from the herd and start off on his own account at right angles thereto, it followed, as a matter of course, that Armitage, being nearest to him, should spur away in pursuit. The bull's vicious little eyes began to roll wickedly, and from a trot he broke into a wild gallop. Then madcap Jack, madder than ever with the excitement of the day's events, was seen to range his horse alongside, and bending over in the saddle and placing his bugle almost against the animal's ear he blew a hideous and terrific blast. There was a ferocious bellow—down went the brute's head, and, lo, in a twinkling horse and man were rolling on the ground, and the bull galloped away unimpeded.

Roars of laughter arose from the discomfited one's comrades, which did not decrease as they watched the savage brute in the distance charging one of the retreating Kafirs, who seemed almost as much disconcerted by this new enemy as he had been by the missiles of his human foes. Finally both disappeared within the bush.

"Hurt, old man?" cried Hoste, riding up as the fallen one found his feet again, and stood rubbing his shoulder and looking rather dazed with the shock. The horse had already struggled up. Fortunately for it, the bull's horns were short and blunt, and it seemed none the worse for the tumble.

"No. Had a devil of a shake-up, though. A bottle of doctor's stuff's a fool to it."

"Music hath charms to soothe the savage beast—sings the poet. In this case it hadn't," said Eustace. "Those ancients must have been awful liars. Eh, Armitage?"

"You bet. Hallo! Where's my old post-horn?" he went on, looking round for his instrument, which he discovered about a dozen yards off, unharmed, save for a slight dent. Putting it to his lips he blew a frightful fanfare.

"I say, Jack, you'll have the old bull back again," said Brathwaite. "Better shut up. He's dead nuts on that old trumpet of yours. And now, the farther we get into the open, the better. We mustn't camp anywhere that'll give Johnny Kafir a chance of cutting out the cattle again."

"We've done a good day's work, anyhow," said Shelton. "This isn't half a bad haul—and it's fairly decent stock for Kafir stock."

"Kafir stock be damned!" growled Carhayes. "Whatever is decent among it is stolen stock, you bet. Not much sleep for any of us to-night, boys. We shall mostly all have to keep our eyes skinned, if we are to take in this lot safe. Whoever of us are not on horse guard will be on cattle guard."

They were joined by the few men who had remained behind to guard the corpse of their slain comrade. This was conveyed in a sort of litter, improvised of blankets and slung between two quiet horses; and now to the dash and excitement of the conflict and pursuit, there succeeded a subdued quiet, almost a gloom, by reason of the presence of the dead man in their midst. Still—it was the fortune of war.

Chapter Twenty One.

Under Orders for Home.

The Kaffrarian Rangers were ordered home.

To be strictly accurate, that redoubtable corps had applied to be withdrawn. There was not enough to do to render it worth the while of the men who composed it—men mostly with a substantial stake in the country—to remain any longer wasting their time in a series of fruitless patrols on the off-chance of an occasional very long distance shot at a stray Gcaléka scout or two; for the enemy no longer attempted to meet them in battle. He had suffered severely, both in men and possessions, and there were those who declared that he had had nearly enough of it. The Frontier Armed and Mounted Police and, if necessary, the regular troops now stationed along the border, would be sufficient to cope with any further disturbance; so most of the volunteer forces applied to be withdrawn.

They had been several weeks in the *veldt*—several weeks absent from their farms and businesses. They had rendered excellent service; had, in fact, constituted the very backbone of the offensive operations. It was only fair, now that there remained no more to be done, to allow them to return. Brathwaite's Horse had already withdrawn, so had most of the mounted corps. The Kaffrarian Rangers were nearly the last.

The men were in excellent health and spirits. They had lost one of their number—the poor young fellow who had met his fate with the patrol under Shelton, and had been buried near where he fell—a few had received wounds, none of these being, however, of a very serious nature. But they had left their mark upon the enemy, and were returning, withal, in possession of a large number of the latter's cattle. Yet they had a grievance, or fancied they had.

They had not nearly enough fighting. The combined plan of the campaign had not been carried out according to their liking. The enemy had been suffered to escape just at the very moment when it was within their power to inflict upon him a decisive and crushing blow. There had been too much of the old womanly element among those intrusted with the conduct of affairs. In a word, the whole business had been bungled. And in this thoroughly characteristic and British growl none joined more heartily than Tom Carhayes.

There was one, however, who in no wise joined in it at all, and that one was Eustace Milne. He had had enough of campaigning to last him for the present, and for every reason mightily welcomed the news that they were ordered home. Of late an intense longing had corrie upon him to return, but now that that ardently desired consummation had been attained he realised that it was dashed with the sickening and desolating consciousness of hopes shattered. The campaign, so far as he was concerned, had been barren of result.

But for him—but for his intervention—Tom Carhayes would have been a dead man, and Eanswyth would be free. The Kafir could not have missed at that distance. But for his interference the bullet of the savage would have sped true, and happiness for him—for her—would have become the blissful, golden, reality of a lifetime. Even now he would be hurrying back to claim her—that is, allowing for a reasonable period exacted by decorum. But no, the cup was shattered in his grasp, and his own was the hand that had shattered it. "A man who interferes in what doesn't concern him deserves all he gets," was the grimly disgusted reflection which lashed his mind again and again.

Why had he intervened to save his cousin's life? When Fortune was playing directly into his hands he, yielding to an idiotic scruple, had deliberately flung back into her face the chance she had held out. She would not proffer it again. His opportunity had occurred and he had let it go by.

Yet he could not have acted otherwise. Could he not? he thought savagely, as at that moment his cousin's voice struck upon his ear. Not that its utterances contained anything objectionable, but to the listener's then frame of mind, there was something insufferably self-assertive in their very tone. Could he not? Let him only get the chance again. But this he never would. It was thought by many that the war was practically at an end.

If his cousin had been a different stamp of man and one built of finer clay, it is more than probable that Eustace would have acted differently—would have conquered that overmastering and unlawful love which he had so long and so successfully concealed, or at any rate would have fled from temptation. But it was far otherwise. The fellow was such a rough, assertive, thick-headed, inconsiderate boor, utterly unable to appreciate his own splendid good fortune. He deserved no mercy. Yet this was the being to whom Eanswyth was bound—whom, moreover, she had managed to tolerate with every semblance of, at any rate, contentment, until he himself had laid siege to the castle of her outwardly calm, but glowingly passionate nature, and had carried it by storm, by a single *coup de main*.

And now? How could she ever resume that old contented toleration, how relegate himself to an outside place. Every look—every word of hers—during that last walk, when he had come upon her so unexpectedly—every sweet and clinging caress during that last parting, was burnt into his memory as with red-hot irons. And now it seemed that the curtain must be rung down on everything. Tom Carhayes was returning in rude health; louder, more boastful, a more aggressive personality than ever. Let the very heavens fall!

A change had come over Eustace. He became moody and taciturn, at times strangely irritable for one of his equable temperament. This was noticed by many; wondered at by some.

"Why, what's the row with you, old chap!" said Carhayes one day in his bluff, off-hand manner. "Sick and sorry that we can't scare up another fight, eh?"

"Milne's conscience is hitting him hard over the number of his 'blanket friends' he has shot already. Ha, ha!" cut in another man, with an asinine guffaw.

The Kaffrarian Rangers were ordered home. The order reached them in their camp on the Bashi, and forthwith they acted upon it. No preparations delayed the setting out of such a light-marching-order corps. Accordingly the breakfasts were cooked and eaten, the camp was struck, and the whole troop started upon its homeward way.

"I say, Hoste!" said Carhayes, while they were breakfasting on boiled mealies and ration beef. "What do you say to a shoot before we leave this? We are bound to get a bushbuck ram or two in some of these kloofs."

"Haven't you shot away enough cartridges yet, Tom?" laughed Hoste. "Still I think we might try for a buck if only for a change after the niggers; besides, we can eat the buck, which is part of the change. I'm on. What do you say, Payne? Will you cut in?"

"What do I say? I say it's the most damn idiotic idea I ever heard mooted," answered Payne sententiously. "Still—I'll cut in."

"All right. We'll have some sport then!" said Carhayes. "You'll come, too, Eustace? That's right," as Eustace nodded assent. "That'll make four of us—we don't want any more," he went on. "We can just hunt down the river bank for two or three hours, and catch up the troop in camp to-night. We are bound to get some sport."

"Likely so are the niggers," murmured the more prudent Payne.

The commander of the troop, when applied to, made no decided objection to the above scheme. There was, as we have said, no discipline in the ordinary sense of the word, the offices of command being elective. Besides, they were under orders to return straight home, which was practically disbandment. So, while not forbidding the undertaking, he pointed out to those concerned that it might involve serious risk to themselves; in a word, was rather a crack-brained idea.

"Just what I said," remarked Payne laconically, lighting his pipe.

"Then why do you go, old chap?" asked one of the bystanders with a laugh.

"That's just what I don't know myself," was the reply, delivered so tranquilly and deliberately as to evoke a general roar.

The camp had been pitched upon high ground overlooking the valley of the Bashi, which ran beneath between rugged bush-clad banks. So the troop set forth on its homeward way, while our four friends, turning their horses' heads in the opposite direction, struck downward into the thick bush along the river bank.

Chapter Twenty Two.

"We are Four Fools."

For upwards of two hours they forced their way through the thick scrub, but success did not crown their efforts—did not even wait upon the same. Once or twice a rustle and a scamper in front announced that something had got up and broken away, but whatever it was, owing to the thickness of the bush and the celerity with which it made itself scarce, not one of the hunters could determine—being unable so much as to catch a glimpse of the quarry. At length, wearied with their failure to obtain sport under abnormal difficulties, they gained the edge of the river, and there, upon a patch of smooth greensward beneath the cool shade of a cliff, they decided to off-saddle and have a snack.

"By Jove!" exclaimed Hoste, looking complacently around. "This is a lovely spot for a picnic. But wouldn't John Kafir have us in a hole just, if he were to come upon us now?"

"We are four fools," said Payne sententiously.

"We are," growled Carhayes. "You never said a truer word than that. Four damned fools to think we'd get a shot at anything in a strip of cursed country we've been chevying niggers up and down for the last six weeks. And as the idea was mine, I suppose I'm the champion fool of the lot," he added with a savage laugh. "We haven't fired a shot this blessed morning, and have had all our trouble for nothing."

This was not precisely the reflection that Payne's words were intended to convey. But he said nothing.

"I'm not sure we have had our trouble for nothing," put in Eustace. "It's grand country, anyhow."

It was. Magnificent and romantic scenery surrounded them; huge perpendicular krantzes towering up many hundreds of feet; piles upon piles of broken rocks and boulders, wherein the luxuriant and tangled vegetation had profusely taken root; great rifts and ravines, covered with dense black forest, and the swift murmuring current of the river joining its music with the piping of birds from rock and brake.

But the remark was productive of a growl only from Carhayes. He had not come out to look at scenery. They had had enough and to spare of that during the campaign. He had come out to get a shot at a buck, and hadn't got it.

Pipes were lighted, and the quartette lounged luxuriously upon the sward. The frowning grandeur of the towering heights, the golden glow of the sunlight upon the tree-tops, the soft, sensuous warmth of the summer air, the hum of insects, and the plashing murmur of the river, unconsciously affected all four—even grumbling, dissatisfied Tom Carhayes.

"Whisht!" said Payne suddenly, holding up his hand to enjoin silence, and starting from his lounging attitude. The others were prompt to follow his example.

"What's the row, George?" whispered Hoste below his breath. "Hear anything?"

For answer Payne waved his hand again and went on listening intently.

Up the sunlit river came a sound—a sound audible to all now, a sound familiar to all—the tread of hoofs upon the stones, of unshod hoofs. Mingling with this were other sounds—the low murmur of human voices. Water, as everybody knows, is a great conductor of sound. Though more than half a mile distant, they recognised the deep tones and inflections of Kafir voices, whose owners were evidently coming down to the river on the same side as themselves.

From their resting place the river ran in a long, straight reach. Peering cautiously through the bushes, they were able to command this. Almost immediately several large oxen, with great branching horns, emerged from the forest, and, entering the water, splashed through to the other side. They were followed by their drivers, three naked Kafirs, who plunged into the river in their wake, holding their assegais high over their heads, for the water came fully breast-high. They could even hear the rattle of the assegai hafts as the savages climbed up the opposite bank, laughing like children as they shook the water drops from their sleek, well-greased skins. They counted thirteen head of cattle.

"A baker's dozen, by Jove! Stolen, of course," whispered Hoste. "*Allamaghtaag*! if only we had known of that before we might have gone to *voer-ly* (Waylay) that drift, for it must be a drift. We might have bagged all three niggers and trundled the oxen back to camp. A full span, save three. Suppose they've eaten the rest. That'll be one apiece—the *schelms*!"

"It isn't altogether too late now," said Carhayes. "I smell some fun ahead. Let them get up over the rise, and then we'll go down and look if their spoor seems worth following."

"And what if they are only the advance guard of a lot more?" suggested Hoste.

"They are not," was the confident reply. "There are too few beasts and too few niggers. I tell you there's some fun sticking out for us."

Quickly the horses were saddled. A high, bushy ridge precluded all chance of their presence being discovered by the three marauders as soon as the latter had crossed the river, and it certainly had not been discovered before. Then, having allowed sufficient time to elapse, they forded the river and rode forward on the other side, so as to converge on the spoor leading up from the drift below.

"Here it is—as plain as mud," said Carhayes, bending over in his saddle to examine the ground, which, dry and sandy, showed the hoof-prints and footmarks so plainly that a child might have followed them. "They are well over the rise by now, and the way isn't so rough as I expected. Our plan is to make straight for the top of the hill. We can't get up much quicker than they can, I'm afraid, unless we want to blow our horses, which we don't. But once we are up there we shall find it all open *veldt*, and all we've got to do is to ride them down in the open, shoot the niggers, and head the stock back for the river again. Anyone propose an amendment to that resolution?"

"We are four fools," said Payne laconically, knocking the ashes out of his pipe and pocketing that useful implement.

"*Ja!* That's so," said Carhayes, joining heartily in the laugh which greeted this remark. "And now, boys, are we on for the fun, that's the question?"

"We just are," cried Hoste, whose dare-devil recklessness was akin to that of Carhayes. The other two acquiesced silently, but as they caught each other's glance, a curious satirical twinkle lurked in the eyes of both men.

"A case of the tail wagging the dog," presently whispered Payne to Eustace. "Two wise men led by two fools!"

The track, rough and stony, took longer to follow than they had expected. Moreover they had to exercise extreme care, lest the clink of the hoof-stroke of a shod horse perchance stumbling on the rocky way should be borne to the quick, watchful ears of those they were following. At length, however, the brow of the ridge was gained, and there before them lay a rolling expanse of open country, yet not so open as Carhayes had predicted, for it was pretty thickly dotted with mimosa, and the grass was long, coarse, and tangled, rendering rapid riding dangerous in parts.

Suddenly they came right upon a kraal nestling in a mimosa covered valley. Three old hags were seated against one of the beehive shaped huts, otherwise the place seemed quite deserted. No children were to be seen—not even a half-starved cur skulking around—and of men or cattle there was no sign. The spoor they were following had grown very indistinct, and here seemed to split up into several directions.

The old women, frightful, toothless crones, all wrinkles and flaps, showed no signs of alarm at this unexpected appearance of the invading white men. On the contrary, they began to abuse them roundly in a shrill, quavering treble.

"Macbeth *in excelsis*!" murmured Eustace at sight of them.

"Stop that cackling, you old hell-cats!" said Carhayes with a growl like that of a savage dog, as he drew his revolver and pointed it right at them, a pantomime which they thoroughly understood, for their high-pitched abuse dropped to a most doleful howl. "Here, Eustace. You can patter the lingo better than any of us, and I haven't the patience, damn it! Ask these old rag bags which way the fellows with the oxen took."

"We know nothing about men or oxen," came the prompt and whimpering reply.

"You do know. Tell us quickly!" repeated Eustace warningly.

Sullenly the first disclaimer was reiterated.

A furious expletive burst from Carhayes.

"We can't lose any more time being fooled by these infernal old hags!" he cried. "If they don't tell us before I count five I'll put a bullet through each of them. Now—*Inye—zimbini—zintátu*..." (One—two—three.)

"Hold hard, don't be a fool," warned Payne. "The shots are bound to be heard."

"So they are. I know a better trick than that." And striking a match Carhayes walked his horse up to the nearest hut. This was sufficient. The old crones shrieked for mercy, while one of them quavered out:

"Ride that way, *abelúngu*!" (White men) pointing in a direction they had not intended to take. "But you will have to ride far—very far."

Believing they had inspired sufficient terror to insure the truth of this information, and furiously cursing the time wasted in eliciting it, Carhayes crammed the spurs into his horse's flanks and started off at a gallop, followed by the other three. But the old crone's statement proved correct. A couple of miles further the tracks, which had been more or less scattered and indistinct, converged into one broad spoor. Another ridge, then down into a kloof, and up the other side. Then, as they gained the brow of yet another ridge, an excited ejaculation burst from the lips of all four. Nearly a mile in front, stringing up a long, gradual acclivity, trotted the thirteen oxen, urged forward by three natives.

"Hurrah! Now we'll cut 'em out!" yelled Carhayes, as they dashed forward in pursuit. The Kafirs, loath to abandon their spoil until absolutely forced to do so, redoubled their efforts, as with loud shouts and waving karosses they strove to accelerate the pace of the already overdriven animals.

"We'd better risk a long shot," shouted Hoste, as it became apparent that the pursued were very near the top of the rise, and in another moment would be out of sight. "There may be a lot of bush, on the other side, and we may lose them."

"No. Better not lose time or distance," said the more prudent Payne. "We'll have 'em directly."

Chapter Twenty Three.

"Onward they ply—in Dreadful Race."

The Kafirs, with their spoil, had disappeared, and on the pursuers gaining the ridge, there seemed, as Hoste had suggested, a pretty good chance of losing them altogether; for the mere depression of the ground down which they were racing, narrowed and deepened into a long, winding valley, thickly overgrown with mimosa bushes and tall grass. The marauders could now be seen straining every nerve to gain this—with their booty, if possible—if not, without it. Every shouted summons to them to stand or be shot seemed only to have the effect of causing them to redouble their efforts—winding in and out among the grass and thorn-bushes with the rapidity of serpents.

The pursuers were gaining. Rough and tangled as the ground now became, the speed of horses was bound to tell in the race. A few moments more and the spoil would be theirs. Suddenly, but very quietly, Eustace said:

"I say, you fellows—don't look round, but—turn your horses' heads and ride like the devil! *We are in a trap!*"

The amazed, the startled look that came upon the faces of those three would have been entertaining in the extreme, but for the seriousness of the occasion. However, they were men accustomed to critical situations. Accordingly, they slackened, as directed, and suddenly headed round their horses as if they had decided to abandon the pursuit.

Not a minute too soon had come Eustace's discovery and warning. Like the passing movement of a sudden gust, the grass and bushes rustled and waved, as a long line of ambushed savages sprang up on either side, and with a wild and deafening yell charged forward upon the thoroughly disconcerted and now sadly demoralised four.

The Kafirs had been lying hidden in horseshoe formation. Had our friends advanced a hundred yards further their doom would have been sealed. They would have been hemmed in completely. Happily, however, when Eustace uttered his warning, they had not quite got between the extremities of the "shoe."

As it stood, however, the situation was appalling to the last degree. Terrified to madness, the horses became almost unmanageable, rearing and plunging in a perfect frenzy, of fear, and it was all that their riders could do to steer them through the bristling thorn-bushes, a single plunge into one of which would, at the rate they were going, hurl both steed and rider to the earth. And, again, the wild war-cry pealed through the valley, and every bush and tussock of grass seemed to *grow* enemies—seemed to swarm with dark, sinuous forms, to blaze with the gleam of assegai blades and rolling eyeballs. The race for spoil had become a race for life.

There had been barely a hundred yards between them and their assailants when the latter first sprang up, and this distance had alarmingly decreased, for the nature of the ground, rough and overgrown with long, tangled grass, and the fact that they were being forced up-hill, tended to neutralise whatever advantage might lie with the mounted men. Moreover the horses, in no small degree blown after their recent spurt, were not at their best, whereas the Kafir warriors, active, hard as iron, had the advantage on that rough ground. On they pressed—their lithe, sinuous, ochre-greased bodies flashing through the grass like serpents—whooping, shouting, rending the air with their shrill, ear-splitting war-whistles. Although many of them had guns, yet not a shot was fired. Either those who led did not care to waste time in stopping to aim, and those who were behind feared to injure their friends in front; or for some reason of their own they were anxious to capture the white men alive. On it sped, that fearful race, the pursuers slowly but surely gaining. And now, from the swarming numbers of the main body, "horns" began to spread out at an angle to the line of flight as though to close up and intercept them further on, at some point best known to themselves.

It was a case of every man for himself. Hoste and Payne had gained some slight start, Eustace and Carhayes bringing up the rear. The latter, gripping his revolver, was in the act of delivering a shot into the thick of a mass of warriors who had raced up to within ten yards of them, when his horse stumbled. The animal had put its foot into an ant-bear hole concealed in the long grass. Down it came, plunging heavily forward on its nose, and shooting its rider over its head.

A deafening roar of exultation went up from the pursuers as they flung themselves upon Carhayes. Still, half-stunned as he was, the desperate pluck of the unfortunate man caused him to make an effort to rise. Only an effort though. As he rose to his knees he was beaten to the ground in a moment beneath the savage blows of the kerries of his assailants.

Eustace heard the crash of the fall, and turning his head, in spite of the deadly risk he ran in suffering his attention to wander from his own course even for a second, he took in the whole scene—the crowd of whooping, excited barbarians, clustering round the fallen man, assegais and kerries waving in the air, then the dull, sickening sound of blows. And even in that moment of deadly peril, his own fate as hopeless as that of the slain man, a thrill of fierce exultation shot through him. Fortune had once more played into his hands. Eanswyth was his. He had got his second chance. This time it was out of his power to throw it away even had he wished to do so. Still—the mockery of it! It had come too late.

Meanwhile, Payne and Hoste, being the best mounted, had obtained some little start, but even upon them the extended lines of the fierce pursuers were beginning to close.

"Now, George—both together! Let 'em have it!" yelled Hoste, pointing his revolver at the foremost of a mass of Kafirs who were charging in upon them on his side. The ball sped. The savage, a tall, sinewy warrior, naked as at his birth save for a collar of jackals' teeth and a leather belt round his waist, leaped high in the air and fell stone dead, shot through the heart. At the same time Payne's pistol spoke, and another barbarian fell, his knee shattered by the bullet. Crack! and down went another while in the act of poising his assegai for a fling.

"Up-hill work, but nearly through!" cried Payne as he dropped another of the pursuers in his tracks. The frightened steeds, with ears thrown back and nostrils distended, tugged frantically at their bits as they tore along, but the agile barbarians seemed to keep pace with them, though they refrained from again attempting to close. But now they began to throw their assegais. One of these grazed Payne's shoulder and stuck fast in the ground in front, quivering nervously. Another scored the flank of Hoste's horse, causing the poor animal to snort and bound with the sharp pain. Another stuck into Payne's boot, while a fourth hit Hoste fair between the shoulders, but having been hurled at long range and being withal a somewhat blunt weapon, it failed to penetrate the stout cord jacket.

"Devilish good shot, that," remarked the target. "But I say, George, where are the other fellows?"

"Dunno! It's a case of every man for himself now, and all his work cut out at that."

All this had been the work of but a few minutes, and now the brow of the hill was reached. A furious and bitter curse burst from the pair.

For on the plain beneath, converging upon their line of flight in such wise as to meet and utterly cut them off, extended two strong bodies of the enemy. These had circled round the hill, while the fugitives had been forced to the top of it, and now they would join hands before the latter could hope to pass through the rapidly closing circle.

"Through them, George. It's our only show!" cried Hoste. And with the reins gripped in his left hand and his revolver in his right, he sat down to his saddle for the last and final charge. It was a wildly exciting moment—the issues, life or death.

The lines were rapidly closing in. With maddened yells and assegais uplifted, the Kafir warriors were straining every effort to complete that fatal circle. A few yards more—twenty—ten! it was done. They were hemmed in.

But the headlong, dashing valour of the two men stood them well. Not a moment did they pause. With a wild shout Hoste put his horse straight at a huge barbarian who strove to stop him—knocking the savage sprawling, and through the opening thus breached the two horsemen shot like an arrow from the bow, and having the advantage of a down-hill course they left the fierce and yelling crowd behind in a trice. Far from safe were they yet. A hole concealed in the grass—a strained sinew—a hundred unforeseen circumstances—and they would be at the mercy of their merciless foes.

And now the latter began to open fire upon them, and the crackle of the volley behind mingled with the ugly hum of missiles overhead and around.

"*Allamaghtaag*! My horse is hit!" exclaimed Payne, feeling the animal squirm under him in a manner there was no mistaking.

"So?" was the concerned reply. "He's got to go, though, as long as you can keep him on his legs. If we can't reach the river, or at any rate the thick bush along it, we're done for."

They turned their heads. Though beyond the reach of their missiles now, they could see that the Kafirs had by no means relinquished the pursuit. On they came—a dense, dark mass streaming across the plain—steady of cruel purpose—pertinacious as a pack of bloodhounds. Hoste's steed was beginning to show ominous signs of exhaustion, while that of his companion, bleeding freely from a bullet hole in the flank, was liable to drop at any moment. And the welcome bush was still a great way off—so, too, was the hour of darkness.

Meanwhile Eustace, spurring for dear life, realised to the bitter full that the terrible event which, in spite of himself, he had so ardently desired, could be of no benefit to him now. For he knew that he was doomed. Nothing short of a miracle could save his life—which is to say, nothing could. The very earth seemed to grow enemies. Behind, around, in front, everywhere, those cat-like, sinuous forms sprang up as if by magic. Suddenly his bridle was seized. A mass of warriors pressed around him, assegais raised. Quick as thought he pointed his revolver at the foremost, and pressed the trigger; but the plunging of his horse nearly unseated him, and the ball whistled harmlessly over the Kafir's shoulder. At the same time a blow on the wrist knocked the weapon from his grasp. He saw the gleam of assegai points, the deadly glare of hatred in the sea of rolling eyes closing in upon him. Then a tall warrior, springing like a leopard, struck full at his heart with a large, broad-bladed assegai.

It was done like lightning. The flash of the broad blade was in his eyes. The blow, delivered with all the strength of a powerful, muscular arm, descended. A hard, numbing knock on the chest, a sharp, crashing pain in the head—Eustace swayed in his saddle, and toppled heavily to the earth. And again the fierce death-shout pealed forth over the wild *veldt*, and was taken up and echoed in tones of hellish exultation from end to end of the excited barbarian host.

The night has melted into dawn; the dawn into sunrise. The first rays are just beginning to gild the tops of the great krantzes overhanging the Hashi. At the foot of one of these krantzes lies the motionless figure of a man. Dead? No, asleep. Slumbering as if he would never wake again.

There is a faint rustle in the thick bush which grows right up to the foot of the krantz—a rustle as of something or somebody forcing a way through—cautiously, stealthily approaching the sleeper. The latter snores on.

The bushes part, and a man steps forth. For a moment he stands, noiselessly contemplating the prostrate figure. Then he emits a low, sardonic chuckle.

At the sound the sleeper springs up. In a twinkling he draws his revolver, then rubs his eyes, and bursts into a laugh.

"Don't make such a row, man," warns the new arrival. "The bush may be full of niggers now, hunting for us. We are in a nice sort of a hole, whichever way you look at it."

"Oh, we'll get out of it somehow," is Hoste's sanguine reply. "When we got separated last night, I didn't know whether we should ever see each other again, George. I suppose there's no chance for the other two fellows?"

"Not a shadow of a chance. Both wiped out."

"H'm! Poor chaps," says Hoste seriously. "As for ourselves, here we are, stranded without even a horse between us; right at the wrong end of the country; hostile niggers all over the shop, and all our fellows gone home. Bright look out, isn't it!"

"We are two fools," answers Payne sententiously.

Chapter Twenty Four.

A Dark Rumour in Komgha.

There was rejoicing in many households when it became known in Komgha that the Kaffrarian Rangers had been ordered home, but in none was it greater than in that run conjointly by Mrs Hoste and her family and Eanswyth Carhayes.

The satisfaction of the former took a characteristically exuberant form. The good soul was loud in her expressions of delight. She never wearied of talking over the doughty deeds of that useful corps; in fact, to listen to her it might have been supposed that the whole success of the campaign, nay the very safety of the Colony itself, had been secured by the unparalleled gallantry of the said Rangers in general and of the absent Hoste in particular. That the latter had only effected his temporary emancipation from domestic thrall in favour of the "tented field" through a happy combination of resolution and stratagem, she seemed quite to have forgotten. He was a sort of hero now.

Eanswyth, for her part, received the news quietly enough, as was her wont. Outwardly, that is. Inwardly she was silently, thankfully happy. The campaign was over—*he* was safe. In a few days he would be with her again—safe. A glow of radiant gladness took possession of her heart. It showed itself in her face—her eyes—even in her voice. It did not escape several of their neighbours and daily visitors, who would remark among themselves what a lucky fellow Tom Carhayes was; at the same time wondering what there could be in such a rough, self-assertive specimen of humanity to call forth such an intensity of love in so refined and beautiful a creature as that sweet wife of his—setting it down to two unlikes being the best mated. It did not escape Mrs Hoste, who, in pursuance of her former instinct, was disposed to attribute it to its real cause. But exuberant as the latter was in matters non-important, there was an under-vein of caution running through her disposition, and like a wise woman she held her tongue, even to her neighbours and intimates.

Eanswyth had suffered during those weeks—had suffered terribly. She had tried to school herself to calmness—to the philosophy of the situation. Others had returned safe and sound, why not he? Why, there were men living around her, old settlers, who had served through three former wars—campaigns lasting for years, not for months or weeks—their arms, too, consisting of muzzle-loading weapons, against an enemy more daring and warlike than the Kafirs of to-day. These had come through safe and sound, why not he?

Thus philosophising, she had striven not to think too much—to hope for the best. But there was little enough in that border settlement to divert her thoughts from the one great subject—apart from the fact that that one subject was on everybody's tongue, in everybody's thoughts. She had found an interest in the two young girls, in reading with them and generally helping to improve their minds, and they, being bright, well-dispositioned children, had appreciated the process; had responded warmly to her efforts. But in the silent night, restless and wakeful, all sorts of grisly pictures would rise before her imagination, or she would start from frightful dreams of blood-stained assegais and hideous hordes of ochre-painted barbarians sweeping round a mere handful of doomed whites standing back to back prepared to sell their lives dearly.

Every scrap of news from the seat of war she had caught at eagerly. She had shuddered and thrilled over the account of the battle with Shelton's patrol and its stirring and victorious termination. Every movement of the Kaffrarian Rangers was known to her as soon as it became public property, and sometimes before; for there were some in an official position who were not averse to stretching a point to obtain such a smile of welcome as would come into the beautiful face of Mrs Carhayes, if they confidentially hinted to her a piece of intelligence just come in from the front and not yet made known to the general public. She had even tried to establish a kind of private intelligence department of her own among some of the Kafirs who hung around the settlement, but these were so contradictory in their statements, and moreover she began to suspect that the rascals were not above drawing pretty freely upon their imaginations for the sake of the sixpences, or cast-off clothes, or packets of coffee and sugar, with which their efforts were invariably rewarded. So this she discontinued, or at any rate ceased to place any reliance on their stories.

She had heard from her husband once or twice, a mere rough scrawl of half a dozen lines, and those chiefly devoted to explaining that camp life—made up as it was of patrols and horse guards and hunting up the enemy—left no time for any such trivial occupations as mere letter-writing. She had heard from Eustace oftener, letters of great length, entertaining withal, but such as all the world might read. But this in no wise troubled her now, for she understood. Eustace was far too cautious to intrust anything that the world might *not* read to so uncertain a means of transit as was then at his disposal. Express-riders might be cut off by the enemy in the course of their precarious and sometimes extremely perilous mission; occasionally were cut off.

A few days now and she would see him again, would hear his voice, would live in the delight of his presence daily as before. Ah, but—how was it to end? The old thought, put far away into the background during the dull heartache of their separation, came to the fore now. They would go back to their home, to Anta's Kloof, and things would be as before. Ah, but would they? There lay the sting. Never—a thousand times never. Things could never be as they were. For now that her love for the one had been awakened, what had she left for the other? Not even the kindly toleration of companionship which she had up till then mistaken for love. A sentiment perilously akin to aversion had now taken the place of this. Alas and alas! How was it to end?

The return of the Kaffrarian Rangers became a matter of daily expectation. Preparations were made for their reception, including a banquet on a large scale. Still they came not.

Then an ugly report got wind in Komgha—whispered at first. A disaster had befallen. Several men belonging to the expected corps had been killed. They had constituted a patrol, report said—then a shooting party straying from the main body. Anyway, they had been cut off by the enemy and massacred to a man. It was only the Moordenaar's Kop affair over again, people said.

Later the rumour began to boil down a little. Only four men had come to grief as reported. They had left the main body to get up a bushbuck hunt on the banks of the Bashi. They must have crossed the river for some reason or other, probably in pursuance of their hunt; anyhow, they were surprised by the Kafirs and killed. And the missing men were Hoste, Payne, Carhayes, and Eustace Milne.

The rumour spread like wildfire. The excitement became prodigious. Men stood in eager knots at the street corners, at the bars, everywhere, each trying to appear as if he knew more about it than his fellows; each claiming to be a greater authority upon the probabilities or improbabilities of the case than all the rest put together. But all were agreed on one point—that the errand of breaking the news to those most concerned was the duty of anybody but themselves. And three of the unfortunate men were married; two of their wives—now widows, alas—being actually resident in the place, within a stone's throw, in fact. It was further agreed that, by whoever eventually performed, the longer this duty could be deferred the better. Further information might arrive any moment. It would be as well to wait.

For once, public opinion was sound in its judgment. Further information did arrive, this time authentic, and it had the effect of boiling down rumour considerably—in fact, by one-half. The four men had set out and crossed the Bashi into the Bomvana country, as at first stated. They had been attacked by the Kafirs in overwhelming numbers, and after a terrible running fight Hoste and Payne had escaped. Their horses had been mortally wounded and themselves forced to lie hidden among the thick bush and krantzes along the Bashi River for two nights and a day, when they were found in a half-starved condition by a strong patrol of the Rangers, which had turned back to search for them. The other two men were missing, and from the report of the survivors no hope could be entertained of their escape. In fact, their fate was placed beyond the shadow of a doubt, for the Rangers had proceeded straight to the scene of the conflict, and though they did not discover the bodies— which the jackals and other wild animals might have accounted for meanwhile—they found the spots, not very far apart, where both men had been slain, and in or near the great patches of dried-up blood were fragments of the unfortunate men's clothing and other articles, including a new and patent kind of spur known to have belonged to Milne.

This was better. The killed had been reduced from four to two, the number of widows from three to one. Still, it was sufficiently terrible. Both men had lived in their midst—one for many years, the other for a shorter time—and were more or less well-known to all. This time the news was genuine, for three of the Rangers themselves had ridden in with all particulars. The sensation created was tremendous. Everybody had something to say.

"Tell you what it is, boys," a weather-beaten, grizzled old farmer was saying— haranguing a gathering of idlers on the *stoep* of the hotel. "There's always something of that sort happens every war. Fellers get so darn careless. They think because Jack Kafir funks sixty men he's in just as big a funk of six. But he ain't. They reckon, too, that because they can't see no Kafirs that there ain't no Kafirs to see. Jest as if they weren't bein' watched every blessed step they take. No, if you go out in a big party to find Jack Kafir you won't find him, but if you go out in a small one, he'll be dead sure to find you. You may jest bet drinks all round on that. Hey? Did you say you'd take me, Bill?" broke off the old fellow with a twinkle in his eye as he caught that of a crony in the group.

"Haw, haw! No, I didn't, but I will though. Put a name to it, old *Baas*."

"Well, I'll call it 'French.' Three star for choice."

The liquid was duly brought and the old fellow, having disposed of two-thirds at a gulp, resumed his disquisition.

"It's this way," he went on. "I'm as certain of it as if I'd seen it. Them oxen were nothin' more or less than a trap. The Kafirs had been watching the poor devils all along and jest sent the oxen as a bait to draw them across the river. It's jest what might have been expected, but I'm surprised they hadn't more sense than to be took so easily. Hoste and Payne especially—not being a couple of Britishers—"

"Here, I say, governor—stow all that for a yarn," growled one of a brace of fresh-faced young Police troopers, who were consuming a modest "split" at a table and resented what they thought was an imputation.

"Well, I don't mean no offence," returned the old fellow testily. "I only mean that Britishers ain't got the experience us Colonial chaps has, and 'll go runnin' their heads into a trap where we should know better."

"All the more credit to their pluck," interrupted another patriotically disposed individual.

"Oh, shut up, Smith. Who the deuce is saying anything against their pluck?" cried someone else.

"Well, I'm sure I wasn't," went on the original speaker. "Tom Carhayes, now, is as plucky a fellow as ever lived—was, rather—and—"

"You don't call Tom Carhayes a Britisher, do you?" objected another man.

"Yes, I do. At least, perhaps not altogether. He's been here a good number of years now and got into our ways. Still, I remember when he first came out. And Milne only came out the other day."

"Well, Milne's 'blanket friends' have paid him off in a coin he didn't bargain for. Wonder what he thinks of 'em now—if he *can* think," said someone, with an ill-natured sneer—for Eustace, like most men with any character in them, was not beloved by everybody.

"Ah, poor chap," went on the old man. "Milne was rather too fond of the Kafirs and Carhayes was a sight too much down on 'em. And now the Kafirs have done for them both, without fear, favour, or—"

"Tsh—tsh—tsh! Shut up, man alive, shut up!"

This was said in a low, warning whisper, and the speaker's sleeve was violently plucked.

"Eh? What's the row?" he asked, turning in amazement.

"Why, that's her!" was the reply, more earnest than grammatical.

"Her? Who?"

"His wife, of course."

A Cape cart was driving by, containing two ladies and two young girls. Of the former one was Mrs Hoste, the other Eanswyth. As they passed quite close to the speakers, Eanswyth turned her head with a bow and a smile to someone standing in front of the hotel. A dead, awkward silence fell upon the group of talkers.

"I say. She didn't hear, did she?" stage-whispered the old man eagerly, when the trap had gone by.

"She didn't look much as though she had—poor thing!" said another whom the serene, radiant happiness shining in that sweet face had not escaped.

"Poor thing, indeed," was the reply. "She ought to be told, though. But I wouldn't be the man to do it, no—not for fifty pounds. Why, they say she can hardly eat or sleep since she heard Tom Carhayes was coming back, she's so pleased. And now, poor Tom—where is he? Lying out there hacked into Kafir mince-meat." And the speaker, jerking his hand in the direction of the Transkei, stalked solemnly down the steps of the *stoep*, heaving a prodigious sigh.

Chapter Twenty Five.

"The Curse has come upon me..."

The party in the Cape cart were returning from a drive out to Draaibosch, a roadside inn and canteen some ten or a dozen miles along the King Williamstown road. Two troops of Horse, one of them Brathwaite's, were encamped there the night before on their way homeward, and a goodly collection of their friends and well-wishers had driven or ridden over to see them start.

It was a lovely day, and the scene had been lively enough as the combined troops—numbering upwards of two hundred horsemen, bronzed and war-worn, but "fit" and in the highest of spirits, had struck their camp and filed off upon their homeward way, cheering and being cheered enthusiastically by the lines of spectators. An enthusiasm, however, in no wise shared by groups of Hlambi and Gaika Kafirs from Ndimba's or Sandili's locations, who, in all the savagery of their red paint and blankets, hung around the door of the canteen with scowling sneers upon their faces, the while bandying among themselves many a deep-toned remark not exactly expressive of amity or affection towards their white brethren. But for this the latter cared not a jot.

"Hey, Johnny!" sang out a trooper, holding out a bundle of assegais towards one of the aforesaid groups as he rode past, "see these? I took 'em from one of Kreli's chaps, up yonder. Plugged him through with a couple of bullets first."

"Haw! haw!" guffawed another. "You fellows had better behave yourselves or we shall be coming to look you up next. Tell old Sandili that, with our love. Ta-ta, Johnny. So long!"

It was poor wit, and those at whom it was directed appreciated it at its proper value. The scowl deepened upon that cloud of dark faces, and a mutter of contempt and defiance rose from more than one throat. Yet in the bottom of their hearts the savages entertained a sufficiently wholesome respect for those hardened, war-worn sharpshooters.

Handkerchiefs waved and hats were flourished in the air, and amid uproarious and deafening cheers the mounted corps paced forth, Brathwaite's Horse leading. And over and above the clamour and tumult of the voices and the shouting, Jack Armitage's bugle might be heard, wildly emitting a shrill and discordant melody, which common consent, amid roars of laughter, pronounced to be a cross between the National Anthem and "*Vat you goed an trek Ferreia.*" (A popular old Boer song.)

Into the fun and frolic of the occasion Eanswyth entered with zest. She had laughed until she nearly cried over the hundred-and-one comic little incidents inseparable from this scene of universal jollity. Even the boldest flights of wit attempted during the multifold and promiscuous good-byes interchanged had moved her mirth. But it was the light, effervescing, uncontrollable laughter of the heart.

The genial, careless jests of the light-hearted crowd, the good humour on every face, found its echo in her. In the unclouded blue of the heavens, the golden sunlit air, there seemed a vibrating chord of joyous melody, a poetry in the sweeping plains, even in the red lines of ochre-smeared savages filing along the narrow tracks leading to or from their respective locations. Her heart sang within her as once more the horses' heads were turned homeward. Any hour now might bring *him*. Why, by the time they reached home *he* might have arrived, or at any rate an express hurried on in advance to announce the arrival of the corps by nightfall.

"Rangers arrived?" repeated in reply to Mrs Hoste's eager question, one of two acquaintances whom they met upon the road when within a mile of the village. "N-no, not yet. They can't be far off, though. Three or four of their men have come in—Shelton among them."

"Oh, thanks, so much!" cried both the ladies, apparently equally eager. "We had better get on as soon as we can. Good-day."

In the fullness of her joy, the clouded expression and hesitating speech accompanying the information had quite escaped Eanswyth—nor had it struck her friend either. Then laughing and chatting in the highest of spirits, they had driven past the conversing groups upon the *stoep* of the hotel, as we have seen.

The trap had been outspanned, and the horses turned loose into the *veldt*. The household were about to sit down to dinner. Suddenly the doorway was darkened and a head was thrust in—a black and dusty head, surmounted by the remnant of a ragged hat.

"Morrow, missis!" said the owner of this get-up, holding out a scrap of paper folded into a note. Mrs Hoste opened it carelessly—then a sort of gasp escaped her, and her face grew white.

"Where—where is your *Baas*!" she stammered.

"*La pa*," replied the native boy, pointing down the street.

Flurried, and hardly knowing what she was about, Mrs Hoste started to follow the messenger. Eanswyth had gone to her room to remove her hat, fortunately.

"Oh, Mr Shelton—is it true?" she cried breathlessly, coming right upon the sender of the missive, who was waiting at no great distance from the house.

"Is it really true? Can it be? What awful news! Oh, it will kill her! What shall we do?"

"Try and be calm, Mrs Hoste," said Shelton gravely. "There is no doubt about its truth, I am sorry to say. It is fortunate you had not heard the first report of the affair which arrived here. All four of them were rumoured killed, I'm told. But—No, don't be alarmed," he added, hastily interrupting an impending outburst. "Your husband is quite safe, and will be here this evening. But poor Tom is killed—not a doubt about it—Milne too. And, now, will you break it to Mrs Carhayes? It must be done, you know. She may hear it by accident any moment; the whole place is talking about it, and just think what a shock that will be."

"Oh, I can't. Don't ask me. It will kill her."

"But, my dear lady, it *must* be done," urged Shelton. "It is a most painful and heart-breaking necessity—but it is a necessity."

"Come and help me through with it, Mr Shelton," pleaded Mrs Hoste piteously. "I shall never manage it alone."

Shelton was in a quandary. He knew Eanswyth fairly well, but he was by nature a retiring man, a trifle shy even, and to find himself saddled with so delicate and painful a task as the breaking of this news to her, was simply appalling. He was a well-to-do man, with a wife and family of his own, yet it is to be feared that during the three dozen paces which it took them to reach the front door, he almost wished he could change places with poor Tom Carhayes.

He wished so altogether as they gained the *stoep*. For in the doorway stood a tall figure—erect, rigid as a post—with face of a ghastly white, lips livid and trembling.

"What does this mean?" gasped Eanswyth. "What 'bad news' is it? Please tell me. I can bear it."

She was holding out a scrap of pencilled paper, Shelton's open note, which Mrs Hoste, in her flurry and horror, had dropped as she went out. It only contained a couple of lines:

> Dear Mrs Hoste:
>
> There is very bad news to tell, which regards Mrs Carhayes.
> Please follow the bearer at once.
>
> Yours truly, Henry Shelton.

"Quick—what is it—the 'bad news'? I can bear it—Quick—you are killing me," gasped Eanswyth, speaking now in a dry whisper.

One look at his accomplice convinced Shelton that he would have to take the whole matter into his own hands.

"Try and be brave, Mrs Carhayes," he said gravely. "It concerns your husband."

"Is he—is he—is it the worst!" she managed to get out.

"It is the worst," he answered simply, deeming it best to get it over as soon as possible.

For a minute he seemed to have reason to congratulate himself on this idea. The rigid stony horror depicted on her features relaxed, giving way to a dazed, bewildered expression, as though she had borne the first brunt of the shock, and was calming down.

"Tell me!" she gasped at length. "How was it? When? Where?"

"It was across the Bashi. They were cut off by the Kafirs, and killed."

"'They'? Who—who else?"

Shelton wished the friendly earth would open beneath his feet then and there.

"Mrs Carhayes, pray be calm," he said unsteadily. "You have heard the worst, remember—the worst, but not all. You cousin shared poor Tom's fate."

"Eustace?"

The word was framed, rather than uttered, by those livid and bloodless lips. Yet the listener caught it and bent his head in assent.

She did not cry out; she did not swoon. Yet those who beheld her almost wished she had done both—anything rather than take the blow as she was doing. She stood there in the doorway—her tall form seeming to tower above them—her large eyes sparkling forth from her livid and bloodless countenance—and the awful and set expression of despair imprinted therein was such as the two who witnessed it prayed they might never behold on human countenance again.

She had heard the worst—the worst, but not all—her informant had said. Had she? The mockery of it! The first news was terrible; the second—death; black, hopeless, living death. Had heard the worst! Ah, the mockery of it! And as these reflections sank into her dazed brain—driven in, as it were, one after another by the dull blows of a hammer, her lips even shaped the ghost of a smile. Ah, the irony of it!

Still she did not faint. She stood there in the doorway, curdling the very heart's blood of the lookers on with that dreadful shadow of a smile. Then, without a word, she turned and walked to her room.

"Oh! I must go to her!" cried Mrs Hoste eagerly. "Oh, this is too fearful."

"If you take my advice—it's better not! Not at present, at any rate," answered Shelton. "Leave her to get over the first shock alone. And what a shock it is. Bereaved of husband and cousin at one stroke. And the cousin was almost like a brother, wasn't he?"

"Yes," and the recollection of her recent suspicions swept in with a rush upon the speaker's mind, deepening her flurry and distress. "Yes. That is—I mean—Yes, I believe she was very fond of him. But how bravely she took it."

"Rather too bravely," answered the other with a grave shake of the head. "I only hope the strain may not be too much for her—affect her brain, I mean. Mrs Carhayes has more than the average share of strong-mindedness, yet she strikes me as being a woman of extraordinarily strong feeling. The shock must have been frightful, and although she didn't scream or faint, the expression of her face was one that I devoutly hope never to see upon any face again. And now, good-bye for the present. I'll call around later and hear how she's getting on. Poor thing!"

The sun of her life had set—had gone down into black night—yet the warm rays of the summer sunshine glanced through the open window of her room, glowing down upon the wide *veldt* outside and upon the distant sparkle of the blue sea. Never again would laughter issue from those lips—yet the sound of light-hearted chat and peals of mirth was ever and anon borne from without. The droning hum of insects in the afternoon air—the clink of horse-hoofs, the deep-toned conversation of natives passing near the window—all these familiar sounds of everyday life found a faint and far-away echo in her benumbed brain. What, though one heart was broken—the world went on just the same.

Stay! Was it but a few minutes ago that she passed out through that door trilling the cheerful fragments of the airiest of songs—but a few minutes since she picked up that fatal scrap of paper, and then stood face to face with those who brought her news which had laid her life in ruins! Only a few minutes! Why, it seemed years—centuries—aeons. Was it a former state of existence that upon which she now looked back as across a great and yawning gulf? Was she now dead—and was this the place of torment? The fire that burned forever and ever! How should she quench the fire in her heart and brain?

There was a very stoniness about her grief as if the blow had petrified her. She did not fling herself upon the couch in her agony of despair. No tears did she shed—better if she had. For long after she had gained her room and locked herself in alone she stood—stood upright—and finally when she sought a chair it was mechanically, as with the movement of a sleep walker. Her heart was broken—her life was ended. He had gone from her—it only remained for her to go to him.

And then, darting in across her tortured brain, in fiery characters, came the recollection of his own words—spoken that first and last blissful morning at Anta's Kloof. "If we are doing wrong through love for each other we shall have to expiate it at some future time. We shall be made to suffer *through* each other," and to this she had responded "Amen." How soon had those words come true. The judgment had fallen. He had gone from her, but she could not go to him. Their love, unlawful in this world, could never be ratified in another. And then, indeed, there fell upon her the gloom of outer darkness. There was no hope.

Chapter Twenty Six.

"And the Summer's Night is a Winter's Day."

For Eanswyth Carhayes the sun of life had indeed set.

The first numbing shock of the fearful news over, a period of even greater agony supervened. He who had succeeded in setting free the wholly unsuspected volcanic fires of her strong and passionate nature—him, her first and only love—she would never see again in life. If she had sinned in yielding to a love that was unlawful, surely she was expiating it now. The punishment seemed greater than she could bear.

She made no outcry—no wild demonstrations of grief. Her sorrow was too real, too sacred, for any such commonplace manifestations. But when she emerged from her first retirement, it was as a walking ghost. There was something about that strained and unnatural calm, something which overawed those who saw it. She was as one walking outside the world and its incidents. They feared for her brain.

As the days slipped by, people wondered. It seemed strange that poor Tom Carhayes should have the faculty of inspiring such intense affection in anybody. No one suspected anything more than the most ordinary of easy-going attachment to exist between him and his wife, yet that the latter was now a broken-hearted woman was but too sadly obvious. Well, there must have been far more in the poor fellow than he had generally been credited with, said the popular voice, and after all, those outside are not of necessity the best judges as to the precise relationship existing between two people. So sympathy for Eanswyth was widespread and unfeigned.

Yet amid all her heart-torture, all her aching and hopeless sorrow, poor Tom's fate hardly obtruded itself. In fact, had she been capable of a thorough and candid self-analysis she would have been forced to admit that it was rather a matter for gratulation than otherwise, for under cover of it she was enabled to indulge her heart-broken grief to the uttermost. Apart from this, horrible as it may seem, her predominating feeling toward her dead husband was that of intense bitterness and resentment. He it was who had led the others into peril. That aggressive fool-hardiness of his, which had caused her many and many a long hour of uneasiness and apprehension, had betrayed him to a barbarous death, and with it that other. The cruel irony of it, too, would burst upon her. He had avenged himself in his very death—had broken her heart.

Had Tom Carhayes been the only one to fall, it is probable that Eanswyth would have mourned him with genuine—we do not say with durable—regret. It is possible that she might have been afflicted with acute remorse at the part she had played. But now all thoughts of any such thing faded completely from her mind, obliterated by the one overwhelming, stunning stroke which had left her life in shadow until it should end.

Then the Rangers had returned, and from the two surviving actors in the terrible tragedy—Payne and Hoste, to wit—she learned the full particulars. It was even as she had suspected—Tom's rashness from first to last. The insane idea of bushbuck hunting in a small party in an enemy's country, then venturing across the river right into what was nothing more nor less than a not very cunningly baited trap—all was due to his truculent fool-hardiness. But Eustace, knowing that her very life was bound up in his—how could *he* have allowed himself to be so easily led away? And this was the bitterest side of it.

To the philosophic and somewhat cynical Payne this interview was an uncomfortable one, while Hoste subsequently pronounced it to be the most trying thing he had ever gone through in his life.

"Is there absolutely no hope?" Eanswyth had said, in a hard, forced voice.

The two men looked at each other.

"Absolutely none, Mrs Carhayes," said Payne. "It would be sham kindness to tell you anything different. Escape was an impossibility, you see. Both their horses were killed and they themselves were surrounded. Hoste and I only got through by the skin of our teeth. If our horses had 'gone under' earlier it would have been all up with us, too."

"But the—but they were not found, were they? They may have been taken prisoners."

Again the two men looked at each other. Neither liked to give utterance to what was passing through his mind. Better a hundredfold the unfortunate men were dead and at rest than helpless captives in the hands of exasperated and merciless savages.

"Kafirs never do take prisoners," said Payne after a pause. "At least, never in the heat and excitement of battle. And it is not likely that Carhayes or Milne would give them a chance, poor chaps."

"You mean—?"

"They would fight hard to the bitter end—would sell their lives dearly. I am afraid you must face the worst. I wish I could say otherwise, but I can't. Eh, Hoste?"

The latter nodded. He had very willingly allowed the other to do all the talking. Then, as all things come to an end sooner or later—even Wigmore Street—so eventually did this trying interview.

"I say, George. That just was a bad quarter of an hour," said Hoste, as the two companions-in-arms found themselves once more in their favourite element—the open air, to wit. "I don't want to go through it again many times in a lifetime. If ever there was 'broken heart,' writ large in any woman's face, it is on that of poor Mrs Carhayes. I believe she'll never get over it."

Payne, who had shown himself far from unfeeling during the above-mentioned trying interview, regarded this remark as a direct challenge to the ingrained cynicism of his nature.

"You don't, eh?" he replied. "Well, I don't want to seem brutal, Hoste, but I predict she'll be patching up that same 'broken heart' in most effective style at some other fellow's expense, before the regulation two years are over. They all do it. Lend us your 'bacco pouch."

Hoste said nothing. But for that little corner of the curtain of her suspicions which his wife had lifted on the first night of Eanswyth's arrival, he might have been three parts inclined to agree with his friend. As things stood, he wasn't.

But could they at that moment have seen the subject of their conversation, it is possible that even the shelly and cynical Payne might have felt shaken in his so glibly expressed opinion. In the seclusion of her room she sat, soft tears coming to the relief of the hitherto dry and burning eyes as she pressed to her lips, forehead, and heart, a little bit of cold and tarnished metal. It was the broken spur which Eustace had been wearing at the time of the disaster, and which her recent visitors had just given her. And over this last sorry relic she was pouring out her whole soul—sorrowing as one who had no hope.

Chapter Twenty Seven.

The Shield of her Love.

When Eustace Milne fell from his saddle to the earth, the savage who had stabbed him, and who was about to follow up the blow, started back with a loud shout of astonishment and dismay.

It arrested the others. They paused as they stood. It arrested assegai blades quivering to bury themselves in the fallen man's body. It arrested murderous knob-kerries whistling in the air ready to descend and crash out the fallen man's brains. They stood, those maddened, bloodthirsty barbarians, paralysed, petrified, as they took up with one voice their compatriot's dismayed shout.

"*Au! Umtagati! Mawo!*" (Ha! Witchcraft! A wonder!)

They crowded round the prostrate body, but none would touch it. The blow had been dealt hard and fair, by a hand which had dealt more than one such blow before, and always with deadly effect. Yet the wound did not bleed.

The dealer of it stood, contemplating his assegai, with looks of amazement, of alarm. Instead of driving its great broad blade up to the hilt in the yielding body of his victim, and feeling the warm blood gush forth upon his hand, the point had encountered something hard, with the effect of administering quite a shock to wrist and arm, so great was the force of the blow and the resistance. And the point of the spear blade had snapped off by at least an inch.

"Witchcraft!" they cried again. "He is dead, and yet he does not bleed. *Mawo!*"

He was. Not a movement stirred his limbs; not a breath heaved his chest ever so faintly. The lips, slightly parted, were as livid as the features.

For a few moments they stood contemplating their victim in speechless amazement. Then one, more daring or less credulous than his fellows, reached forward as if about to plunge his assegai into the motionless body. The rest hung breathlessly watching the result of the experiment. But before it could be carried into effect the deep tones of a peremptory voice suspended the uplifted weapon. Every head turned, and the circle parted to make way for the new arrival.

He was a tall, muscular Kafir, as straight as a dart, and carried his head with an air of command which, with the marked deference shown him, bespoke him a man of considerable rank. His bronzed and sinewy proportions were plentifully adorned with fantastic ornaments of beadwork and cow-tails, and he wore a headpiece of monkey skin surmounted by the long waving plumes of the blue crane.

Without a word he advanced, and, bending over the prostrate body, scrutinised the dead man's features. A slight start and exclamation of astonishment escaped him, then, recovering himself, he carefully examined, without touching it, the place where the assegai had struck. There it was, visible to all, a clean cut in the cord jacket—yet no sign of blood.

"*Au*! He does not bleed! He does not bleed!" ejaculated the crowd again.

By this time the numbers of the latter had augmented. Having given up the chase of the other two whites, or leaving it to their advance guards, the Kafirs swarmed back by twos and threes to where the gathering crowd showed that something unusual was going on.

The chief drew a knife from his girdle and bent once more over the prostrate form. But his purpose was not at present a bloodthirsty one, for he only held the broad blade across the livid lips. Then raising it he scrutinised it keenly. The bright steel was ever so slightly dimmed.

"Ha!" he exclaimed in a tone of satisfaction, rising to his feet after repeating the operation. Then he issued his orders, with the result that poor Eustace was lifted on to a stout blanket, and four men, advancing, shouldered a corner apiece and thus, with their living burden in their midst, the whole band moved away down the kloof.

After about two hours' marching, during which the country grew wilder and more wooded, they halted at a water-hole—one of a chain of several in the otherwise dried-up bed of a stream. Eustace was gently lowered to the ground, and, squatting around him, his bearers began to watch him with a great and gathering curiosity, for he was beginning to show signs of returning life.

At a rapid signal from the chief, water was fetched from the hole and his brow and face bathed. A tremor ran through his frame and a sigh escaped him. Then he opened his eyes.

"*Hau*!" exclaimed the Kafirs, bending eagerly forward.

At sight of the ring of dark faces gazing upon him in the gathering dusk, Eustace raised his head with a slight start. Then, as recollection returned to him, he sank wearily back. His head was aching, too, as if it would split. He would be fortunate if the blow which had deprived him of consciousness did not end in concussion of the brain.

With the return of consciousness came a feeling of intense gratification that he was still alive. This may seem a superfluous statement, yet not. Many a man waking to the consciousness that he was a helpless captive in the power of fierce and ruthless barbarians, has prayed with all his soul for the mercy of a swift and certain death, and has done so with a grim and terrible earnestness.

Not so, however, Eustace Milne. He had something to live for now. While there was life there was hope. He was not going to throw away a single chance.

To this end, then, he lay perfectly still, closing his eyes again, for he wanted to think, to clear his terribly aching and beclouded brain. And while thus lying, seemingly unconscious, his ears caught the subdued hum of his captors' conversation—caught the whispered burden of their superstitious misgivings, and he resolved to turn them to account.

"It is a powerful 'charm,'" one of them was saying. "We ought to find it—to take it away from him."

"We had better not meddle with it," was the reply. "Wait and see. It may not be too powerful for Ngcenika, or it may. We shall see."

"Ha! Ngcenika—the great prophetess. *Ewa, ewa!*" (Yes—yes) exclaimed several.

A powerful charm? Ngcenika, the prophetess? What did they mean. Then it dawned upon him as in a flash. The uplifted assegai, the great leaping barbarian, grinning in bloodthirsty glee as the weapon quivered in his sinewy grasp: then the blow—straight at his heart. It all came back lo him now.

Yet how had he escaped? The stroke had been straight, strong, and surely directed. He had felt the contact. Checking an impulse to raise his hand to his heart, he expanded his chest ever so slightly. No sharp, pricking pang, as of a stab or cut. He was unwounded. But how?

And then as the truth burst upon him, such a thrill of new-born hope radiated throughout his being that he could hardly refrain from leaping to his feet then and there. The silver box—Eanswyth's gift at parting—this was what had interposed between him and certain death! The silver box—with its contents, the representation of that sweet face, those last lines, tear stained, "warm from her hand and heart," as she herself had put it—this was what had turned the deadly stroke which should have cleft his heart in twain. What an omen!

A "charm," they had called it—a powerful "charm." Ha! that must be his cue. Would it prove too potent for Ngcenika? they had conjectured. The name was familiar to him as owned by Kreli's principal witch-doctress, a shadowy personage withal, and known to few, if any, of the whites, and therefore credited with powers above the average. Certain it was that her influence at that time was great.

More than ever now had he his cue, for he could guess his destination. They were taking him to the hiding place of the Paramount Chief, and with the thorough knowledge he possessed of his captors, the chance of some opportunity presenting itself seemed a fairly good one. But, above all, he must keep up his character for invulnerability. Neither peril nor pain must wring from him the faintest indication of weakness.

In furtherance of this idea—the racking, splitting pain in his head notwithstanding—he sat up and looked deliberately around as though just awakening from an ordinary sleep. He noticed a start run round the circle of swarthy, wondering countenances. As he did so, his glance fell upon one that was familiar to him.

"*Hau*, Ixeshane!" cried its owner, stepping forth from the circle. "You have come a long way to visit us!" and the ghost of a mocking smile lurked round the speaker's mouth.

"That is so, Hlangani. Here—tell one of them to dip that half-full of water at the hole." He had drawn a flask from his pocket and held out the metal cup. One of the Kafirs took it and proceeded to execute his request without a word. Then, adding some spirit to the water, he drank it off, and half-filling the cup again—with raw brandy—he handed it to the chief. Hlangani drained it at a single gulp.

"*Silúngile!*" (Good) he said briefly, then stood waiting as if to see what the other would say next. Calmly Eustace returned the flask to his pocket. But he said nothing.

After about an hour's halt the band arose, and, gathering up their weapons and such scanty *impedimenta* as they possessed, the Kafirs prepared to start.

"Can you walk, Ixeshane?" said the chief.

"Certainly," was the reply. His head was splitting and it was all he could do to keep on his feet at all. Still his new character must be kept up, and the night air was cool and invigorating. But just as he was about to step forth with the others, his arms were suddenly forced behind him and quickly and securely bound. There was no time for resistance, even had he entertained the idea of offering any, which he had not.

"Am I a fool, Hlangani?" he said. "Do I imagine that I, unarmed and alone, can escape from about two hundred armed warriors, think you? Why, then, this precaution?"

"It is night," replied the chief laconically.

It was night, but it was bright moonlight. The Kafirs were marching in no particular order, very much at ease in fact, and as he walked, surrounded by a strong body guard, he could form some idea of the strength of the band. This numbered at least a couple of hundred, he estimated; but the full strength of the party which had so disastrously surprised them must have consisted of nearly twice that number. Then he questioned them concerning the fate of his comrades. For answer they grinned significantly, going through a pantomimic form of slaying a prostrate enemy with assegais.

"All killed?" said Eustace, incredulously.

"No. Only the one who is with you," was the answer. "But the other two will be dead by this time. Their horses were used up, and our people are sure to have overtaken them long before they got to the river. *Au umlúngu!*" went on the speaker, "Were you all mad, you four poor whites, that you thought to come into the country of the Great Chief, Sarili, the Chief Paramount, and eat the cattle of his children?"

"But this is not his country. It belongs to Moni, the chief of the Amabomvane."

"Not his country. Ha!" echoed the listeners, wagging their heads in disdain. "Not his country! The white man's 'charm' may be potent, but it has rendered him mad."

"Ho, Sarili—father!" chorused the warriors, launching out into an impromptu song in honour of the might and virtues of their chief. "Sarili—lord! The Great, Great One! The deadly snake! The mighty buffalo bull, scattering the enemy's hosts with the thunder of his charge! The fierce tiger, lying in wait to spring! Give us thy white enemies that we may devour them alive. Ha—ah!"

The last ejaculation was thundered out in a prolonged, unanimous roar, and inspired by the fierce rhythm of the chant, the warriors with one accord formed up into columns, and the dark serried ranks, marching through the night, swelling the wild war-song, beating time with sticks, the quivering rattle of assegai hafts mingling with the thunderous tread of hundreds of feet, and the gleam of the moonlight upon weapons and rolling eyeballs, went to form a picture of indescribable grandeur and awe.

Again and again surged forth the weird rhythm:

> Ho, Sarili, son of Hintza!
> Great Chief of the House of Gcaléka!
> Great Father of the children of Xosa!
> Strong lion, devourer of the whites!
> Great serpent, striking dead thine enemies!
> Give us thy white enemies
>   that we may hew them into small pieces.
> Ha - Ah! Great Chief! whose kraals overflow with fatness!
> Great Chief! whose cornfields wave to feed a people!
> Warrior of warriors,
>   whom weapons surround like the trees of a forest!

We return to thee drunk with the blood of thine enemies.
"Há - há - há!"

With each wild roar, shouted in unison at the end of each of these impromptu strophes, the barbarians immediately surrounding him would turn to Eustace and flash their blades in his face, brandishing their weapons in pantomimic representation of carving him to pieces. This to one less versed in their habits and character would have been to the last degree terrifying, bound and at their mercy as he was. But it inspired in him but little alarm. They were merely letting off steam. Whatever his fate might eventually be, his time had not yet come, and this he knew.

After a great deal more of this sort of thing, they began to get tired of their martial display. The chanting ceased and the singers subsided once more into their normal state of free and easy jollity. They laughed and poked fun among themselves, and let off a good deal of chaff at the expense of their prisoner. And this metamorphosis was not a little curious. The fierce, ruthless expression, blazing with racial antipathy, depicted on each dark countenance during that wild and headlong chase for blood, had disappeared, giving way to one that was actually pleasing, the normal light-hearted demeanour of a keen-witted and kindly natured people. Yet the chances of the prisoner's life being eventually spared were infinitesimal.

Chapter Twenty Eight.

The Silver Box.

Throughout the night their march continued. Towards dawn, however, a short halt was made, to no one more welcome than to the captive himself; the fact being that poor Eustace was deadly tired, and, but for the expediency of keeping up his character for invulnerability, would have requested the chief, as a favour, to allow him some rest before then. As it was, however, he was glad of the opportunity; but, although he had not tasted food since the previous midday, he could not eat. He felt feverish and ill.

Day was breaking as the party resumed its way. And now the features of the country had undergone an entire change. The wide, sweeping, mimosa-dotted dales had been left behind—had given place to wild forest country, whose rugged grandeur of desolation increased with every step. Great rocks overhung each dark ravine, and the trunks of hoary yellow-wood trees, from whose gigantic and spreading limbs depended lichens and monkey ropes, showed through the cool semi-gloom like the massive columns of cathedral aisles. An undergrowth of dense bush hemmed in the narrow, winding path they were pursuing, and its tangled depths were ever and anon resonant with the piping whistle of birds, and the shrill, startled chatter of monkeys swinging aloft among the tree-tops, skipping away from bough to bough with marvellous alacrity. Once a sharp hiss was heard in front, causing the foremost of the party to halt abruptly, with a volley of excited ejaculations, as a *huge rinkhaals*, lying in the middle of the narrow track, slowly unwound his black coils, and, with hood inflated, raised his head in the air as if challenging his human foes. But these, by dint of shouting and beating the ground with sticks, induced him to move off—for, chiefly from motives of superstition, Kafirs will not kill a snake if they can possibly help it—and the hideous reptile was heard lazily rustling his way through the jungle in his retreat.

They had been toiling up the steep, rugged side of a ravine. Suddenly an exclamation of astonishment from those in front, who had already gained the ridge, brought up the rest of the party at redoubled speed.

"*Hau! Istiméle!*" (The steamer) echoed several, as the cause of the prevailing astonishment met their eyes.

The ridge was of some elevation. Beyond the succession of forest-clad valleys and rock-crowned divides lay a broad expanse of blue sea, and away near the offing stretched a long line of dark smoke. Eustace could make out the masts and funnel of a large steamer, steering to the eastward.

And what a sense of contrast did the sight awaken in his mind. The vessel was probably one of the Union Company's mail steamships, coasting round to Natal. How plainly he would conjure up the scene upon her decks, the passengers striving to while away the tediousness of their floating captivity with chess and draughts—the latter of divers kinds—with books and tobacco, with chat and flirtation; whereas, here he was, at no very great distance either, undergoing, in this savage wilderness, a captivity which was terribly real—a prisoner of war among a tribe of sullen and partially crushed barbarians, with almost certain death, as a sacrifice to their slain compatriots, staring him in the face, and a strong probability of that death being a cruel and lingering one withal. And the pure rays of the newly risen sun shone forth joyously upon that blue surface, and a whiff of strong salt air seemed borne in upon them from the bosom of the wide, free ocean.

For some minutes the Kafirs stood, talking, laughing like children as they gazed upon the long, low form of the distant steamship, concerning which many of their quaint remarks and conjectures would have been amusing enough at any other time. And, as if anything was wanting to keep him alive to the peril of his position, Hlangani, stepping to the prisoner's side, observed:

"The time has come to blind you, Ixeshane."

The words were grim enough in all conscience—frightful enough to more than justify the start which Eustace could not repress, as he turned to the speaker. But a glance was enough to reassure him. The chief advanced toward him, holding nothing more formidable than a folded handkerchief.

To the ordeal of being blindfolded Eustace submitted without a word. He recognised its force. They were nearing their destination. Even a captive, probably foredoomed to death, was not to be allowed to take mental notes of the approaches to the present retreat of the Paramount Chief. Besides, by insuring such ignorance, they would render any chance of his possible escape the more futile. But as he walked, steered by one of his escort, who kept a hand on his shoulder, he concentrated every faculty, short of the sight of which he was temporarily deprived, upon observations relating to the lay of the ground. One thing he knew. Wherever they might be they were at no great distance from the sea coast. That was something.

Suddenly a diversion occurred. A long, loud, peculiar cry sounded from some distance in front. It was a signal. As it was answered by the returning warriors, once more the wild war-song was raised, and being taken up all along the line, the forest echoed with the thunderous roar of the savage strophe, and the clash of weapons beating time to the weird and thrilling chant. For some minutes thus they marched; then by the sound Eustace knew that his escort was forming up in martial array around him; knew moreover, from this circumstance, that the forest had come to an end. Then the bandage was suddenly removed from his eyes.

The abrupt transition from darkness to light was bewildering. But he made out that he was standing in front of a hut, which his captors were ordering him to enter. In the momentary glance which he could obtain he saw that other huts were standing around, and beyond the crowd of armed men which encompassed him he could descry the faces of women and children gazing at him with mingled curiosity and wonder. Then, stooping, he crept through the low doorway. Two of his guards entered with him, and to his unspeakable gratification their first act was to relieve him of the *reim* which secured his arms. This done, a woman appeared bearing a calabash of curdled milk and a little reed basket of stamped mealies.

"Here is food for you, *Umlúngu*," said one of them. "And now you can rest until—until you are wanted. But do not go outside," he added, shortly, and with a significant grip of his assegai. Then they went out, fastening the wicker screen that served as a door behind them, and Eustace was left alone.

The interior of the hut was cool, if a trifle grimy, and there were rather fewer cockroaches than usual disporting themselves among the domed thatch of the roof—possibly owing to the tenement being of recent construction. But Eustace was dead tired and the shelter and solitude were more than welcome to him just then. The curdled milk and mealies were both refreshing and satisfying. Having finished his meal he lighted his pipe, for his captors had deprived him of nothing but his weapons, and proceeded to think out the situation. But nature asserted herself. Before he had taken a dozen whiffs he fell fast asleep.

How long he slept he could not tell, but it must have been some hours. He awoke with a start of bewilderment, for his slumber had been a heavy and dreamless one: the slumber of exhaustion. Opening his eyes to the subdued gloom of the hut he hardly knew where he was. The atmosphere of that primitive and ill-ventilated tenement was stuffy and oppressive with an effluvium of grease and smoke, and the cockroaches were running over his face and hands. Then the situation came back to him with a rush. He was a prisoner.

There was not much doing outside, to judge by the tranquillity that reigned. He could hear the deep inflections of voices carrying on a languid conversation, and occasionally the shrill squall of an infant. His watch had stopped, but he guessed it to be about the middle of the afternoon.

He was about to make an attempt at undoing the door, but remembering the parting injunction of his guard, he judged it better not. At the same time it occurred to him that he had not yet investigated the cause of the saving of his life. Here was a grand opportunity.

Cautiously, and with one ear on the alert for interruption, he took the silver box from the inside pocket in which it was kept. Removing the chamois leather covering, which showed a clean cut an inch long, he gazed with astonishment upon, the box itself. The assegai had struck it fair, and there in the centre of the lid its point, broken off flush, remained firmly embedded. He turned the box over. The point had just indented the other side but not sufficiently to show through.

For some minutes he sat gazing upon it, with a strange mixture of feeling, and well he might. This last gift of Eanswyth's had been the means of saving his life—it and it alone. It had lain over his heart, and but for its intervention that sure and powerfully directed stroke would have cleft his heart in twain. That was absolutely a fact, and one established beyond any sort of doubt.

Her hand had averted the death-stroke—the shield of her love had stood between him and certain destruction. Surely—surely that love could not be so unlawful—so accursed a thing. It had availed to save him—to save him for itself. Eustace was not a superstitious man, but even he might, to a certain extent, feel justified in drawing a highly favourable augury from the circumstance. Yet he was not out of his difficulties—his perils—yet. They had, in fact, only just begun; and this he knew.

So far his captors had not ill-treated him, rather the reverse. But this augured next to nothing either way. The Gcalékas had suffered severe losses. Even now they were in hiding. They were not likely to be in a very merciful mood in dealing with a white prisoner, one of the hated race which had shot down their righting men, driven them from their country, and carried off most of their cattle. The people would clamour for his blood, the chiefs would hardly care to run counter to their wish—he would probably be handed over to the witch-doctors and put to some hideous and lingering death.

It was a frightful thought, coming upon him alone and helpless. Better that the former blow had gone home. He would have met with a swift and merciful death in the excitement of battle—whereas now? And then it crossed his mind that the interposition of the silver box might not have been a blessing after all, but quite the reverse. What if it had only availed to preserve him for a death amid lingering torments? But no, he would not think that. If her love had been the means of preserving him thus far, it had preserved him for itself. Yet it was difficult to feel sanguine with the odds so terribly against him.

What would she do when she heard that Tom had been killed and himself captured by the savages? "Were anything to befall you, my heart would be broken," had been almost her last words, and the recollection of them tortured him like a red-hot iron, for he had only his own fool-hardiness to thank that he was in this critical position at all. Fortunately it did not occur to him that he might be reported dead, instead of merely missing.

His reflections were interrupted. A great noise arose without—voices—then the steady tramp of feet—the clash of weapons—and over and above all, the weird, thrilling rhythmical chant of the war-song. He had just time to restore the silver box to its place, when the door of the hut was flung open and there entered three Kafirs fully armed. They ordered him to rise immediately and pass outside.

Chapter Twenty Nine.

The Paramount Chief.

The spectacle which met Eustace's eyes, on emerging from the dark and stuffy hut, struck him as grand and stirring in the extreme.

He saw around him an open clearing, a large natural amphitheatre, surrounded by dense forest on three sides, the fourth being constituted by a line of jagged rocks more or less bush-grown. Groups of hastily constructed huts, in shape and material resembling huge beehives, stood around in an irregular circle, leaving a large open space in the centre. And into this space was defiling a great mass of armed warriors.

On they came, marching in columns, the air vibrating to the roar of their terrible war-song. On they came, a wild and fierce array, in their fantastic war dresses—the glint of their assegai blades dancing in the sunlight like the ripples of a shining sea. They were marching round the great open space.

Into this muster of fierce and excited savages Eustace found himself guided. If the demeanour of his guards had hitherto been good-humoured and friendly, it was so no longer. Those immediately about him kept turning to brandish their assegais in his face as they marched, going through the pantomime of carving him to pieces, uttering taunts and threats of the most blood-curdling character.

"*Hau umlúngu*! Are you cold? The fire will soon be ready. Then you will be warm—warm, ha-ha!" they sang, rubbing their hands and spreading them out before an imaginary blaze. "The wood is hot—ah-ah! It burns! ah-ah!" And then they would skip first on one foot, then on another, as if trying to avoid a carpeting of glowing coals. Or, "The fighting men of the Ama-Gcaléka are thirsty. But they will soon have to drink. Blood—plenty of blood—the drink of warriors—the drink that shall make their hearts strong. *Hau*!" And at this they would feign to stab the prisoner—bringing their blades near enough to have frightened a nervous man out of his wits. Or again: "The ants are hungry. The black ants are swarming for their food. It shall soon be theirs. Ha-ha! They want it alive. They want eyes. They want brains. They want blood! Ha-ha! The black, ants are swarming for their food." Here the savages would squirm and wriggle as in imitation of a man being devoured alive by insects. For this was an allusion to a highly popular barbarity among these children of Nature; one not unfrequently meted out to those who had incurred the envy or hostility of the chiefs and witch-doctors, and had been "smelt out" accordingly.

When all were gathered within the open space the war chant ceased. The great muster of excited barbarians had formed up into crescent rank and now dropped into a squatting posture. To the open side of this, escorted by about fifty warriors, the prisoner was marched.

As he passed through that sea of fierce eyes, all turned on him with a bloodthirsty stare, between that great crowd of savage forms, squatted around like tigers on the crouch, Eustace felt his pulses quicken. The critical time had arrived.

Even at that perilous moment he took in the place and its surroundings. He noted the faces of women, behind the dark serried ranks of the warriors, peering eagerly at him. There were, however, but few, and they wore a crushed and anxious look. He noted, further, that the huts were of recent and hasty construction, and that the cattle inclosure was small and scantily stocked. All this pointed to the conclusion that the kraal was a temporary one. The bulk of the women and cattle would be stowed away in some more secure hiding place. Only for a moment, however, was he thus suffered to look around. His thoughts were quickly diverted to a far more important consideration.

His guards had fallen back a few paces, leaving him standing alone. In front, seated on the ground, was a group consisting of a dozen or fourteen persons, all eyeing him narrowly. These he judged to be the principal chiefs and councillors of the Gcaléka tribe. One glance at the most prominent figure among these convinced him that he stood in the presence of the Paramount Chief himself.

Kreli, or Sarili, as the name is accurately rendered—the former being, however, that by which he was popularly, indeed, historically known—the chief of the Gcalékas and the suzerain head of all the Xosa race, was at that time about sixty years of age. Tall and erect in person, dignified in demeanour, despising gimcrack and chimney-pot hat counterfeits of civilisation, he was every inch a fine specimen of the savage ruler. His shrewd, massive countenance showed character in every line, and the glance of his keen eyes was straight and manly. His beard, thick and bushy for a Kafir, was only just beginning to show a frost of grey among its jetty blackness. Such was the man before whom Eustace Milne stood—so to speak—arraigned.

For some moments the august group sat eyeing the prisoner in silence. Eustace, keenly observing those dark impassive faces, realised that there was not one there which was known to him. He had seen Hlangani's gigantic form, resplendent or the reverse in the most wildly elaborate war costume, seated among the fighting men. Here in the group before him all were strangers.

While some of his chiefs were arrayed in costumes of plumes and skins and cow-tails exceeding fantastic, Kreli himself had eschewed all martial adornments. An ample red blanket swathed his person, and above his left elbow he wore the thick ivory armlet affected by most Kafirs of rank or position. But there was that about his personality which marked him out from the rest. Eustace, gazing upon the arbiter of his fate, realised that the latter looked every inch a chief—every inch a man.

"Why do you come here making war upon me and my people, *umlúngu*!" said the chief, shortly.

"There is war between our races," answered Eustace. "It is every man's duty to fight for his nation, at the command of his chief."

"Who ordered you to take up arms against us? You are not a soldier, nor are you a policeman."

This was hard hitting. Eustace felt a trifle nonplussed. But he conceived that boldness would best answer his purpose.

"There were not enough regular troops or Police to stand against the might of the Gcaléka nation," he replied. "Those of us who owned property were obliged to take up arms in defence of our property."

"Was your property on the eastern side of the Kei? Was it on this side of the Bashi?" pursued the chief. "When a man's house is threatened does he go four days' journey away from it in order to protect it?" A hum of assent—a sort of native equivalent for "Hear, hear," went up from the councillors at this hard hit.

"Do I understand the chief to mean that we whose property lay along the border were to wait quietly for the Gcaléka forces to come and 'eat us up' while we were unprepared?" said Eustace quietly. "That because we were not on your side of the Kei we were to do nothing to defend ourselves; to wait until your people should cross the river?"

"Does a dog yelp out before he is kicked?"

"Does it help him, anyway, to do so after?" replied the prisoner, with a slight smile over this new rendering of an old proverb. "But the chief cannot be talking seriously. He is joking."

"*Hau!*" burst forth the *amapakati* in mingled surprise and resentment.

"You are a bold man, *umlúngu*," said Kreli, frowning. "Do you know that I hold your life in my hand?"

This was coming to the point with a vengeance. Eustace realised that, like Agag, he must "walk delicately." It would not do to take up a defiant attitude. On the other hand to show any sign of trepidation might prove equally disastrous. He elected to steer as near as possible a middle course.

"That is so," he replied. "I am as anxious to live as most people. But this is war-time. When a man goes to war he does not lock up his life behind him at home. What would the Great Chief gain by my death?"

"His people's pleasure," replied Kreli, with sombre significance, waving a hand in the direction of the armed crowd squatted around. Then turning, he began conferring in a low tone with his councillors, with the result that presently one of the latter directed that the prisoner should be removed altogether beyond earshot.

Eustace accordingly was marched a sufficient distance from the debating group, a move which brought him close to the ranks of armed warriors. Many of the latter amused themselves by going through a wordless, but highly suggestive performance illustrative of the fate they hoped awaited him. One would imitate the cutting out of a tongue, another the gouging of an eye, etc., all grinning the while in high glee.

Even Eustace, strong-nerved as he was, began to feel the horrible strain of the suspense. He glanced towards the group of chiefs and *amapakati* much as the prisoner in the dock might eye the door of the room where the jury was locked up. He began talking to his guards by way of diversion.

"Who is that with Hlangani, who has just joined the *amapakati*?" he asked.

"Ukiva."

He looked with new interest at the warrior in question, in whose name he recognised that of a fighting chief of some note, and who was reported to have commanded the enemy in the fight with Shelton's patrol.

"And the man half standing up—who is he?"

"Sigcau—the great chief's first son. *Whau umlúngu!*" broke off his informant. "You speak with our tongue even as one of ourselves. Yet the chiefs and principal men of the House of Gcaléka are unknown lo you by sight."

"Those of the House of Gaika are not. Tell me. Which is Botmane?"

"Botmane? Lo!" replied several of the Kafirs emphatically. "He next to the Great Chief."

Eustace looked with keen interest upon the man pointed out—an old man with a grey head, and a shrewd, but kindly natured face. He was Kreli's principal councillor and at that time was reported to be somewhat in disfavour by reason of having been strenuously opposed to a war with the whites. He was well-known to Eustace by name; in fact the latter had once, to his considerable chagrin, just missed meeting him on the occasion of a political visit he had made to the Komgha some months previously.

Meanwhile the prisoner might well feel anxious as he watched the group of *amapakati*, for they were debating nothing less than the question whether he should be put to death or not.

The chief Kreli was by no means a cruel or bloodthirsty ruler—and he was a tolerably astute one. It is far from certain that he himself had ever been in favour of making war at that time. He was too shrewd and far-seeing to imagine that success could possibly attend his arms in the long run, but on the other hand he bore a deep and latent grudge against the English by reason of the death at their hands of his father, Hintza, who had been made a prisoner not altogether under circumstances of an unimpeachable kind and shot while attempting to escape. This had occurred forty years earlier.

So when the young bloods of the tribe, thirsting for martial distinction, had forced the hands of their elders and rulers, by provoking a series of frictions with their Fingo neighbours then under British protection, the old chief had exercised no very strenuous opposition to their indulging themselves to the top of their bent.

Having, however, given way to the war spirit, he left no stone unturned to insure success. Runners were sent to the Gaika and Hlambi tribes located in British Kaffraria, viz.: within the Colonial limits—but although plenty of young men owning those nationalities drifted across the Kei in squads to join his standard, the bulk of the tribes themselves were slow to respond to his appeal. Had it been otherwise, the position of the border people would have been more serious. With the enemy at their very doors they would have found plenty of occupation at home, instead of being free to pour their forces into the Transkei. Things, however, had turned out differently. The Gcaléka country had been ravaged from end to end, and the old chief was at that moment practically a fugitive. It may readily be imagined, therefore, that he was in rather an ugly humour, and not likely to show much clemency towards the white prisoner in his power.

There was another consideration which militated against the said clemency. Although he had made no allusion to it, it must not be supposed that Kreli was all this time unaware of the identity of his prisoner. The latter's friendship with many of the Gaika rulers was a rank offence in the eyes of the Paramount Chief just then. Had he not sent his "word" to those chiefs, and had not his "word" fallen on ears dull of hearing? Instead of rising at his call they were yet "sitting still." What more likely than that white men, such as this one, were influencing them—were advising them contrary to their allegiance to him, the Paramount Chief?

Some of the *amapakati* were in favour of sparing the prisoner at present. He might be of use to them hereafter. He seemed not like an ordinary white man. He spoke their tongue and understood their customs. There was no knowing but that he might eventually serve them materially with his own people. Others, again, thought they might just as well give him over to the people to be put to death in their own way. It would please the fighting men—many of whom had lost fathers and brothers at the hands of the whites. Yet again, one or two more originated another proposal. They had heard something of this white man being a bit of a wizard—that he owned a "charm" which had turned the blade of a broad assegai from his heart. Let him be handed over to Ngcenika, the great witch-doctress. Let her try whether his "charm" was too strong for her.

This idea met with something like universal acceptance. Shrewd and intelligent as they are in ordinary matters, Kafirs are given to the most childish superstitions, and, in adopting the above suggestion, these credulous savages really did look forward to witnessing something novel in the way of a competition in magic. In their minds the experiment was likely to prove a thing worth seeing.

"*Ewa! Ewa!*" ("Yes—yes") they cried emphatically. "Let Ngcenika be called."

"So be it," assented Kreli. "Let the witch-doctress be sought."

But almost before the words had left his lips—there pealed forth a wild, unearthly shriek—a frightful yell—emanating from the line of rugged and bush-grown rocks which shut in one side of the clearing. Chiefs, *amapakati*, warriors—all turned towards the sound, an anxious expression upon every face—upon many, one of apprehension, of fear. Even to the white prisoner the interruption was sufficiently startling. And then there bounded forth into their midst a hideous, a truly appalling apparition.

Chapter Thirty.

The Witch-Doctress.

Man, woman, or demon—which was it?

A grim, massive face, a pair of fierce, rolling eyes, which seemed to sparkle with a cruel and blood thirsty scintillation, a large, strongly built trunk, whose conformation alone betrayed the sex of the creature. Limbs and body were hung around thickly with barbarous "charms" in hideous and disgusting profusion—birds' heads and claws, frogs and lizards, snakes' skins, mingling with the fresh and bloody entrails of some animal. But the head of this revolting object was simply demoniacal in aspect. The hair, instead of being short and woolly, had been allowed to attain some length, and hung down on each side of the frightful face in a black, kinky mane, save for two lengths of it, which, stiffened with some sort of horrid pigment, stood erect like a couple of long red horns on each side of the wearer's ears. Between these "horns," and crowning the creature's head, grinned a human skull, whose eyeless sockets were smeared round with a broad circle in dark crimson. And that nothing should be wanting to complete the diabolical horror of her appearance, the repulsive and glistening coils of a live serpent were folding and unfolding about the left arm and shoulder of the sorceress.

Something like a shudder of fear ran through the ranks of the armed warriors as they gazed upon this frightful apparition. Brave men all—fearless fighters when pitted against equal forces—now they quailed, sat there in their armed might, thoroughly cowed before this female fiend. She would require blood—would demand a life, perhaps several—that was certain. Whose would it be?

The wild, beast-like bounds of the witch-doctress subsided into a kind of half-gliding, half-dancing step—her demoniacal words into a weird nasal sort of chant—as she approached the chief and his councillors.

"Seek not for Ngcenika, O son of Hintza, father of the children of Xosa!" she cried in a loud voice, fixing her eyes upon Kreli. "Seek not for Ngcenika, O *amapakati*, wise men of the House of Gcaléka, when your wisdom is defeated by the witchcraft of your enemies. Seek not Ngcenika, O ye fighting men, children of the Great Chief, your father, when your blood is spilled in battle, and your bullets fly harmless from the bodies of the whites because of the evil wiles of the enemy within your ranks. Seek her not, for she is here—here to protect you—here to 'smell out' the evil wizard in your midst. She needs no seeking; she needs no calling. She is here!"

"Ha! ha!" ejaculated the warriors in a kind of gasping roar, for those ominous words told but too truly what would presently happen. Not a man but dreaded that he might be the victim, and in proportion as each man stood well in rank or possessions, so much the greater was his apprehension.

"I hear the voices of the shadowy dead!" went on the sorceress, striking an attitude of intense listening, and gazing upwards over the heads of her audience. "I hear their voices like the whispering murmur of many waters. I hear them in the air? No. I hear them in the roar of the salt waves of yonder blue sea? No. I hear them in the whispering leaves of the forest—in the echoing voices of the rocks? No. In the sunshine? No. I am in the dark—in the dark!" she repeated, raising her tone to a high, quavering shriek, while her features began to work, her eyes to roll wildly. "I am in the gloom of the far depths, and the world itself is rolling above me. The air is thick. I choke. I suffocate. I am in the tomb. The rock walls close me in. There are faces around me—eyes—myriads of eyes—serpent eyes—hissing tongues. They come about me in the black gloom. They scorch—they burn. Ah-ah!"

An awful change had come over the speaker. Her features were working convulsively—she foamed at the mouth—her eyes were turned literally inward so that nothing but the white was visible. Her body swayed to and fro in short, irregular jerks, as though avoiding the attack of unseen enemies. The live serpent, which, grasped by the neck, she held aloft in the air, writhed its sinuous length, and with hood expanded and eyes scintillating, was hissing ferociously. The effect upon the savage audience was striking. Not a word was uttered—not a finger moved. All sat motionless, like so many statues of bronze, every eye bent in awesome entrancement upon the seer. Even Eustace felt the original contemptuous interest with which he had watched the performance deepen into a blood-curdling sort of repulsion. From the stage of mere jugglery the case had entered upon one which began to look uncommonly like genuine diabolical possession.

"I am in the gloom of the depths," shrieked the hideous sorceress, "even the Home of the Immortal Serpents, which none can find save those who are beloved of the spirits. The air is black and thick. It is shining with eyes—eyes, eyes—everywhere eyes. The ground is alive with serpents, even the spirits of our valiant dead, and they speak. They speak but one word and that is 'Blood! Blood—blood—blood!'" repeated the frightful monster. "Blood must flow! blood! blood!" And uttering a series of deafening howls she fell prone to the earth in frightful convulsions.

Not one of the spectators moved. The hideous features working, the eyes rolling till they seemed about to drop from their sockets, the foam flying from the lips—the body of Ngcenika seeming to stiffen itself like a corpse, bounded many feet in the air, and falling to the earth with a heavy thud, bounded and rebounded again—the festoons of barbarous and disgusting ornaments which adorned her person, twisting and untwisting in the air like clusters of snakes. The live *rinkhaals*, which had escaped from her grasp, lay coiled in an attitude of defence, its head reared threateningly.

For some minutes this appalling scene continued. Then the horrible contortions of the body ceased. The witch-doctress lay motionless; the swollen eyes, the terrible face, set and rigid, staring up to Heaven. She might have been dead. So, too, might have been the spectators, so still, so motionless were they.

The suspense was becoming horrible, the silence crushing. There was just a whisper of air among the leaves of the surrounding forest, causing a faint rustle, otherwise not a sound—not even the distant call of a bird. Eustace, gazing upon the motionless dark forms that surrounded him and upon the immeasurably repulsive figure of the prostrate demoniac, felt that he could stand it no longer—that he must do something to break that awful silence even though it should cost him his life, when an interruption occurred, so sudden, so startling in its unexpectedness, that he could hardly believe his eyes.

The witch-doctress, who had seemed prone in the powerlessness of extreme exhaustion for hours at least, suddenly sprang to her feet with a blood-curdling yell.

"The white wizard!" she shrieked. "The white wizard!"

"Ha! The white wizard! The white wizard!" echoed the warriors, relieved that the storm had passed them by this time. "Let us see. Is his charm too strong for Ngcenika?"

The time had come. Though unarmed, Eustace was still unbound. Instinctively and warily he glanced around, eager to grasp at some means of doing battle for his life. But no such means rewarded his glance.

Ngcenika walked up to one of the guards, and laid her hand on the bundle of assegais which he carried. The man surrendered it with alacrity, striving to conceal the apprehension which came over his features as he came face to face with the terrible witch-doctress. She chose a short-handled, broad-bladed stabbing assegai, examined it critically, and returned to her former position.

Placing the weapon on the ground she proceeded to dance round it in a circle, chanting a weird, droning incantation. The prisoner watched her keenly. No attempt had been made to bind him. At last her song ceased. Grasping the assegai in her powerful right hand, she advanced towards Eustace.

At a sign from Ngcenika the guards fell back some twenty yards. Behind them were the dense ranks of armed warriors, all craning eagerly forward to watch what was to follow. At about the same distance in front sat the group of chiefs and councillors, so that the prisoner and the sorceress were completely hemmed in.

"White wizard—white dog!" she began, standing within striking distance. "Wizard indeed! What is thy magic worth? Dost thou not fear me?"

Eustace, seeing through the repulsive mass of gew-gaws which represented the juggling line of business, realised that he had to deal with a powerful, broadly built, middle-aged woman of about five foot ten. She looked hard and muscular, and as strong as any two men—in fact, no mean antagonist, even had he been similarly armed, and he was unarmed.

"No, I do not fear you," he replied quietly, keeping his eyes upon hers, like a skilful fencer. The answer seemed rather to amuse than irritate her.

"He does not fear me!" she repeated. "Ha! *Inyoka*, (Serpent), does he fear thee!" she cried, darting the serpent's head within a couple of inches of the prisoner's face. The reptile hissed hideously, but Eustace, who knew that it had been rendered harmless, and that it must long since have spat its venom glands empty, did not allow himself to be disconcerted by this. A murmur of wonder arose from the spectators.

(The *rinkhaal*, a variety of cobra, has the faculty of being able, when angry, to eject an acrid, venomous saliva, to a distance of about six feet.)

"He is not afraid! The white wizard is not afraid!" they cried.

"Dost thou dare to stand before me while I strike thee? Is thy charm potent enough, O white wizard?" said Ngcenika, raising the assegai in the air.

"I dare."

"Present thy breast, then. Give thy heart to my stroke. Let thy 'charm' protect thee if it can."

A desperate plan had occurred to Eustace—to wrench the assegai from the hag's hand and make a dash for the forest. But even concurrently with the idea, he realised the absolute impracticability of it. He more, than doubted his ability to disarm his adversary; he had no doubt at all as to the certainty of his being seized long before he could accomplish that feat. No—he must stand up to the blow. It was his only chance, and at any rate his death would be a swift and painless one.

The dark, brawny arm of the sorceress was upraised, her muscular fingers gripped the assegai haft a few inches from the blade. The shining spear-head gleamed aloft.

Not once did his glance wander from that cruel demon-face confronting him. Yet between it and him floated the sweet, oval contour of another very different countenance.

"Love of my life—preserve that life once more for thyself!" he murmured with the impassioned fervour of an invocation of faith. His lips moved.

"Ha! Thou repeatest thy charm, O white wizard," said Ngcenika. "Is it stronger than mine? Is it stronger than mine?"

One might have heard a pin drop. That fierce, excitable crowd, bending forward, straining their eyes upon this unwonted scene, held their very breath as they gazed.

The prisoner stood with chest expanded—erect—facing the witch-doctress. There was a flash of light through the air, and the spear descended. No writhing body, gushing with blood, sank to the earth. The prisoner stood, erect and smiling.

"*Hau*!" cried the warriors. "The 'charm' is too strong. The white man is unhurt—*Mawo*!"

Ngcenika could be seen examining the point of her assegai in scowling concern. It was completely flattened and turned.

It must not be supposed that Eustace was so simple as to imagine that the sorceress would strike at the spot where she knew the impediment was concealed—over his heart, to wit. That cunning she-devil, as he well knew, would aim just to the right of this, and would reckon infallibly upon transfixing him. Accordingly, while watching the stroke, with incredible quickness and dexterity he timed himself to swerve slightly in that direction thus actually catching the point of the weapon upon the silver box. Again had the love of Eanswyth stepped between himself and death.

"Where is the man who owns this spear?" cried the witch-doctress, suddenly.

With much inward trepidation a warrior stepped forward.

"Thy weapon is bewitched!" cried the hag, in a terrible voice.

The man made no reply. He thought his doom was sealed.

"Yes, thy weapon is bewitched." Then raising her voice: "Where is the man who struck this white wizard in battle?"

A moment's hesitation—and there advanced from the ranks of the fighting men a tall, powerful warrior. He grasped in his hand a broad-bladed assegai, with the point broken short off.

"I am Mfulini, the son of Mapute," he began, not waiting to be addressed first. "I am a fighting man of the race of Gcaléka! I love war. *Hau*! I have struck more than one enemy, but have never struck him twice. *Hau*! I struck this white man and my weapon broke, my strong *umkonto* (The broad headed close-quarter assegai) that has drunk the heart's blood of five Fingo dogs. The weapon is bewitched. He who has done this thing must be found. The wizard must be found. *Hau*!"

"*Ewa, Ewa*!" shouted the warriors. "The wizard must be found. The great witch-doctress must find him. Then will the white man's magic be no longer too strong for her. He must be killed! Find him! Find him! He must be killed!"

Chapter Thirty One.

The "Smelling Out."

"He must be killed! He must be killed!"

The cry was taken up. The bloodthirsty shout rolled through the ranks fiercer and fiercer till the wild roaring chorus was deafening. That crouching, armed multitude, a moment before so motionless and silent, sprang erect, swaying to and fro, frenzied with uncontrollable excitement; a legion of dark demons roaring and howling under the promptings of superstition and ferocity; bellowing for blood—blood, blood, no matter whose. Weapons waved wildly in the air, and the deep-throated shout volleyed forth. "He must be killed!"

The warriors were seated in an immense double semicircle. Gliding with her half-dancing step to the upper end of this, the witch-doctress began chanting an incantation in a high nasal key, an invocation to the great *Inyoka* (Serpent) who held the kraal and its inhabitants under its especial favour. As she commenced her round, the shouting of the warriors was hushed. All stood upright and silent. Different emotions held sway in each grim, dark countenance. The hearts of many were sinking with deadly fear, yet each strove to meet the eye of the terrible witch-doctress boldly and without quailing. They knew that that fatal round would prove of deadly import to one or more of them ere it was completed.

"Ho—*Inyoka 'nukulu*!" (Great serpent) chanted the hag, with a significant shake of the body of the hideous reptile, which she held by the neck. "Find the wizard! Find the wizard!"

"Find the wizard!" echoed those whom she had already passed by as she commenced her passage along the line.

"Find the wizard!" they shouted, rapping the ground with their sticks. Those who had yet to undergo the ordeal kept stem silence.

The chorus grew in volume as the number qualified to swell it increased. Not merely a lust for blood did that horrid shout represent—it embodied also a delirious relief on the part of those already safe.

Suddenly Ngcenika made a half pause, raising her voice in the midst of her yelling chant. The serpent, its black coils writhing and twisting around her arm, opened its jaws and hissed horribly. Those still expectant held their breaths; those already relieved shouted and hammered with their sticks harder than ever. Those directly opposite the sorceress, at this ill-omened juncture, stood turned to stone.

"Find him, Inyoka!" snarled the hag.

"Find him! Find him!" echoed the deep-toned chorus.

But the pause was only momentary. Not yet was the victim singled out. Ngcenika resumed her way, only to repeat the process further along the line. And this she would do at intervals, sometimes coming to a dead stop in such significant and purpose-fraught fashion that the whole body of spectators stood ready to hurl themselves like lightning upon the unlucky one denounced. The hellish hag was enjoying the terror she inspired, and as strong men of tried bravery one after another quailed before her she gloated over their fears to such a pitch that her voice rose to a deafening shriek of demoniacal glee.

The other end of the great human crescent was nearly reached and still no victim. And now those who had escaped so far began to feel their apprehensions return. It would be no unprecedented affair were a second trial to occur, or even a third. The sorceress might elect to make her fatal progress through the ranks again and again. There were barely fifty men left. Unless the victim or victims should be found among those, a second progress was inevitable.

The bloodthirsty chorus rose into a deafening roar. The tension was fearful to witness. The hideous possession of the repulsive witch-doctress had communicated itself in some degree to the mass of excitable savages. Many were foaming at the mouth and apparently on the eve of convulsions. Not satisfied with the shouting, the infuriated mob beat time with their feet in addition to their sticks, as they joined in the hell-hag's demoniacal incantations, and the perspiration streamed from every pore till the very air was heavy with a sickening and musky odour. It was a repellent and appalling scene, and even the white spectator, apart from the extreme peril of his own situation, felt his blood curdle within him at this vision of what was very like a diabolical power let loose. But there was worse to follow.

Suddenly the sorceress was seen to halt. Her voice rose to a frightful yell, as with blazing eyes, and pouring forth a torrent of denunciation, she raised the great black serpent aloft in such wise that its writhing neck and hissing jaws made a dart straight at the face of a man in the rear rank of the line and near the end of the latter.

"Thou hast found him, *Inyoka*! Thou hast found him! Show us the wizard!" screeched the hideous witch-doctress. The grinning skull and the two devil-like horns of hair which surmounted her head quivered convulsively. Her eyes started from the sockets, and the weird and barbaric amulets hung about her person rattled like castanets. She was once more the mouthing demoniac of a short half-hour ago.

The writhings and hisses of the serpent had become perfectly frantic. Suddenly the reptile was seen to spring free of her grasp and to fling itself straight at the man whose face it had first struck at.

"The wizard! The wizard!" roared the warriors. "*Hau*! It is Vudana! Vudana, the son of Sekweni, *Hau*!"

"Vudana, the wizard! Seize him!" shrieked the sorceress. "Seize him, but slay him not. He must confess! He must confess! On your lives, slay him not!"

The first part of her mandate had already been obeyed. Those in his immediate neighbourhood had flung themselves upon the doomed man and disarmed him almost before the words of denunciation had left the hag's lips. The second part was in no danger of being disobeyed now. Better for the victim if it had.

The latter was a man just past middle age, with a quiet and far from unpleasing cast of features. He was not a chief, but had a reputation for shrewdness and foresight beyond that of many an accredited leader.

"Ha, Vudana! Vudana, the wizard!" cried Ngcenika mockingly. "Vudana, who did not believe in the efficacy of my magic. Vudana, who pretended to manufacture 'charms' as effective as mine. Vudana, whose poor attempts at magic have been effective to destroy mine in the case of all who believed in them. Call the names of those who fell," she cried, addressing the crowd. "They are all believers in Vudana, not in me! Where are they now? Ask the Amanglezi—even the Amafengu, before whose bullets they fell. Ask the jackal and the vulture, who have picked their bones. Ask Mfulini, the son of Mapute, whose weapon was turned by the magic of the white man! Was he a believer in Vudana's 'charms'?" she added in a menacing voice, rolling her eyes around.

"He was not," shouted the warrior named, springing forward. "Where is the man who bewitched my broad *umkonto*. Let him confess and say how he did it."

"It is well, Mfulini," said the witch-doctress grimly, knowing that the other trembled for his personal safety now that she had dexterously turned suspicion upon him. "Thou shall be the man to make him confess."

"I have nothing to confess," said Vudana. He lay on his bark, held powerless by several men while waiting for a *reim* to be brought wherewith to bind him. He knew that he was doomed—doomed not merely to death, but to one of the differing forms of frightful torment meted out to those accused of his offence. He knew moreover that whether he accused himself or not the result would be the same, and a warrior light blazed from his eyes as he replied.

"If the Great Chief wants my cattle, my possessions, they are his; let him take them. If he wants my life, it too is his; let him take it. But I will not accuse myself of that which I have never committed."

If Kreli had heard this appeal he made no sign. Witchcraft was an offence—theoretically at any rate—outside the secular province. "Smelling out" was a good old custom which had its uses, and one not lightly to be interfered with. It was doubtful, however, whether he did hear, for a shout of execration, led by the witch-doctress, drowned the victim's words.

"He will not confess! *Au*! Where are the hot stones? To the fire! To the fire!" roared the crowd. The witch-doctress uttered a fiendish laugh.

"No. To the ants!" she cried.

"*Ewa! Ewa*! To the ants!" they echoed. "Bring him along. *Hau*! The ants are hungry!"

A noosed *reim* was thrown round the doomed man's neck, and another made fast to each of his wrists, and thus, with the whole crowd surging and yelling around him, he was dragged into the adjoining forest.

"*Hamba-ké, umlúngu*!" ("Go on, white man") said several of the warriors guarding Eustace, motioning him to proceed. "We are going to show you a sight. Quick, or we shall be late!"

By no means free from apprehension on his own account, Eustace obeyed. When they arrived among the eager and excited crowd, the entertainment had already begun. All made way for the white prisoner and his guards, and there was a fiendish leer on many a dark face which needed not a muttered remark or two to explain. The horrible scene he was about to witness was extremely likely to be his own fate.

The doomed man lay spread eagled on his back; his hands and feet, stretched to their utmost tension, were fastened to stout pegs driven into the ground. Two of the Kafirs were busily anointing his naked body with a sticky compound, which was, in fact, a mixture of honey and native beer. This they smeared over him with bits of rag: ears, eyes, nose, coming in for a plentiful share. Already his flesh seemed alive with moving objects, and then the cause became apparent. The wretched man was tied down right across a huge ant's nest, which had been broken in order to receive his body. Already the infuriated insects were making their bites felt. *He was to be devoured alive by black ants.*

"Confess, Vudana," cried Ngcenika. "Confess thy witchcraft and how thy 'charms' were obtained. The black ants bite hard. Ha!"

"Confess? Ha-ha!" jeered the sufferer, his eyes blazing. "Not to thee, vulture. Not to thee, jackal. Not to thee, spawn of a Fingo dog. Ha! That is the witch-doctress of the Amagcaleka! Such a thing as that! What magic can she make? A cheat—a liar! I can die—I can die as I have lived—a man, a warrior."

"*Hau*! A wizard! A traitor!" vociferated the crowd. "Confess thy witchcraft, lest we put thee to the flaming torment. The fire bites deeper than the black ants. *Hau*!"

"I laugh at the fire," roared the victim. "I laugh at all that you can do. The fire is but a pleasant warmth. The bite of the ants is but the softest tickling. Thou dog, Mfulini, were I free, I would whip thee round the kraal."

"Is thy bed a comfortable one, Vudana?" replied the barbarian thus apostrophised, with a sneer. And picking up a handful of the venomous insects he scattered them upon the tortured man's face with a brutal laugh.

For all his defiant fortitude the latter was undergoing agonies. The ants were swarming all over his body, crawling into his nostrils and ears, biting everywhere, eating the rims of his eyelids, his lips, his throat, and he was powerless to move a hand or foot. The spectators crowded around, mocking and jeering at him. A few minutes ago he was a man of consideration—now all pushed and fought for the front places to witness his sufferings, all heaped execrations upon him as they gloated over the horrible punishment of one who had been denounced as a wizard.

"Whose magic is the greatest, Vudana—thine or mine?" jeered Ngcenika, bending over her victim until her face was close to his. But the proximity of that repulsive countenance infuriated even the helpless victim. With a roar of rage he spat full into it, vociferating:

"Thou spawn of a Fingo dog! Thine hour is come. I have put my mark upon thee. Before many moons are dead thou too shalt die, and thy death shall be even as mine. I, Vudana, say it. Hear ye my words all!"

"He has confessed," shouted the crowd. "He is a wizard. He has confessed. Let him die the death!"

With a yell of fury Ngcenika started back, and glared vengefully around as if inquest of some means whereby to add to the sufferer's agony. Then she remembered that it would hardly bear adding to under the circumstances, and contented herself with a satanic laugh.

Nor would it. In a short time the miserable man's body was black with the repulsive insects. They swarmed into his ears and nostrils. His struggles became fearful, as he writhed in the excruciating torment of their poisonous bites. He foamed at the mouth. His eyeballs rolled and strained in their

sockets, and he shook his head and roared like a beast. It would be impossible to exaggerate the agonies he was undergoing. His frantic struggles availed not to shake off a single one of the myriad insects swarming upon him. Already his eyes were half eaten away.

It was a fiendish and appalling spectacle. The man was now raving mad. He gnashed his teeth and howled. His contortions were fearful to witness. Yet no spark of pity or compunction did the sight awaken in the ferocious hearts of the spectators, many of whom were, up to the moment of the fatal denunciation, his kindred and his friends. But since his treatment of the witch-doctress all were chary of venturing too close. Many of the superstitious barbarians had already began to look upon Ngcenika with decreased respect. Vudana, suffering as a wizard, had spat in her face, accompanying the act with a prophecy and a curse. On no consideration would they run the risk of exposing themselves to like treatment.

Eustace, forced to be a spectator of this blood-curdling scene, felt his head swim with horror and disgust. The chastened gloom of the forest, the gibing crowd of armed savages, the weird shrill singing of the witch-doctress, and the frightful contortions and beast-like roars of the miserable victim, who was being literally devoured alive, made up a picture likely to haunt a man in his dreams for the rest of his life, to start him suddenly awake in a cold sweat of terror. Still he remembered that any exhibition of feeling would be in the highest degree dangerous, and controlled himself accordingly.

All this had taken some time and now the frantic struggles of the sufferer had subsided. A convulsive shudder would now and then run through his limbs, and his sightless eyeballs would roll in a manner hideous to behold, and ever the disgusting insects swarmed over him in a horrible moving mass, now red with blood, and smothered beneath gouts of saliva which had flown from the maniac's lips. Upon his violent struggles had followed exhaustion—mercifully, the exhaustion of approaching death.

"He is dying!" cried several, bending over the victim. "*Hau*! A man like Vudana should have taken much longer to die."

This was said in a disappointed tone. The barbarous appetite of these savages was thoroughly roused—whetted for further atrocities. A shout arose.

"The white man! The white man! What shall we do with him?"

Well might Eustace start, in horror and dismay. But a glance served to show that the object of attention was not himself, but somebody at the other end of the crowd, in which direction all heads were turned. Then as the crowd parted a moment he caught a glimpse of something—somebody rather—which evoked a second start, this time one of very unequivocal amazement. Could he believe his eyes?

Chapter Thirty Two.

A Strange Duel.

In the midst of the savage throng was another white man, also a prisoner, who had been forced to assist at the barbarous scene just detailed. His lot, however, had been cast in far worse lines than that of Eustace, for his hands were tightly fastened behind his back and a *reim* connected his ankles in such wise that he could only take short steps—which painful fact he would every now and then forget, with the result of just so many ignominious "croppers." Whereat his dusky tormentors would shout with gleeful laughter.

In addition to his bonds the unfortunate man appeared to have undergone considerable maltreatment. His hair and beard were matted with dust and blood, and his head was rudely bandaged with rags of the filthiest description. He was clad in a greasy and tattered shirt, and trousers to match—his own clothes having been impounded by his captors. Moreover there were livid wales upon his face and hands, and such parts of his person as were visible through his ragged apparel, which showed that he had been unmercifully beaten. Well might Eustace start in amazement, absolute and unfeigned. In this pitiable object he recognised Tom Carhayes.

He gazed at him speechless—as at one who has risen from the dead. If ever he could have sworn to any man's death it would have been to that of the man before him. He had seen the assegais flash in the air and descend—had heard the dull, sickening blows of the kerries which had beaten the life out of his unfortunate cousin. Yet, here stood the latter—not exactly unhurt, but yet full of life.

"*Hau*, Umlilwane!" said Hlangani, who was standing beside the latter—grinning hideously into his victim's face. "You are not near enough to see well. The black ants bite—harder than the shot from your gun," he went on, with grim meaning, beckoning to those who stood by to drag the prisoner nearer to the body of the unfortunate Vudana, which lay, raw and bloody, the veins exposed in many places by the bites of the myriad swarming insects. Carhayes gazed upon the horrid sight with a shudder of disgust. Then raising his eyes he encountered those of Eustace. A shout of astonishment escaped him.

"How did you get here?" he cried. "Thought you were rubbed out if ever any fellow was. Suppose you thought the same of me. Well, well. It'll come to that soon. These damned black devils have bested me, just as I reckoned I was besting them. They've been giving me hell already. But I say, Eustace, you seem to be in clover," noticing the other's freedom from bonds or ill-treatment. Then he added bitterly, "I forgot; you always did stand in well with them."

"That isn't going to help me much now, I'm afraid," answered Eustace. "I've just made a fool of the witch-doctress and she won't let things rest there, depend upon it. My case isn't much more hopeful than yours. Have you tried the bribery trick?"

"No. How do you mean?"

"Offer some big-wig, like our particular friend there—I won't mention names—a deuce of a lot of cattle to let you escape. Try and work it—only you must be thundering careful."

The Kafirs, who had been attentively listening to the conversation between the two white men, here deemed that enough had been said. Dialogue in an unknown tongue must represent just so much plotting, argued their suspicious natures. So they interposed.

"See there," said Hlangani, with a meaning glance at the fearfully contorted features of the miserable victim of the witch-doctress. "See there, Umlilwane, and remember my 'word' to you the day you shot my white hunting dog and wounded me in the shoulder. *You had better first have cut off your right hand, for it is better to lose a hand than one's mind. Hau*! You laughed then. Who laughs now?"

To Eustace those words now stood out in deadly significance. The wretched Vudana had died raving mad. This, then, was the promised vengeance. Whatever his own fate might be, that of his cousin was sealed. Nothing short of a miracle could save him. Carhayes, noting the deadly and implacable expression upon the dark countenance of his enemy, realised something of this, and fearless as he habitually was, it was all he could do to keep from betraying some misgiving.

At this juncture a mandate arrived from Kreli that the warriors should once more assemble within the temporary kraal, and that the white prisoners should again be brought before him. Singing, chatting, laughing, administering many a sly kick or cuff to poor Carhayes, the savages swarmed back to the open space, dragging that unfortunate along in rough, unceremonious fashion. Soon the glade was empty, save for the body of the miserable victim of their blindly superstitious ferocity. It lay there, stark, mangled, and hideous.

The Paramount Chief and his councillors still sat in a group apart. They had borne no part in, betrayed no interest in, the barbarous tragedy which had just taken place. Such a matter as the punishment of a wizard was entirely beneath their notice—in theory at any rate. They still sat in grave and dignified impassiveness.

Eustace, noting the difference between his own treatment and that of his cousin—the one bound with unnecessary rigour, hustled and kicked, the other, though disarmed, treated with a certain amount of consideration—began to entertain strong hopes on his own account. But tending materially to dash them was the fact that Ngcenika, standing before the chief and the *amapakati*, was favouring that august assemblage with a very fierce and denunciatory harangue.

There were two white men, she said—two prisoners. One of these was a man of some power, who had been able to oppose her magic with his own; only for a time, however—the hag took care to add. This man it might be well to keep for a little while longer at any rate; there were several experiments which she herself intended to try upon him. But the other—he had always been a bitter enemy of their race. Many had fallen at his hands. Had he not cut a notch upon his gun-stock for every fighting man of the race of Xosa whom he had slain? There was the gun-stock and there were the notches. There were many of them, let the Great Chief—let the *amapakati* count.

At the production of this damning "*pièce de conviction*," a shout of fury rose from the ranks of the warriors.

"To the fire!" they cried. "To the fire with him!"

The situation was appalling, yet Carhayes never quailed. The desperate pluck of the man bore him up even then. He scowled contemptuously upon the lines of dark and threatening faces, then turned erect and fearless towards the chief.

For a few moments they confronted each other thus in silence. The Englishman, somewhat weak and unsteady from exhaustion and ill-treatment, could still look the arbiter of his fate straight in the eyes without blenching. They might do their worst and be damned, he said to himself. He, Tom Carhayes, was not going to whine for mercy to any nigger—even if that "nigger" was the Chief Paramount of all the Amaxosa tribes.

The latter, for his part, was not without respect for the white man's intrepidity, but he had no intention of sparing him for all that. He had been debating with his chiefs and councillors, and they had decided that Carhayes ought to be sacrificed as an uncompromising and determined enemy of their race. The other it might be expedient to keep a little longer and see how events would turn.

"What have you to say, *umlúngu?*" said Kreli at length.

"Nothing. Not a damn thing," broke in Carhayes, in a loud, harsh tone.

"Tom, for God's sake don't be such a fool," whispered Eustace, who was near enough to be heard. "Can't you be civil for once?"

"No, I can't; not to any infernal black scoundrel," roared the other savagely. "It's different with you, Eustace," changing his tone to a bitter sneer. "Damn it, man, you're about half a Kafir already. Why don't you ask old Kreli for a couple of his daughters and set up a kraal here among them, eh?"

A sounding whack across the ear with the haft of an assegai choked the words in his throat. He stood, literally foaming with fury.

"Attend, thou white dog," cried a great deep-toned voice. "Attend when the Great Chief is talking to thee. *Au*!"

An infuriated mastiff straining at his chain is a pretty good exemplification of impotent wrath, but even he is nothing to the aspect and demeanour of Carhayes as he turned to the perpetrator of this indignity. The veins rolled in his forehead as if they would burst. The muscles stood out upon his neck like cords as he strove by a superhuman effort to burst his bonds. But Hlangani only sneered.

"Listen when the Great Chief is talking to thee, thou jackal, or I will strike thee again," he said.

"God damn the Great Chief!" roared poor Tom, his voice rising to a hurricane shriek of fury under this shameful indignity, which he was powerless to resent. "And you, Hlangani, you dog, if I stood unbound I would kill you at this moment—kill you all unarmed as I am. Coward! Dare you try it!"

"What is this *indaba*?" interrupted Kreli sternly. "This white man has a very long tongue. Perhaps it may be shortened with advantage." A hum of applause greeted this remark, and the chief went on. "You are asked a question, *umlúngu*, and instead of answering you rave and bellow and throw yourself about like a cow that has lost her calf. And now what have you to say? You have invaded our country and shot our people with your own hand. If a man thrusts his head into a hornet's nest, whom shall he blame but himself if he gets stung—if he treads upon a serpent, how shall he complain if made to feel the reptile's fangs?"

"Well, you see, it's war-time," answered Carhayes bluntly, beginning to think he might just as well say something to save his life, if words could save it, that is. "I have met your people in fair fight, and I challenge any man, black or white, to deny that I have acted fair, square, and above board. And when we do take prisoners we don't treat them as I have been treated since I was brought here. They are taken care of by the doctors if wounded, as I am; not tied up and starved and kicked, as I have been."

"Their doctors are the Fingo dogs," interrupted the chief darkly, "their medicine a sharp assegai. Freeborn men of the House of Gcaléka to die at the hand of a Fingo slave! *Hau*!"

A roar of execration went up at this hit. "To the fire with him!" howled the savage crowd. "Give him to us, Great Chief, that we may make him die a hundred deaths!"

"That is the sort of healing my children get when they fall into the hands of Amanglezi. And you, *umlúngu*, you have offered an insult to the House of Gcaléka in the person of Hlangani, my herald, a man of the House of Hintza, my father. Was it war-time when you shed his blood? Did you meet in fair fight when you shot him suddenly and at close-quarters, he having no gun?"

"Was it war-time when Hlangani entered the Gaika location to stir up strife? Was it right that he should bring his dogs on to my farm to hunt my bucks?" answered Carhayes fearlessly. "Again, was it fair play for four men, armed with assegais, to attack one, who had but two shots? Or was it self-defence? Listen to my words, Kreli, and you chiefs and *amapakati* of the House of Gcaléka," he went on, raising his voice till it was audible to the whole assemblage. "In the presence of you all I proclaim Hlangani a coward. He has struck and insulted me because I am bound. He dare not meet me free. I challenge him to do so. Loosen these bonds. I am weak and wounded. I cannot escape—you need not fear—and let him meet me if he dares, with any weapon he chooses. I challenge him. If he refuses he is nothing but a cowardly dog, and worse than the meanest Fingo. If you, Kreli, refuse my request, it is because you *know* this bragging herald of yours to be a coward."

The fierce rapidity of this harangue, the audacity of the request embodied within it, took away the auditors' breath. Yet the idea appealed to them—appealed powerfully to their ardently martial sympathies. The very novelty of such a duel as that proposed invested it with a rare attractiveness.

"What does Hlangani say?" observed Kreli, with a partly amused glance at his subordinate.

"This, O Great Chief of my father's house," replied the warrior, the light of battle springing into his eyes. "Of what man living was Hlangani ever afraid? What man ever had to call him twice? Yet, O Great Chief, the head of my father's house, I would ask a boon. When I have whipped this miserable white dog, I would claim possession of his wretched carcase absolutely, alive or dead."

"It is granted, Hlangani," said the chief.

"And I?" cried Carhayes. "What shall be given to me when I have sent this cur, who strikes helpless men, howling to his hut? My liberty, of course?"

"No," replied Kreli, shortly.

"No?" echoed the prisoner. "My life then?"

"No," answered the chief again. "Be content, *umlúngu*. If you conquer you shall have a swift and merciful death. If you fail, Hlangani claims you."

Carhayes stared at the chief for a moment, then, as he realised that he had nothing to hope for, whether he won in the combat or not—an expression of such deadly ferocity, such fell and murderous purpose swept across his face, that many of those who witnessed it realised that their countryman was going to snatch no easy victory.

The stout rawhide *reims* which bound his hands behind him were loosened—and that which secured his feet was removed. He stood swinging his arms and stamping to hasten the circulation—then he asked for some water, which was brought him.

"*Ha, umlúngu!*" jeered Ngcenika, addressing Eustace, as the two white men stood talking together. "Give this valiant fighter some white magic to strengthen him. He will need it."

"Well, Eustace, I'm going to kill that dog," said Carhayes. "I'm going to die fighting anyway, so that's all right. Now—I'm ready. What are we going to fight with?"

"This," said one of the bystanders, handing him a pair of hard-wood kerries.

Hlangani now made his appearance similarly armed. The crescent formation of warriors had narrowed their ranks, the chiefs and councillors and Eustace and his guards composing the upper arc of the circle. The prisoner could not have broken through that dense array of armed men which hemmed him in on every side, had he entertained the idea.

Both the principals in that strange impromptu duel were men of splendid physique. The Kafir, nearly naked, looked like a bronze giant, towering above his adversary in his magnificent height and straight and perfect proportions. The Englishman, thick-set, deep-chested, concentrated a vast amount of muscular power within his five-foot-eight. He had thrown off his ragged shirt, and the muscles of his chest and arms stood out like ropes. He looked a terribly awkward antagonist, and moreover on his side the conflict would be fought with all the ferocity of despair. He was a man bent on selling his life dearly.

Hlangani, for his part, was confident and smiling. He was going to fight with his natural weapons, a pair of good, trusty kerries. This blundering white man, though he had the strength and ferocity of an enraged bull, had more than that quadruped's stupidity. He would knock him out of shape in no time.

When blood is up, the spirit of Donnybrook is very strong among Kafirs. The next best thing to taking part in a fight is to witness one—and now, accordingly, every head was bent forward with the most eager interest as the two combatants advanced towards each other in the open space. There was no "ring" proper, nor were there any recognised rules; no "time" either. Each man's business was to kill or disable the other—as effectually as possible, and by any means in his power.

Now a smart Kafir, armed with two good kerries whose use he thoroughly understands, is about as tough a customer to tackle as is a professional pugilist to the average Briton who knows how to use his hands but indifferently. Of this Carhayes was perfectly aware. Consequently his plan was to meet his antagonist with extreme wariness; in fact, to stand rather on the defensive, at any rate at first. He was a fair single stick player, which tended not a little to equalise the chances.

As they drew near each other and reached striking distance, they looked straight into each other's eyes like a pair of skilful fencers. The savage, with one kerrie raised in the air, the other held horizontally before his breast, but both with a nervous, supple grasp, ready to turn any way with lightning rapidity—his glance upon that of his foe—his active, muscular frame poised lightly on one foot, then on another, with feline readiness, would have furnished a perfect subject for an instantaneous photograph representing strength and address combined. The Englishman, his bearded lips compressed, his blue eyes sparkling and alert, shining with suppressed eagerness to come to close-quarters with his crafty and formidable foe, was none the less a fine specimen of courage and undaunted resolution.

Hlangani, a sneering laugh upon his thick lips, opened the ball by making a judicious feint. But his adversary never moved. He followed it up by another, then a series of them, whirling his striking kerrie round the Englishman's head in the most startling proximity, now on this side, now on that, holding his parrying one ready for any attack the other might make upon him. Still Carhayes stood strictly on the defensive. He knew the Kafir was trying to "draw him"—knew that his enemy's quick eye was prepared for any opportunity. He was not going to waste energy gratuitously.

Suddenly, and with lightning-like celerity, Hlangani made a sweep at the lower part of his adversary's leg. It would have been the ruin of a less experienced combatant, but Carhayes' kerrie, lowered just two inches, met that of his opponent with a sounding crash just in time to save his skull somewhere in the region of the ear. It was a clever feint, and a dexterous follow-up, but it had failed. Hlangani began to realise that he had met a foeman worthy of his steel—or, rather, of his wood. Still he knew the other's impetuous temper, and by wearing out his patience reckoned on obtaining a sure and tolerably easy victory.

And it seemed as if he would gain the result of his reasoning even sooner than he expected. Bristling with rage, literally smarting with the indignity recently put upon him, Carhayes abandoned the defensive. With a sudden rush, he charged his antagonist, and for a few moments nothing was heard but the clash of hard-wood in strike and parry. Hlangani was touched on the shoulder, while Carhayes got a rap on the knuckles, which in cold blood would have turned him almost sick with pain. But his blood was at boiling point now, and he was fighting with the despairing ferocity of one who has no hope left in life. He pressed his gigantic adversary with such vigour and determination that the other had no alternative but to give way.

The fun was waxing fast and furious now. The warriors crowding in nearer and nearer, pressed forward in breathless attention, encouraging their champion with many a deep-toned hum of applause when he scored or seemed likely to score a point. The few women then in the kraal stood on tiptoe, trying to peer over the heads and shoulders of the armed men. Even the chiefs and councillors condescended to show considerable interest in this impromptu tournament, while Eustace Milne, animated by various motives, watched its progress narrowly.

For a few moments it really seemed that the white man would prove the victor. Before the impetuosity of his furious attacks Hlangani was constrained to give way more and more. A Beserk ferocity seemed to have taken possession of Carhayes. His eyes glared through the blood and dust which clung to his unwashen visage. Every hair of his beard seemed to bristle and stand upright, like the mane of a wild boar. His chest heaved, and the dexterity with which he whirled his kerrie around his adversary's ears—always quick to ward the latter's blows from himself—was wonderful to behold.

Crash—scroosh! The blow told. A sound as of the crunching of bone. Hlangani staggered back half a dozen paces, the blood pouring from a wound in his skull. It was a blow that would probably have shattered the skull of a white man.

But before Carhayes could follow it up, the wily savage adopted a different plan. By a series of astonishing leaps and bounds, now backward, now from side to side, he endeavoured to bewilder his enemy, and very nearly succeeded. Mad with rage, desperation, and a consciousness of failing strength, Carhayes was fast losing control over himself. He roared like a wild animal. He began to strike out wildly, leaving his guard open. This the cunning barbarian saw and encouraged. Those looking on had no doubt now as to who held the winning cards; even Eustace could see it, but his cousin was too far off now to hear a word of warning or advice, which, however, was just as well for himself.

Again the combatants closed. The splinters began to fly in all directions as the hard-wood sticks whirled and crashed. Then suddenly a crushing blow on the wrist sent Carhayes' kerrie flying from his grasp and almost simultaneously with it came a sickening "scrunch." The white man dropped like an ox at the shambles, the blood pouring from his head.

Echoing the mighty roar of exultation that went up from the spectators, Hlangani stood with his foot on the chest of his prostrate adversary, his kerrie raised to strike again. But there was no necessity. Poor Tom lay like a corpse, stunned and motionless. The ferocious triumph depicted on the countenance of the savage was horrible to behold.

"He is mine," he cried, his chest heaving, his eyes blazing, "mine absolutely. The Great Chief has said it. Bring *reims*."

In a trice a few stout rawhide thongs were procured, and Carhayes was once more bound hand and foot. Then acting under the directions of his fierce conqueror—three or four stalwart Kafirs raised the insensible form of the unfortunate settler and bore it away.

"He has only begun to taste the fury of Hlangani's revenge," said a voice at Eustace's side. Turning he beheld the witch-doctress, Ngcenika. The hag pointed to the retreating group with a mocking leer.

"He will wake," she went on. "But he will never be seen again, Ixeshane—never. *Hau*!"

"Where will he wake, Ngcenika?" asked Eustace, in a voice which he strove to render unconcerned.

"*Kwa, Zinyoka*," (At the Home of the Serpents) replied the hag with a brutal laugh.

"And where is that?"

"Where is it? Ha, ha!" mocked the witch-doctress. "Thou art a magician, too, Ixeshane. Wouldst thou indeed like to know?"

"Perhaps."

"Invoke thy magic then, and see if it will tell thee. But better not. For they who look upon the Home of the Serpents are seen no more in life. Thou hast seen the last of yon white man, Ixeshane; thou and these standing around here. Ha, ha! Better for him that he had never been born." And with a Satanic laugh she turned away and left him.

Strong-nerved as he was, Eustace felt his flesh creep. The hag's parting words hinted at some mysterious and darkly horrible fate in store for his unfortunate cousin. His own precarious position brought a sense of this doubly home to him. He remembered how jubilant poor Tom had been over the outbreak of the war. This, then, was to be the end of it. Instead of paying off old scores with his hated and despised foes, he had himself walked blindfold into the trap, and was to be sacrificed in some frightful manner to their vengeance.

Chapter Thirty Three.

"I walk in Shadow."

Eanswyth was back again in her old home—living her old life, as in the times that were past—but alone.

When she had announced her intention of returning to Anta's Kloof, her friends had received the proposition with incredulity—when they saw that she was determined, with dismay.

It was stark lunacy, they declared. She to go to live on an out-of-the-way farm, alone! There was not even a neighbour for pretty near a score of miles, all the surrounding stock-farmers having trekked into *laager*. The Gaikas were reported more restless than ever, nor were symptoms wanting that they were on the eve of an outbreak. The Gcaléka campaign had fired their warlike spirits, but had failed to convey its accompanying warning, and those "in the know" asserted that the savages might rise any minute and make common cause with their countrymen across the Kei. And in the face of all this, here was Eanswyth proposing to establish herself on a lonely farm bordering on the very location of the plotting and disaffected tribesmen. Why, it was lunacy—rank suicide!

The worst of it was that nobody on earth had the power to prevent her from doing as she chose. Her own family were Western Province people and lived far up in the Karroo. Had they been ever so willing, it would take them nearly three weeks to arrive—by which time it might be too late. But Eanswyth did not choose to send for any one. She wanted to be alone.

"You need not be in the least alarmed on my account," she had said to the Hostes in answer to their reiterated expostulations. "Even if the Gaikas should rise, I don't believe they would do me the slightest harm. The people on Nteya's location know me well, and the old chief and I used to be great friends. I feel as if I must go to my old home again—and—don't think me ungracious, but it will do me good to be entirely alone."

"That was how poor Milne used to argue," said Hoste gravely. "But they killed him all the same."

"Yes," she replied, mastering the quick sharp spasm which the allusion evoked. "But they were Gcalékas—not our people, who knew him."

Hoste shook his head.

"You are committing suicide," he said. "And the worst of it is we have no power on earth to prevent you."

"No, you haven't," she assented with the shadow of a smile. "So let me go my own way with a good grace. Besides, with old Josane to look after me, I can't come to much harm."

She had telegraphed to her late husband's manager at Swaanepoel's Hoek, requesting him to send the old cattle-herd to her at once. Three days later Josane arrived, and having commissioned Hoste to buy her a few cows and some slaughter sheep, enough to supply her modest household. Eanswyth had carried out her somewhat eccentric plan.

The utter loneliness of the place—the entire absence of life—the empty kraals and the silent homestead, all this is inexpressibly grateful to her crushed and lacerated spirit. And in the dead silence of those uninhabited rooms she conjures up the sweetest, the holiest memories. Her solitude, her complete isolation, conveys no terror—no spark of misgiving, for it is there that her very life has been lived. The dead stillness of the midnight hour, the ghostly creaking of a board, the hundred and one varying sounds begotten of silence and darkness, inspire her with no alarm, for her imagination peoples these empty and deserted rooms with life once more.

She can see him as she saw him in life, moving about the place on different errands bent. There is his favourite chair; there his place at the table. His personality seems still to pervade the whole house, his spirit to hover around her, to permeate her whole being, here as it could nowhere else. But it was on first entering his room, which still contained a few possessions too cumbersome or too worthless to carry away—a trunk or two and a few old clothes—here it was that that awful and vivid contrast struck her in overwhelming force.

What an expression there is in such poor and useless relics—a glove, a boot, a hat, even an old pipe—when we know we shall never see the owner again, parted perhaps by circumstances, by distance, by death. Do not such things seem verily to speak—and to speak eloquently—to bring before our eyes, to sound within our ears, the vision, the voice of one whom we shall never behold again? Ah! do they not!

Standing for the first time alone in that room, Eanswyth felt as though her heart had been broken afresh. She fell prone among those poor and worthless relics, pressing them passionately to her lips, while her tears fell like rain. If ever her lover's spirit could come back to her, surely it would be in that room.

"O Eustace, my darling, my first and only love!" murmured the stricken creature, lying face to the very floor in the agony of her grief. "Come to me from the shadowy spirit land! O God, send him to me, that I may look upon him once more!"

The shadows deepened within the room. Raising her head she gazed around, and the expression of pitiable eagerness on the white drawn face was fearful to behold.

"Oh, dear Lord, if our love is so wicked are we not punished enough! O God, show him to me again if but for a moment! The ghastliest terrors of the grave are sweetness to me, if I may but see him once—my dear dead love! Eustace, Eustace! You cannot come to me, but I shall soon go to you! Is it a loving God or a fiend that tortures us so? Ah-ah!"

Her heart-broken paroxysm could go no further. No apparition from another world met her eyes as they strove to penetrate the deepening shadows as though fully expecting one. The exhaustion that supervened was beneficial to a degree, in that it acted as a safety valve to her fearfully overwrought brain. Her very mind was in danger.

For nearly a fortnight has Eanswyth thus dwelt, and so far from beginning to tire of her solitude, she hugs it closer to her. She has received visits from the Hostes and other friends who, reckoning that a couple of days of solitude would sicken her of it altogether, had come with the object of inducing her to return to the settlement. Besides, Christmas was close at hand and, her bereavement notwithstanding, it did not somehow seem good that she should spend that genial season alone and in a position not altogether free from danger. But their kindly efforts proved futile; indeed, Eanswyth could hardly disguise the fact that their visits were unwelcome. She preferred solitude at such a time, she said. Then Mrs Hoste had undertaken to lecture her. It could not be right to abandon one's self so entirely, even to a great sorrow, purred that complacent matron. It seemed somehow to argue a want of Christian resignation. It was all very well up to a certain point, of course; but beyond that, it looked like flying in the face of Providence. And Eanswyth had turned her great eyes with such a blank and bewildered look upon the speaker's face, as if wondering what on earth the woman could be talking about, that Mrs Hoste, good-hearted though shallow, had dropped her rôle of preacher then and there.

One thing that struck Eanswyth as not a little strange was that hardly a Kafir had been near the place, whereas formerly their dusky neighbours had been wont to visit them on one pretext or another enough and to spare, the latter especially, in poor Tom's opinion. She had sent word to Nteya, inviting him to visit her and have a talk, but the old chief had made some excuse, promising, however, to come over and see her later. All this looked strange and, taken in conjunction with the fact that there had been war-dancing again in Nteya's location, suspicious. So thought at any rate Josane, who gave vent to his misgivings in no uncertain tone. But Eanswyth treated his warnings with perfect unconcern. She would not move, she declared. She was afraid of nobody. If Josane was, he might go if he liked. To which the staunch old fellow would reply that he feared no man, black or white; that he was there to take care of her, and there he would stay, adding, with a growl, that it might be bad for Nteya's, or anybody else's, people should they attempt to molest her.

It wanted but a day or two to Christmas—but an hour to sunset. It was one of those marvellous evenings not uncommon in South Africa, as well as in the southern parts of Europe—one of those evenings when sky and earth alike are vivid with rich colouring, and the cloudless blue of the heavens assumes a deeper azure still, and there is a dreamy enchantment in the air, and every sight, every sound, toned and mellowed by distance, blends in perfect harmony with the changing glories of the dying day. Then the sun goes down in a flaming rainbow of rare tints, each more subtle than the other, each more gorgeous, and withal more delicate than the last.

The enchantment of the hour was upon Eanswyth to the full—the loneliness, the sense of absolute solitude, cut off from the outer world, alone with her dead. Wandering down to the gate of the now tenantless ostrich camp she is going over the incidents of that last day—that first and that last day, for it was that upon which they had discovered to each other their great and all-absorbing love. "The last day we shall have together," he had said—and it was so. She can vividly conjure up his presence at her side now. Every word he said, every careless gesture even, comes back to her now. Here was the gate where they had stood feeding the great birds, idly chatting about nothing in particular, and yet how full were both their hearts even then. And that long sweet embrace so startlingly interrupted! Ah! what a day that had been! One day out of a whole lifetime. Standing here on this doubly hallowed spot, it seems to her that an eternity of unutterable wretchedness would not be too great a price to pay for just that one day over again. But he is gone. Whether their love had been the most sacred that ever blessed the lot of mortal here below, or the unhallowed, inexorably forbidden thing it really is, matters nothing now. Death has decided, and from his arbitration there is no appeal.

She throws herself upon the sward: there in the shade of the mimosa trees where they had sat together. All Nature is calm and at peace, and, with the withdrawal of man, the wild creatures of the earth seem to have reclaimed their own. A little duiker buck steps daintily along beneath the thorn fence of the ostrich camp, and the grating, metallic cackle of the wild guinea-fowl is followed by the appearance of quite a large covey of those fine game birds, pecking away, though ever with an air of confirmed distrust, within two score yards of the pale, silent mourner, seated there. The half-whistling, half-twanging note of the yellow thrush mingles with the melodious call of a pair of blue cranes stalking along in the grass, and above the drowsy, measured hum of bees storing sweetness from the flowering aloes, there arises the heavier boom of some great scarabaeus winging his way in blundering, aimless fashion athwart the balmy and sensuous evening air.

The sun sinks to the western ridge—the voices of animal and insect life swell in harmonious chorus, louder and louder, in that last hour of parting day. His golden beams, now horizontal, sweep the broad and rolling plains in a sea of fire, throwing out the rounded spurs of the Kabousie Hills into so many waves of vivid green. Then the flaming chariot of day is gone.

And in the unearthly hush of the roseate afterglow, that pale, heart-broken mourner wends her way home. Home! An empty house, where the echo of a footfall sounds ghostly and startling; an abode peopled with reminiscences of the dead—meet companionship for a dead and empty heart.

Never so dead—never so empty—as this evening. Never since the first moment of receiving the awful news has she felt so utterly crushed, so soul-weary as here to-night. "How was it all to end?" had been their oft-spoken thought—here on this very spot. The answer had come now. Death had supplied it. But—how was *this* to end?

The glories of departing day were breaking forth into ever varying splendours. The spurs of the mountain range, now green, now gold, assumed a rich purple against the flaming red of the sky. The deepening afterglow flushed and quivered, as the scintillating eyes of heaven sprang forth into the arching vault—not one by one, but in whole groups. Then the pearly shades of twilight and the cool, moist fragrance of the falling night.

Why was the earth so wondrously lovely—why should eyes rest upon such semi-divine splendour while the heart was aching and bursting? was the unspoken cry that went up from that heart-weary mourner standing there alone gazing forth into the depths of the star-gemmed night.

Stay! What is that tongue of flame suddenly leaping forth into the darkness? Another and another—and lo! by magic, from a score of lofty heights, red fires are gushing upward into the black and velvety gloom, and as the ominous beacons gather in flaming volume roaring up to a great height, the lurid glow of the dark firmament is reflected dully upon the slumbering plains.

A weird, far-away chorus floats upon the stillness, now rising, now falling. Its boding import there is no mistaking. It is the gathering cry of a barbarian host. The Gaika location is up in arms. Heavens! What is to become of this delicate woman here, alone and unprotected, exposed to the full brunt of a savage rising—and all that it means?

Eanswyth is standing on the *stoep*, her eyes fixed upon the appalling phenomenon, but in their glance is no shadow of fear. Death has no terrors for her now; at peril she can afford to laugh. Her lips are even curving into a sweet, sad smile.

"Just as it was that night," she exclaims. "The parallel is complete. Blaze on red signals of death—and when destruction does break forth let it begin with me! I will wait for it, welcome it, for I walk in shadow now—will welcome it here on this spot where we stood that sweet and blessed night—here where our hearts first met—here where mine is breaking now!"

Her voice dies away in a sob. She sinks to the ground. The distant glare of the war-fires of the savages falls fully upon that prostrate figure lying there in the abandonment of woe. It lights up a very sacrifice. The rough stones of the *stoep* are those of an altar—the sacrifice a broken heart.

"Here is where we stood that night together," she murmurs, pressing her lips to the hard, cold stones. "It is just as it was then. Oh, my love—my love, come back to me! Come back—even from the cold grave!"

"Eanswyth!"

The word is breathed in a low, unsteady voice. Every drop of blood within her turns to ice. It is answered at last, her oft-repeated prayer. She is about to behold him. Does she not shrink from it? Not by a hair's-breadth.

"Let me see you, my love," she murmurs softly, not daring to move lest the spell should be broken. "Where—where are you?"

"Where our hearts first met—there they meet again. Look up, my sweet one. I am here."

She does look up. In the red and boding glare of those ominous war-fires she sees him as she saw him that night. She springs to her feet—and a loud and thrilling cry goes forth upon the darkness.

"Eustace—Eustace! Oh, my love! Spirit or flesh—you shall not leave me! At last—at last!"

Chapter Thirty Four.

From Death and—to Death.

She realised it at length—realised that this was no visitant from the spirit-world conjured up in answer to her impassioned prayer, but her lover himself, alive and unharmed. She had thrown herself upon his breast, and clung to him with all her strength, sobbing passionately—clung to him as if even then afraid that he might vanish as suddenly as he had appeared.

"My love, my love," he murmured in that low magnetic tone which she knew so well, and which thrilled her to the heart's core. "Calm those poor nerves, my darling, and rest on the sweetness of our meeting. We met—our hearts met first on this very spot. Now they meet once more, never again to part."

Still her feeling was too strong for words; she could only cling to him in silence, while he covered her face and soft hair with kisses. A moment ago she was mourning him as dead, was burying her heart in his unknown and far-away grave, and lo, as by magic, he stood before her, and she was safe in his embrace. A moment ago life was one long vista of blank, agonising grief; now the joys of heaven itself might pale before the unutterable bliss of this meeting.

Unlawful or not as their love might be, there was something solemn, almost sacred, in its intense reality. The myriad eyes of heaven looked down from the dark vault above, and the sullen redness of the war-fires flashing from the distant heights shed a dull, threatening glow upon those two, standing there locked in each other's embrace. Then once more the wild, weird war-cry of the savage hosts swelled forth upon the night. It was an awesome and fearful background to this picture of renewed life and bliss.

Such a reunion can best be left to the imagination, for it will bear no detailment.

"Why did you draw my very heart out of me like this, Eustace, my life?" she said at last, raising her head. "When they told me you were dead I knew it would not be long before I joined you. I could not have endured this living death much longer."

There were those who pronounced Eanswyth Carhayes to be the most beautiful woman they had ever beheld—who had started with amazement at such an apparition on an out-of-the-way Kaffrarian farm. A grand creature, they declared, but a trifle too cold. They would have marvelled that they had ever passed such a verdict could they but have seen her now, her splendid eyes burning into those of her lover in the starlight as she went on:

"You are longing to ask what I am doing here in this place all alone and at such a time. This. I came here as to a sanctuary: a sacred spot which enshrined all the dearest memories of you. Here in silence and in solitude I could conjure up visions of you—could see you walking beside me as on that last day we spent together. Here I could kneel and kiss the floor, the very earth which your feet had trod; and—O Eustace, my very life, it was a riven and a shattered heart I offered up daily—hourly—at the shrine of your dear memory."

Her tones thrilled upon his ear. Never had life held such a delirious, intoxicating moment. To the cool, philosophical, strong-nerved man it seemed as if his very senses were slipping away from him under the thrilling love-tones of this stately, beautiful creature nestling within his arms. Again their lips met—met as they had met that first time—met as if they were never again to part.

"Inkose!"

The sudden sonorous interruption caused Eanswyth to start as if she had been shot, and well it might. Her lover, however, had passed through too many strange and stirring experiences of late to be otherwise than slightly and momentarily disconcerted.

A dark figure stood at the lowest step of the *stoep*, one hand raised in the air, after the dignified and graceful manner of native salutation.

"Greeting, Josane," he replied.

"Now do mine eyes behold a goodly sight," went on the old Kafir with animation, speaking in the pleasing figurative hyperbole of his race. "My father and friend is safe home once more. We have mourned him as dead and he is alive again. He has returned to gladden our hearts and delight our eyes. It is good—it is good."

"How did you know I had returned, Josane?"

Had there been light enough they would have detected the most whimsical smile come over the old Kafir's face as he replied:

"Am I not the *Inkosikazi's* watch-dog? What sort of a watch-dog is it that permits a footstep to approach from outside without his knowledge?"

"You are, indeed, a man, Josane—a man among men, and trust to those who trust you," replied Eustace, in that tone of thorough friendship and regard which had enabled him to win so effectually the confidence of the natives.

The old cattle-herd's face beamed with gratification, which, however, was quickly dashed with anxiety.

"Look yonder," he said. "There is trouble in the Gaika location to-night. Take the *Inkosikazi* and leave—this very night. I know what I say." Then, marking the other's hesitation, "I know what I say," he repeated impressively. "Am I not the *Inkosikazi's* watch-dog? Am I not her eyes and ears? Even now there is one approaching from Nteya's kraal."

He had struck a listening attitude. Eustace, his recent experiences fresh in his mind, felt depressed and anxious, gazing expectantly into the darkness, his hand upon the butt of his revolver.

"Halt! Who comes there?" he cried in the Xosa tongue.

"A friend, Ixeshane!" came the prompt reply, as a dark form stepped into view.

Now that life was worth living again, Eanswyth felt all her old apprehensions return; but she had every confidence in her lover's judgment and the fidelity of her trusted old retainer.

"*Hau*, Ixeshane! You are here; it is good," said the new arrival in the most matter-of-fact way, as though he were not wondering to distraction how it was that the man who had been reported slain in the Bomvana country by the hostile Gcalékas, should be standing there alive and well before him. "I am here to warn the *Inkosikazi*. She must leave, and at once. The fire-tongues of the Amaxosa are speaking to each other; the war-cry of the Ama Ngqika is cleaving the night."

"We have seen and heard that before, Ncanduku," answered Eustace, recognising the new arrival at once. "Yet your people would not harm us. Are we not friends?"

The Kafir shook his head.

"Who can be called friends in war-time?" he said. "There are strangers in our midst—strangers from another land. Who can answer for them? I am Ncanduku, the brother of Nteya. The chief will not have his friends harmed at the hands of strangers. But they must go. Look yonder, and lose no time. Get your horses and take the *Inkosikazi*, and leave at once, for the Ama Ngqika have responded to the call of their brethren and the Paramount Chief, and have risen to arms. *The land is dead.*"

There was no need to follow the direction of the Kafir's indication. A dull, red glare, some distance off, shone forth upon the night; then another and another. Signal fires? No. These shone from no prominent height, but from the plain itself. Then Eustace took in the situation in a moment. The savages were beginning to fire the deserted homesteads of the settlers.

"Inspan the buggy quickly, Josane," he said. "And, Ncandúku, come inside for a moment. I will find *basela* (Best rendered by the familiar term 'backshish') for you and Nteya." But the voice which had conveyed such timely warning responded not. The messenger had disappeared.

The whole condition of affairs was patent to Eustace's mind. Nteya, though a chief whose status was not far inferior to that of Sandili himself, was not all-powerful. Those of his tribesmen who came from a distance, and were not of his own clan, would be slow to give implicit obedience to his "word," their instincts for slaughter and pillage once fairly let loose, and so he had sent to warn Eanswyth. Besides, it was probable that there were Gcalékas among them. Ncanduku's words, "strangers from another land," seemed to point that way. He put it to Josane while harnessing the horses. The old man emitted a dry laugh.

"There are about six hundred of the Gcaléka fighting men in Nteya's location to-night," he replied. "Every farmhouse in the land will be burned before the morning. *Whau*, Ixeshane! Is there any time to lose now?"

Eustace realised that assuredly there was not. But inspanning a pair of horses was, to his experienced hand, the work of a very few minutes indeed.

"Who is their chief?" he asked, tugging at the last strap. "Sigcau?"

"No. Ukiva."

An involuntary exclamation of concern escaped Eustace. For the chief named had evinced a marked hostility towards himself during his recent captivity; indeed, this man's influence had more than once almost turned the scale in favour of his death. No wonder he felt anxious.

Eanswyth had gone into the house to put a few things together, having, with an effort, overcome her reluctance to let him out of her sight during the few minutes required for inspanning. Now she reappeared. "I am ready, Eustace," she said.

He helped her to her seat and was beside her in a moment.

"Let go, Josane!" he cried. And the Kafir, standing away from the horses' heads, uttered a sonorous farewell.

"What will become of him, dear?" said Eanswyth, as they started off at a brisk pace.

"He is going to stay here and try and save the house. I'm afraid he won't be able to, though. They are bound to burn it along with the others. And now take the reins a moment, dearest. I left my horse hitched up somewhere here, because I wanted to come upon you unawares. I'll just take off the saddle and tie it on behind."

"But what about the horse? Why not take him with us?"

"Josane will look after him. I won't take him along now, because—well, it's just on the cards we might have to make a push for it, and a led horse is a nuisance. Ah—there he is," as a low whinnying was heard on their left front and duly responded to by the pair in harness.

In less than two minutes he had the saddle secured at the back of the buggy and was beside her again. It is to be feared Eustace drove very badly that night. Had the inquiry been made, candour would have compelled him to admit that he had never driven so badly in his life.

Eanswyth, for her part, was quite overcome with the thrilling, intoxicating happiness of the hour. But what an hour! They were fleeing through the night—fleeing for their lives—their way lighted by the terrible signal beacons of the savage foe—by the glare of flaming homesteads fired by his ravaging and vengeful hand. But then, he who was dead is alive again, and is beside her—they two fleeing together through the night.

"Darling," she whispered at last, nestling up closer to him. "Why did they try to kill me by telling me you were dead?"

"They had every reason to suppose so. Now, what do you think stood between me and certain death?"

"What?"

"Your love—not once, but twice. The silver box. See. Here it is, where it has ever been—over my heart. Twice it turned the point of the assegai."

"Eustace!"

"It is as I say. Your love preserved me for yourself."

"Oh, my darling, surely then it cannot be so wicked—so unlawful!" she exclaimed with a quiver in her voice.

"I never believed it could," he replied.

Up till then, poor Tom's name had not been mentioned. Both seemed to avoid allusion to it. Now, however, that Eustace had to narrate his adventures and escape, it could not well be avoided. But in describing the strange impromptu duel between the Gcaléka warrior and his unfortunate cousin, he purposely omitted any reference to the latter's probable hideous fate, leaving Eanswyth to suppose he had been slain then and there. It was impossible that she should have been otherwise than deeply moved.

"He died fighting bravely, at any rate," she said at last.

"Yes. Want of courage was never one of poor Tom's failings. All the time we were out he was keener on a fight than all the rest of the command put together."

There was silence after this. Then at last:

"How did you escape, Eustace, my darling? You have not told me."

"Through paying ransom to that same Hlangani and paying pretty stiffly too. Four hundred and fifty head of good cattle was the figure. Such a haggle as it was, too. It would have been impolitic to agree too quickly. Then, I had to square this witch-doctress, and I daresay old Kreli himself will come in for some of the pickings. From motives of policy we had to carry out the escape as if it was a genuine escape and not a put-up job—but they managed it all right—took me across the river on some pretext or other and then gave me the opportunity of leg-bail. As soon as the war is over Hlangani will come down on me for the cattle."

"How did you know I was back at Anta's Kloof, dearest? Did the Hostes tell you?" said Eanswyth at last.

"No. I met that one-eyed fellow Tomkins just outside Komgha. I only waited while he called up two or three more to back his statement and then started off here as hard as ever I could send my nag over the ground."

The journey was about half accomplished. The buggy bowled merrily along—and its occupants—alone together in the warm balmy southern night—began to wish the settlement was even further off. They were ascending a long rise.

"Hallo, what's up?" exclaimed Eustace suddenly, whipping up his horses, which he had been allowing to walk up the hill.

The brow of the hill was of some altitude and commanded a considerable view of the surrounding country. But the whole of the latter was lit up by a dull and lurid glow. At intervals apart burned what looked like several huge and distant bonfires.

"They mean business this time," said Eustace, reining in a moment to breathe his horses on the brow of the rise. "Look. There goes Hoste's place. That's Bradfield's over there—and beyond that must be Oesthuisen's. Look at them all blazing merrily; and—by jingo—there goes Draaibosch!"

Far and wide for many a mile the country was aglow with blazing homesteads. Evidently it was the result of preconcerted action on the part of the savages. The wild yelling chorus of the barbarous incendiaries, executing their fierce war-dances around their work of destruction, was borne distinctly upon the night.

"The sooner we get into Komgha the better now," he went on, sending the buggy spinning down the long declivity which lay in front. At the bottom of this the road was intersected by a dry water course, fringed with bush; otherwise the *veldt* was for the most part open, dotted with straggling clumps of mimosa.

Down went the buggy into the dry sandy drift. Suddenly the horses shied violently, then stopped short with a jerk which nearly upset the vehicle. A dark firm, springing panther-like, apparently from the ground, had seized the reins.

Instinctively Eustace recognised that this was no time for parleying. Quick as thought he drew his revolver and fired. The assailant relaxed his hold, staggered, spun round, then fell heavily to the earth. The horses, thus released, tore wildly onward, mad with terror.

A roar and a red, sheeting flash split the darkness behind. The missiles hummed overhead, one of them tearing a hole in the wide brim of Eanswyth's hat. This aroused all the demon in the blood of her companion. Standing up in his seat, regardless of prudence, he pointed his revolver at the black onrushing mass discernible in the starlight, and fired three shots in rapid succession. A horrible, shrill, piercing scream, showed that they had told with widespread and deadly effect.

"Ha! *Bulala abelúngu!*" (Death to the whites) howled the exasperated barbarians. And dropping flat on the ground they poured another volley into the retiring vehicle.

But the latter had gained some distance now. The horses, panic-stricken and well-nigh unmanageable, were tearing up the hill on the other side of the drift, and it was all their driver could do in the darkness to keep them in the track. The buggy swayed fearfully, and twice catching a wheel in an ant-heap was within an ace of turning over.

Suddenly one of the horses stumbled heavily, then fell. All his driver's efforts to raise him were useless. The poor beast had been struck by a bullet, and lay, feebly struggling, the blood pouring from a jagged wound in his flank.

The black bolt of despair shot through Eustace's heart. There was a feeble chance of escape for Eanswyth, but a very feeble one. Of himself he did not think. Quickly he set to work to cut loose the other horse.

But the traditional sagacity of that quadruped, as is almost invariably the case, failed in an emergency. He plunged and kicked in such wise as to hinder seriously, if not defeat, every effort to disengage him from the harness. Eustace, his listening powers at their utmost tension, caught the light pit-pat of the pursuers' footsteps racing up the hill in the darkness. They would be upon him before—

Ha! The horse was loose.

"Quick, Eanswyth. Mount! It is your only chance!" he said, shortening the reins into a bridle and holding them for her.

"I will not."

"Quick, quick! Every moment lost is a life!"

"I will not. We will die together. I will not live without you," and the heroic flash in the grand eyes was visible in the starlight.

The stealthy footsteps were now plainly audible. They could not have been two hundred yards distant. Suddenly the horse, catching a renewed access of panic, plucked the reins from Eustace's hand, and careered wildly away into the *veldt*. The last chance of escape was cut off. They must die together now. Facing round, crouching low behind the broken-down vehicle, they listened for the approach of the pursuers.

All the bitterness of the moment was upon those two—upon him especially—crouching there in the dark and lonely *veldt*. Their reunion was only to be a reunion in death.

The last dread act was drawing on. The stealthy steps of the approaching foe were now more distinctly audible. With a deadly and vengeful fire at his heart, Eustace prepared to sell their lives as dearly as ever life was sold.

"We need not fear, my sweet one," whispered the heroine at his side. "We are dying together."

Nearer—nearer, came those cat-like footfalls. Then they ceased. The pulses of the two anxious listeners beat with an intense and surging throb of expectation in the dead silence.

But instead of those stealthy feet, swift to shed blood, there was borne upon the night the sound of horses' hoofs. Then a crash of fire-arms, and a ringing cheer. No savage war-cry that, but a genuine British shout.

"That you, Milne?" cried a familiar voice. "All right: keep cool, old man. We shan't hit you by mistake. How many are there?"

"I don't know. Better not tackle them in the dark, Hoste. Who is with you?"

"Some Police. But where are the niggers?"

Where indeed? Savages have no stomach for facing unknown odds. Their late assailants had prudently made themselves scarce.

"We seem to be only just in time, anyway?" said Hoste, with a long whistle of consternation as he realised the critical position of affairs. "Is Mrs Carhayes all right?" he added anxiously.

"Quite, thanks, Mr Hoste," replied Eanswyth. "But you are, as you say, only just in time."

Two of the Police horses were inspanned to the buggy, the men mounting behind comrades, and the party set forth. It would not do to linger. The enemy might return in force at any moment.

Their escape had indeed been a narrow one. It was only late in the afternoon that Hoste had, by chance, learned from a trustworthy source that the Gaikas meant to rise that night. Horror-stricken, he had rushed off to the officer in command of the Mounted Police to beg for some troopers as a protective escort in order to bring Eanswyth away from her lonely and perilous situation. An experienced sergeant and twenty-five men had been immediately ordered out—arriving in the very nick of time, as we have seen.

"Well, we are all burnt out now, anyway," said Hoste as they journeyed along as rapidly as possible. "Look at my old place, what a flare-up it's making. And the hotel at Draaibosch! It's making a bigger blaze than all."

"That's McDonald's 'Cape Smoke,'" (An inferior quality of Cape brandy is thus popularly termed) laughed the police sergeant.

It was a weird and awesome sight. The whole country was literally in a blaze—the murk of the reddened smoke of burning homesteads obliterating the stars. And ever and anon the fierce, tumultuous thunder of a distant war-dance was borne upon the air, with the vengeful shouts of excited savages, beginning their orgy of torch and assegai.

Chapter Thirty Five.

Eustace becomes Unpopular.

The state of excitement prevailing in Komgha during the period of hostilities within the Transkei, was as nothing to that which prevailed now that the tide of war was rolling around the very outposts of the settlement itself.

The once sleepy little village had become a vast armed camp, garrisoned by regular troops, as well as being the halting place for numerous bodies of irregulars—mounted burghers or Fingo levies—once more called out or volunteering for active service, the latter with more zest this time, inasmuch as the enemy was within their very gates. It was the headquarters of operations, and all day long—frequently all night too—what with expeditions or patrols setting out, or returning, or preparing; the arrival of reinforcements; the flash and trappings of the military element; the exaggerated and conflicting rumours varying with every half-hour that went by. With all these things, we say, the sojourners in that favoured settlement found things as lively as they could wish.

There was no mistaking the position of affairs now. The Gaikas, whose locations occupied the whole northern half of British Kaffraria, the Hlambi clans, who held the rugged country along the eastern slopes of the Amatola Mountains, were all up in arms. All, that is, save an insignificant fraction, who applied to the Government for protection as 'loyals'; their loyalty consisting in taking no part in hostilities themselves, but aiding with supplies and information those who did—as well as affording a refuge in time of need to the women and cattle belonging to their hostile countrymen. Communication with the Colony was practically cut off—for, except to strong parties, the King Williamstown road was closed. A strong escort, consisting of Police and military, was attacked within a few miles of the settlement itself, only getting through by dint of hard fighting; and ever in their bushy hiding places, on the surrounding hills, hovered dark clouds of armed Savages ready to swoop down upon lonely express-rider or waggon train insufficiently guarded. The smoke of ruined homesteads rose from the fair plains of British Kaffraria, and by night the lurid signals of the hostile barbarians flamed forth from many a lofty peak.

In the Transkei matters were rather worse than before the previous three months of campaigning. Very far from crushed, the Gcalékas swarmed back into their oft-swept country, and with the aid of their new allies set to work with redoubled ardour to make things as lively for the white man as they possibly could. This kept nearly all the forces then at the front actively employed in that direction, leaving the field open to the residue of the Gaikas and Hlambis to burn and pillage throughout British Kaffraria at their own sweet will. The destruction of property was great and widespread.

Still, on the whole, men seemed rather to enjoy the prevailing state of things than otherwise, even those who were severe losers, strange to say. The colonial mind, adventurous at bottom, dearly loves excitement, once it has drunk at that enchanted fountain. Perhaps one of the best illustrations of this is to be found in the numbers who remained, and do remain, on at Johannesburg after the collapse, in a state of semi-starvation—rather than exchange the liveliness and stir of that restless and mushroom town for the surer but more sober conditions of life offered by the scenes of their birth. In British Kaffraria, the renewed outbreak of hostilities afforded plenty of excitement, which went as a set-off against the aforesaid losses—for the time being at any rate. Those who had already taken part in the first campaign either volunteered for the second or stayed at home and talked about both. Though whether he had been out or not made no difference as regarded the talking part of it, for every man jack you might meet in a day's wandering was open to give you his opinion upon what had been done, and what hadn't been done; above all upon what *should* have been done; in a word, felt himself entirely competent to direct the whole of the field operations there and then, and without even the traditional minute's notice.

But however enjoyable all this may have been to society at large, as there represented, there was one to whom it was intolerably irksome, and that one was Eustace Milne. The reasons for this were diverse. In the first place, in the then crowded state of the community, he could hardly ever obtain an opportunity of talking, with Eanswyth alone; which was not wholly without advantage in that it enabled the latter to keep up her *rôle*; for if her former sorrowing and heart-wrung condition had now become the hollowest mockery, there was no reason why everybody should be informed thereof, but very much the reverse. He could not see her alone in the house, for it was always full of people, and when it was not, still, the walls were thin. He could not take her for a ride outside the settlement, for in those early days the enemy was daring, and did not always keep at a respectful distance. It would not do to run any more risks. In the next place, all the "talking big," and indeed the talking at all, that went on, morning, noon, and night, on the well-worn, and threadbare topic was wearisome to him. The thing had become, in fact, a bore of the first water. But the most distasteful side of it all was the notoriety which he himself had, all involuntarily, attained. A man who had been reported slain, and then turned up safe and sound after having been held a prisoner for some weeks by the savage and ordinarily ruthless enemy they were then fighting, was sure to attract considerable attention throughout the frontier community. Friends, neighbours, intimates, people they had never seen or heard of before, would call on the Hostes all day and every day—literally in swarms, as the victim of these attentions put it—in order to see Eustace, and haply, to extract a "yarn" as to his late captivity. If he walked through the township some effusive individual was bound to rush at him with an "I say, Mister, 'scuse me, but we're told you're the man that was taken prisoner by old Kreli. Now, do us the favour to step round and have a drink. We don't see a man who has escaped from them black devils every day." And then, under pain of being regarded as churlish to a degree, he would find himself compelled to join a group of jovial, but under the circumstances excessively unwelcome, strangers, and proceed to the nearest bar to be cross questioned within an inch of his life, and expected to put away sundry "splits" that he did not want. Or those in charge of operations, offensive and defensive, would make his acquaintance and ask him to dine, always with the object of eliciting useful information. But to these Eustace was very reticent and proved, in fact, a sore disappointment. He had been treated fairly well by his captors. They were savages, smarting under a sense of defeat and loss. They might have put him to death amid cruel torments; instead of which they had given him his liberty. For the said liberty he had yet to pay—to pay pretty smartly, too, but this was only fair and might be looked upon in the light of ransom. He was not going to give any information to their detriment merely because, under a doubtfully administered system of organisation, they had taken up arms against the Colony. Besides, as a matter of fact, it was doubtful whether he had any information to give.

So his entertainers were disappointed. Everyone who accosted him upon the objectionable topic was disappointed. He became unpopular.

The infinitesimal intellect of the community felt slighted. The far from infinitesimal sense of self-importance of the said community was wounded to the core. Here was a man who had passed through strange and startling experiences which everyone else was dying to share—at second hand. Yet he kept them to himself. Who was he, indeed, they would like to know? Other men, had they gone through the same experiences, would have had them on tap all day long, for the benefit of all comers, good measure and brimming over. This one, on the contrary, was as close as death itself. Who was he that he should affect a singularity?

When a man is unpopular in a small community, he is pretty sure before long to be made aware of that fact. In this instance there were not wanting individuals the ingenuity of whose inventive powers was equal to the occasion. No wonder Milne was reticent as to what he had gone through—hinted these—for it was almost certainly not to his credit. It was a singular thing that he should have emerged from the ordeal unhurt and smiling, while poor Tom Carhayes had been mercilessly butchered. It looked, fishy—uncommonly so. The more you looked at it, the more it began to take on the aspect of a put-up job. Indeed it would not be surprising if it turned out that the expedition across the Bashi was a cunningly devised trap, not originating with the Kafirs either. The escape of Hoste and Payne was part of the programme—no motive existing why these two should be put out of the way.

Motive? Motive for desiring Tom Carhayes' death? Well, any fool could see that, one might have thought. Was there not a young and beautiful widow in the case—who would succeed lo the dead man's extremely comfortable possessions, and whom, by this time, any one could see with half an eye, was desperately in love with the plotting and unscrupulous cousin? That was motive enough, one would think.

It was easy, moreover, now to see through the predilection of that arch-schemer for their native neighbours and now enemies. It was all part of the plot. Doubtless he was even no sending them secret information and advice in return for what they had done for him. It would be surprising if he turned out anything better than a Kafir spy, were the real truth known.

These amiable hints and innuendoes, sedulously buzzed around, were not long in reaching the object of them. But they affected his impenetrable self-possession about as much as the discharge of a pea-shooter might affect the back of the mail-plated armadillo. His philosophical mind saw no earthly reason for disturbing itself about any rumours which a pack of spiteful idiots might choose to set afloat. Hoste's advice to him, to run two or three of these amiable gentry to earth and visit them with a good sound kicking, only made him laugh. Why should he mind what anybody said? If people chose to believe it they might—but if they didn't they wouldn't, and that was all about it.

True, he was tempted, on one or two occasions, to follow his friend's advice—and that was when Eanswyth was brought into the matter. But he remembered that you cannot strangle a widespread slander by force, and that short of the direst necessity the association in an ordinary row of any woman's name is justifiable neither by expediency nor good taste. But he resolved to get her to move down to Swaanepoel's Hoek at the very earliest opportunity.

Chapter Thirty Six.

A Row in the Camp.

There was just this much to bear out the ill-natured comments of the scandal-mongers, in that the re-appearance of the missing cousin had gone very far towards consoling the young widow for the loss of the dead husband.

The fact was that where her strongest, deepest feelings were concerned, Eanswyth, like most other women, was a bad actress. The awful poignancy of her suffering had been too real—the subsequent and blissful revulsion too overpowering—for her to be able to counterfeit the one or dissemble the other, with anything like a satisfactory result. Those who had witnessed the former, now shook their heads, feeling convinced that they had then mistaken the object of it. They began to look at Eanswyth ever so little, askance.

But why need she care if they did? She was independent, young and beautiful. She loved passionately, and her love was abundantly returned. A great and absorbing interest has a tendency to dwarf all minor worries. She did not, in fact, care.

Eustace, thanks to his cool and cautious temperament, was a better actor; so good, indeed, that to those who watched them it seemed that the affection was mainly, if not entirely, on one side. Sometimes he would warn her.

"For your own sake, dearest," he would say on such rare occasions when they were alone together. "For your own sake try and keep up appearances a little longer; at any rate until we are out of this infernal back-biting, gossipy little hole. Remember, you are supposed to be plunged in an abyss of woe, and here you are looking as absurdly happy as a bird which has just escaped from a cage."

"Oh, darling, you are right as usual," she would reply, trying to look serious. "But what am I to do? No wonder people think I have no heart."

"And they think right for once, for you have given it away—to me. Do keep up appearances, that's all. It won't be for much longer."

Eustace had secured a couple of rooms for his own use in one of the neighbouring cottages. The time not spent with Eanswyth was got through strolling about the camp, or now and then taking a short ride out into the *veldt* when the *entourage* was reported safe. But this, in deference to Eanswyth's fears, he did but seldom.

"Why on earth don't you go to the front again, Milne?" this or that friend or acquaintance would inquire. "You must find it properly slow hanging on in this hole. I know I do. Why, you could easily get a command of Fingo or

Hottentot levies, or, for the matter of that, it oughtn't to be difficult for a fellow with your record to raise a command on your own account."

"The fact is I've had enough of going to the front," Eustace would reply. "When I was there I used often to wonder what business it was of mine anyway, and when the Kafirs made a prisoner of me, my first thought was that it served me devilish well right. I give you my word it was. And I tell you what it is. When a man has got up every day for nearly a month, not knowing whether he'd go to bed between his blankets that night or pinned down to a black ants' nest, he's in no particular hurry to go and expose himself to a repetition of the process. It tells upon the nerves, don't you know."

"By Jove, I believe you," replied the other. "I never knew Jack Kafir was such a cruel devil before, at least not to white men. Well, if I'd gone through what you have, I believe I'd give the front a wide berth, too. As it is, I'm off in a day or two, I hope."

"I trust you may meet with better luck," said Eustace.

One day a considerable force of mounted burghers started for the Transkei—a good typical force—hardened, seasoned frontiersmen all, well mounted, well armed; in fact, a thoroughly serviceable looking corps all round. There was the usual complement of spectators seeing them off—the usual amount of cheering and hat-waving. On the outskirts of the crowd was a sprinkling of natives, representing divers races and colours.

"*Au!*" exclaimed a tall Gaika, as the crowd dispersed. "*That* will be a hard stone for Kreli to try and crush. If it was the *Amapolise* (Police) he could knock them to pieces with a stick. Mere boys!"

"What's that you say, Johnny?" said a hard-fisted individual, turning threateningly upon the speaker.

"Nothing. I only made a remark to my comrade," replied the man in his own language.

"Did you?" said the other walking up to the Kafir and looking him straight in the eye. "Then just keep your damned remarks to yourself, Johnny, or we shall quarrel. D'you hear?"

But the Kafir never quailed, never moved. He was a tall, powerful native and carried his head grandly. The white man, though shorter, looked tough and wiry as whip cord. The crowd, which had been scattering, gathered round the pair with the celerity of a mob of London street-cads round a fallen cab-horse.

"What's the row? A cheeky nigger? Give him fits, Mister! Knock him into the middle of next week!" were some of the cries that burst from the group of angry and excited men.

"I have committed no offence," said the Kafir. "I made a remark to a comrade, saying what a fine lot of men those were."

"Oh, yes? Very likely!" shouted several ironically.

"See here now. You get out of this," said the first man. "Do you hear, get out. Don't say another word—or—"

He did not finish. Stung by a contemptuous look in the Kafir's eyes, he dashed his fist full into his face.

It was a crushing blow—but the native did not fall. Like lightning he aimed a blow at his assailant's head with his heavy kerrie—a blow which would have shattered the skull like an egg shell. But the other threw up his arm in time, receiving nearly the full force of the blow on that member, which dropped to his side completely paralysed. Without attempting to follow up his success the savage sprang back, whirling his kerrie round his head. The crowd, taken by surprise, scattered before him.

Only for a moment, though. Like a pack of hounds pressed back by a stag at bay they gave way but to close up again. In a trice the man's kerrie was struck from his grasp, and he was thrown down, beaten, kicked, and very roughly handled.

"Tie up the *schelm*!"

"Give him six dozen well-laid on!" "Six dozen without counting!" "Cheeky brute!" were some of the shouts that accompanied each kick and blow dealt or aimed at the prostrate Kafir, who altogether seemed to be having a pretty bad time of it.

"That's a damned shame!" exclaimed a voice behind them.

All started and turned their heads, some astonished—all angry—some perhaps a little ashamed of themselves—towards the owner of the voice, a horseman who sat calmly in his saddle some twenty yards away—an expression of strong disgust upon his features.

"What have you got to say to it anyhow, I'd like to know?" cried the man who had just struck the native.

"What I said before—that it's a damned shame," replied Eustace Milne unhesitatingly.

"What's a shame, Mister?" sneered another. "That one o' your precious black kids is getting a hidin' for his infernal cheek?"

"That it should take twenty men to give it him, and that, too, when he's down."

"I tell you what it is, friend," said the first speaker furiously. "It may take rather less than twenty to give you one, and that, too, when you're up!" which sally provoked a blatant guffaw from several of the hearers.

"I'm not much afraid of that," answered Eustace tranquilly. "But now, seeing that British love of fair play has been about vindicated by a score of Englishmen kicking a prostrate Kafir, how would it be to let him get up and go?"

The keen, biting sarcasm told. The group, which mainly consisted of the low element, actually did begin to look a trifle ashamed of itself. The better element composing it gave way and took itself off, as Eustace deliberately walked his horse up to the fallen native. There were a few muttered jeers about "the nigger's friend" and getting into the Assembly on the strength of "blanket votes," (The native franchise, derisively so termed) and so forth, but none offered any active opposition except one, however, and that was the man who had originated the disturbance.

"Look here," he shouted savagely. "I don't know who you are and I don't care. But if you don't take yourself off out of this mighty quick, I'll just about knock you into a jelly; you see if I don't."

"*Ja*, that's right. Serve him as you did the nigger!" yelled the bystanders, a lot of rowdy hobbledehoys and a contingent of town loafers whom the prospect of an easy-going, devil-may-care life in the *veldt* had drawn from the more sober avocations of bricklaying and waggon-building within the Colony, and who, it may be added, distinguished themselves at the seat of hostilities by such a line of drunken mutinous insubordination as rendered them an occasion of perennial detestation and disgust to their respective commanders. These now closed up around their bullying, swash-bucklering champion, relieving their ardently martial spirits by hooting and cat's calls. It was only one man against a crowd. They felt perfectly safe.

"Who sold his mate to the blanked niggers!" they yelled. "Ought to be tarred and feathered. Come on, boys; let's do it. Who's for tarring and feathering the Kafir spy?"

All cordially welcomed this spicy proposal, but curiously enough, no one appeared anxious to begin, for they still kept some paces behind the original aggressor. That worthy, however, seemed to have plenty of fight in him, for he advanced upon Eustace unhesitatingly.

"Come now. Are you going to clear?" he shouted. "You're not? All right. I'll soon make you."

A stirrup-iron, wielded by a clever hand, is a terribly formidable weapon. Backing his horse a pace or two Eustace wrenched loose his stirrup. Quick as lightning, it whirled in the air, and as his assailant sprang wildly at him down it came. The aggressive bully went to earth like a felled ox.

"Any more takers for the tar-and-feather line of business?" said Eustace quietly, but with the light of battle in his eyes.

The insulting jeers and the hooting still continued. But no one advanced. No one seemed anxious to tackle that particularly resolute looking horseman.

"Get out of this, you cowardly skunks!" sung out a voice behind him, which voice proceeded from another horseman, who had ridden up unseen during the *émeute*. "Twenty to one! Faugh! For two pins we'll sjambok the lot of you."

"Hallo, Errington! Where have you dropped from? Thought you were away down in the Colony," said Eustace, turning to the new arrival, a fine soldierly looking man of about his own age, in whom he recognised a former Field-Captain in Brathwaite's Horse. The crowd had already begun to melt away before this new accession of force.

"Yer—send yer winder to be cleaned! Stick it in yer breeches pocket!" were some of the witticisms yelled back by the retreating rowdies, in allusion to the eye-glass worn by the newcomer.

"By jove, Milne. You seem to have been in the wars," said the latter looking from one to the other of the injured parties. "What's the row, eh?"

"It speaks for itself. Nothing much, though. I've only been reminding our valiant friends there that fair play is a jewel even when its only a Kafir that's concerned."—"Which unsavoury Ethiop seems to have been knocked about a bit, however," rejoined the other, sticking his glass into his eye to examine the fallen native.

The Kafir, who had raised himself to a sitting posture, was now staring stupidly about him as though half dazed. Blood was issuing from his nose and mouth, and one of his eyes was completely closed up. His assailants had all slunk away by now, the arrival upon the scene of this unwelcome ally having turned the scale against any plan they might have entertained of showing further unpleasantness toward the solitary intervener.

Some three or four of the Gaika's countrymen, who had held aloof, now came up to the assistance of their friend. These gave their version of the story. Eustace listened attentively.

"It was a foolish thing to make any remark at such a time and in such a place," he said. "It was sure to provoke strife. Go and get him a tot of grog," throwing them a sixpence, "and then you'd better get away home."

"I tell you what it is, Milne," said Errington in a low tone. "I know that fellow you floored so neatly. He's one of the best bruisers in the country, and I'm afraid you haven't seen the last of him. You'd better keep a bright lookout as long as you're in this part. He's bound to play you some dog's trick at the earliest opportunity."

"Is he? Well I must try and be ready for him. I suppose now we must bring the poor devil round, eh? He seems about stunned."

Errington had a flask in his pocket. Dismounting he raised the fallen man's head and poured some of the contents into his mouth.

The fellow revived—gradually, stupidly. He had received a bad blow, which only a thick slouch hat and a thicker skull had saved from being a worse one.

"Who the hell are you?" he growled surlily, as he sat up. "Oh, I know you," he went on as his glance lit upon Eustace. "All right, my fine feller, wait a bit, till I'm all right again. You'll be sorry yet for that damned coward's whack you've given me. See if you're not."

"You brought it upon yourself. Why did you try and rush me?"

"I didn't rush you with a stirrup-iron, did I?"

"No. But see here. If I'm attacked I'm not going to leave the choice of my means of defence to the enemy. Not much. How would that pan out for an idea in fighting old Kreli, for instance?"

"Of course," struck in Errington. "That's sound sense, and you know it is, Jackson. You and Milne have had a bit of a scrimmage and you've got the worst of it. It might easily have been the other way. So don't let us have any grudge-bearing over it. Take another drink, man," pouring out a liberal modicum of whiskey into the cup of the flask, "and shake hands and make it up."

The man, who was not a bad fellow at bottom, gave a growl as he tossed off the tendered potion. Then he held out his hand to Eustace.

"Well, Mister, I don't bear no grudge. If you'll jest say you're sorry you hit me—"

"I'll say that with pleasure, Jackson," replied Eustace, as they shook hands. "And look here, if you still feel a bit groggy on your pins, jump on my horse and ride home. I'll walk."

"No, thanks. I'm all right now. Besides I ain't going your way. My waggon's outspanned yonder on the flat. Good-night."

"I stand very much indebted to you, Errington, for two services rendered," said Eustace as they rode towards the township. "And I'm not sure that the last isn't by far the most important."

"Pooh! not at all, my dear fellow. That howling rabble wouldn't have come within twenty yards of you."

"I don't know about that. The vagabonds were rather beginning to realise that twenty to one meant long odds in favour of the twenty, when you came up. But the deft way in which you smoothed down our friend with the broken head was diplomatic to a degree. I hate rows, and the knowledge that some fellow is going about day and night seeking an opportunity of fastening a quarrel upon you unawares is tiresome. Besides, I'm nothing of a boxer, and if I were should hate a shindy just as much."

"I quite agree with you," said the other, who *was* something of a boxer. "To form the centre of attraction to a howling, yahooing rabble, making an undignified exhibition of yourself bashing and being bashed by some other fellow like a couple of butcher's boys in the gutter, is bound to be a revolting process whichever way you look at it. Even the law of the pistol seems to be an improvement on it."

"I think so, too. It puts men on better terms of equality. Any man may become a dead shot and a quick drawer, but not one man in ten can fulfil all the conditions requisite to becoming a good boxer. The fact is, however, I hate rows of any kind, even when only a spectator. When fellows say they like them I never altogether believe them."

"Unless they are very young. But the Berserk taint soon wears off as you get on into life a bit," said Errington.

"Well now—I turn off here. Good-evening."

Chapter Thirty Seven.

"It is the Voice of an Oracle."

Swaanepoel's Hoek, poor Tom Carhayes' other farm, was situated in the division of Somerset East, somewhere between the Great and Little Fish Rivers. It was rather an out-of-the-way place, lying in a mountainous district, sparsely inhabited and only reached by rough wheel-tracks through narrow, winding *poorts*. But the scenery was wild and romantic to a degree. The bold sweep of bush-grown slopes, the lofty heights culminating in red iron-bound *krantzes* whose inaccessible hedges afforded nesting place for colonies of *aasvogels*, the thunder of the mountain torrent pent-up between black rocky walls where the maiden-hair fern hung in solid festoons from every crack and cranny, the cheerful and abundant sounds of bird and animal life—all this rendered the place a wonderfully pleasant and attractive, if somewhat out-of-the-way, residence.

To Eanswyth Carhayes, however, this very isolation constituted an additional charm. The solemn grandeur of the soaring mountains, the hush of the seldom trodden valleys, conveyed to her mind, after the bustle and turmoil of the crowded frontier settlement, the perfection of peace. She felt that she could spend her whole life on this beautiful spot. And it was her own.

She had only once before visited the place—shortly after her marriage—and then had spent but three or four days there. Its beauties had failed at that time to strike her imagination. Now it was different. All the world was a Paradise. It seemed that there was nothing left in life for her to desire.

The house was a fair size, almost too large for the overseer and his family. That worthy had asked Eustace whether Mrs Carhayes would prefer that they should vacate it. There was a substantial outbuilding, used—or rather only half of it was used—as a store, and a saddle and harness room. They could make themselves perfectly snug in that, if Mrs Carhayes wished to have the house to herself.

"I can answer for it: Mrs Carhayes wishes nothing of the sort," he had replied. "In fact, we were talking over that very thing on the way down."

"Sure the children won't disturb her, Mr Milne?"

"Well, it hasn't looked like it up till now. Those youngsters of yours don't seem particularly obstreperous, Bentley, and Mrs Carhayes appears rather to have taken a fancy to them than otherwise."

"If there's a kind sweet lady in this world, Mr Milne, it's Mrs Carhayes," said the overseer earnestly. "I know the wife'll make her right comfortable while she's here. She'll save her all bother over housekeeping or anything of that sort. Excuse the question, but is she likely to be making a long stay?"

"I shouldn't wonder. You see, there's nowhere else for her to go, and the quiet of this place suits her after all she has gone through. And she has gone through some pretty lively times, I need hardly tell you."

"I should think so. Why, what a narrow escape she had that time you were bringing her away from Anta's Kloof, when the trap broke down. That was a frightful position for any lady to be in, in all conscience."

"Oh, you heard of that, did you? Ah, I forgot. It was in every paper in the Colony—more or less inaccurately reported, of course," added Eustace drily, and then the two men lit their pipes and chatted for an hour or so about the war and its events.

"By the way, Bentley," said Eustace presently. "Talking about that outbuilding. I've decided to knock out the partition—it's only a wooden one—between the two rooms next to the storeroom, turn them into one, and use it as a bedroom for myself. The house is rather congested with the lot of us in it, after all. We might go to work at it this afternoon."

"Certainly, Mr Milne, certainly," replied the overseer. And forthwith the tool-chest was laid under requisition, and in a couple of hours the necessary alterations were effected.

This move did not altogether meet with Eanswyth's approval, and she expostulated accordingly.

"Why should you be the one turned out in the cold," she said. "There's no earthly necessity for it. You will be horribly uncomfortable over there, Eustace, and in winter the nights will be quite bitter. Then again, the roof is a thatched one, and the first rain we get will start it leaking like a sieve. Besides, there's plenty of room in the house."

"It isn't that, you dear, thoughtful, considerate guardian angel," he answered. "It isn't quite that, though I put it that way for Bentley's behoof. It is something of a concession to Mother Grundy, for even here that arch-hag can make her upas power felt, and I don't want to have all the tongues in the district wagging like the tails of a pack of foxhounds just unkennelled. We had enough of that at Komgha. So I've arranged that at any rate we shan't be under the same roof. See?"

"Yes; but it's ridiculous all the same. As if we weren't relations, too."

"And will be closer relations soon—in fact, the closest. I suppose we must wait a year—but that rests with you."

"I don't know. It's an awfully long time," and she sighed. Then rather hesitatingly: "Darling, you have never yet shown me the little silver box. We are alone now, and—"

"And you are dying to see it. Well, Eanswyth, it is really a most remarkable coincidence—in fact, almost makes a man feel superstitious."

It was near sundown. A soft, golden light rested upon the great slopes, and the cooing of doves floated melodiously from the mealie lands in the valley. The mountain stream roared through its rocky bed at their feet, and among the crannies and ledges of a profusion of piled up boulders forming miniature cliffs around, a whole colony of bright eyed little *dasjes* (The "rock rabbit"— really a species of marmot) were disporting themselves, scampering in and out with a boldness which augured volumes in favour of the peaceable aspect of the two human intruders upon their sequestered haunt.

"As you say, the time and place are indeed fitting," said Eustace, sitting down upon a boulder and taking the box from its place of concealment. "Now, my darling, look at this. The assegai point is broken short off, driven with such force that it has remained embedded in the lid."

It was even as he said. Had the blade been driven with a powerful hammer it could not have been more firmly wedged within the metal.

"That was the blow I received during the fight," he went on. "The dent at the side of it was done when I stood up to the witch-doctress. It did not penetrate much that time; not that the blow wasn't hard enough, for it nearly knocked me down, but the assegai was a rotten one and made of soft iron, and the point flattened out like a Snider bullet. Heavens! but that was an ordeal—something of a nerve-tickler!" he added, with a grave and meditative look in his eyes, as if he were mentally re-enacting that trying and critical scene.

Eanswyth shuddered, but said nothing. She nestled rather closer to his side, as he continued:

"Now to open the box—a thing I haven't done since, partly from superstitious motives—partly that I intended we should do so together—if we ever were to be again together, that is."

He pressed the spring, but it was out of order. It needed the wrench of a strong knife blade before the lid flew open.

"Look at that. The assegai point is so firmly wedged that it would take a hammer to drive it out—but I propose to leave it in—use it as a 'charm' next war perhaps. Now for the letter. It has gone through and through it— through the photograph too—and has just dinted the bottom of the box."

He spread out the letter. Those last tender, loving words, direct from her overflowing heart, were pierced and lacerated by the point of the murderous weapon.

"If this is not an oracle, there never was such a thing," he went on. "Look at this"—reading—"'I dare not say "God bless you." Coming from me it would entail a curse, rather than a blessing...' The point has cut clean through the words 'a curse'—Mfulini's assegai has made short work of that malediction. Is not that the voice of an oracle?"

She made no reply. She was watching the development of the investigation with rapt, eager attention.

"Here again—'Were anything to befall you—were you never to come back to me my heart would be broken...' As the paper is folded it has cut through the word 'heart'—And—by Jove, this is more than a coincidence! Here again, it has gone clean through the same word. Look at the end. *I want you in all your dangers and hardships to have, with you, these poor little lines, coming, as they are, warm from my hand and heart*... And now for the photograph. It is a sweetly lifelike representation of you, my dearest—"

A cry from her interrupted him. The portrait was a three parts length cabinet one, cut round to enable it to fit the box, which it did exactly. Right through the breast of the portrait, the assegai point had pierced.

"O Eustace—this is an oracle, indeed!" she cried. "Do you not see? The spear point has gone right through my 'heart' again for the third time. My dearest love, thrice has my 'heart' stood between you and death—once in the portrait, twice in the letter. At the same time it has obliterated the word 'curse.' It is, indeed, an 'oracle' and—What if I had never given you that box at all?"

"I should be a lot of dry bones scattered about the *veldt* in Bomvanaland at this moment," he rejoined. "Now you see how your love has twice stood between me and death; has preserved my life for itself. My sweet guardian angel, does not that look as if some Fate had always intended us for each other from the very first!"

Chapter Thirty Eight.

At Swaanepoel's Hoek.

Several months had gone by.

The war was nearly over now. Struck on all sides—decimated by the terrible breech-loading weapons of the whites—harried even in their wildest strongholds, their supplies running low, their crops destroyed, and winter upon them—the insurgent tribes recognised that they were irretrievably worsted. They had no heart for further fighting—their principal thought now was to make the best terms they could for themselves. So all along the frontier the disheartened savages were flocking in to lay down their arms and surrender. Those who belonged to independent tribes in the Transkei were treated as belligerents—and after being disarmed were located at such places as the Government thought fit. Those who were British subjects, and whose locations were within the colonial boundaries, such as the Gaikas, Hlambis, and a section of the Tembus, were treated as rebels and lodged in gaol until such time as it should please the authorities to put them on their trial for high treason, treason, felony, or sedition, according to their rank, responsibilities, or deeds. Still the unfortunate barbarians preferred to discount the chances of the future against present starvation—and continued to come in, in swarms. The gaols were soon crammed to overflowing; so, too, were the supplementary buildings hired for the emergency.

Not all, however, had preferred imprisonment with plenty to liberty with starvation. There were still armed bands lurking in the forest recesses of the Amatola, and in the rugged and bushy fastnesses beyond the Kei. While most of the chiefs of the colonial tribes had either surrendered or been slain, the head and Paramount Chief of all was still at large. "Kreli must be captured or killed," was the general cry. "Until this is done the war can never be considered at an end." But the old chief had no intention of submitting to either process if he could possibly help it. He continued to make himself remarkably scarce.

Another character who was very particularly wanted was Hlangani, and for this shrewd and daring leader the search was almost as keen as for Kreli himself. Common report had killed him over and over again, but somehow there was no satisfactory evidence of his identification. Then a wild rumour got about that he had been sent by his chief on a mission to invoke the aid of the Zulu King, who at that time was, rightly or wrongly, credited with keeping South Africa in general, and the colony of Natal in particular, in a state of uneasiness and alarm. But, wherever he was, like his chief, and the "bold gendarmes" of the burlesque song, he continued to be "when wanted never there."

All these reports and many more reached Eustace Milne, who had taken no active part in frontier affairs since we saw him last. He had even been sounded as to his willingness to undertake a post on behalf of the Government which should involve establishing diplomatic relations with the yet combatant bands, but this he had declined. He intended to do what he could for certain of the rebels later on, but meanwhile the time had not yet come.

Moreover, he was too happy amid the peaceful idyllic life he was then leading to care to leave it even for a time in order to serve a potentially ungrateful country. And it was idyllic. There was quite enough to do on the place to keep even his energetic temperament active. The stock which had constituted the capital of their common partnership and had been sent to Swaanepoel's Hoek at the outbreak of the war required considerable looking after, for, owing to the change of *veldt*, it did not thrive as well as could be wished. And then the place afforded plenty of sport; far more than Anta's Kloof had done. Leopards, wild pigs, and bushbucks abounded in the bushy kloofs; indeed, there were rather too many of the former, looking at it from the farming point of view. The valley bottoms and the water courses were full of guinea-fowl and francolins, and high up on the mountain slopes, the vaal rykbok might be shot for the going after, to say nothing of a plentiful sprinkling of quail and now and then a bustard. Eustace was often constrained to admit to himself that he would hardly have believed it possible that life could hold such perfect and unalloyed happiness.

He had, as we have said, plenty of wholesome and congenial work, with sport to his heart's content, and enjoyed a complete immunity from care or worry. These things alone might make any man happy. But there was another factor in this instance. There was the sweet companionship of one whom he had loved passionately when the case was hopeless and she was beyond his reach, and whom he loved not less absorbingly now that all barriers were broken down between them, now that they would soon belong to each other until their life's end. This was the influence that cast a radiant glow upon the doings and undertakings of everyday life, encircling everything with a halo of love, even as the very peace of Heaven.

Not less upon Eanswyth did the same influences fall. The revulsion following upon that awful period of heart-break and despair had given her fresh life indeed. In her grand beauty, in the full glow of health and perfect happiness, no one would have recognised the white, stricken mourner of that time. She realised that there was nothing on earth left to desire. And then her conscience would faintly reproach her. Had she a right to revel in such perfect happiness in the midst of a world of sorrow and strife?

But the said world seemed to keep very fairly outside that idyllic abode. Now and then they would drive or ride into Somerset East, or visit or be visited by a neighbour—the latter not often. The bulk of the surrounding settlers were Boers, and beyond exchanging a few neighbourly civilities from time to time they saw but little of them. This, however, was not an unmixed evil.

Bentley had been as good as his word. His wife was a capital housekeeper and had effectively taken all cares of that nature off Eanswyth's hands. Both were thoroughly good and worthy people, of colonial birth, who, by steadiness and trustworthy intelligence, had worked their way up from a very lowly position. Unlike too many of their class, however, they were not consumed with a perennial anxiety to show forth their equality in the sight of Heaven with those whom they knew to be immeasurably their superiors in birth and culture, and to whom, moreover, they owed in no small degree their own well-being. So the relations existing between the two different factors which composed the household were of the most cordial nature.

There had been some delay in settling up Tom Carhayes' affairs—in fact, they were not settled yet. With a good sense and foresight, rather unexpected in one of his unthinking and impulsive temperament, poor Tom had made his will previous to embarking on the Gcaléka campaign. Everything he possessed was bequeathed to his wife—with no restriction upon her marrying again—and Eustace and a mutual friend were appointed executors.

This generosity had inspired in Eanswyth considerable compunction, and was the only defective spoke in the wheel of her present great happiness. Sometimes she almost suspected that her husband had guessed at how matters really stood, and the idea cost her more than one remorseful pang. Yet, though she had failed in her allegiance, it was in her heart alone. She would have died sooner than have done so otherwise, she told herself.

Twice had the executors applied for the necessary authority to administer the estate. But the Master of the Supreme Court professed himself not quite satisfied. The evidence as to the testator's actual death struck him as inadequate—resting, as it did, upon the sole testimony of one of the executors, who could not even be positive that the man was dead when last seen by him. He might be alive still, though held a prisoner. Against this view was urged the length of time which had elapsed, and the utter improbability that the Gcaléka bands, broken up and harried, as they were, from point to point, would hamper themselves with a prisoner, let alone a member of that race toward which they had every reason to entertain the most uncompromising and implacable rancour. The Supreme Court, however, was immovable. When hostilities were entirely at an end, they argued, evidence might be forthcoming on the part of natives who had actually witnessed the testator's death. That fact incontestably established, letters of administration could at once be granted. Meanwhile the matter must be postponed a little longer.

This delay affected those most concerned not one whit. There was not the slightest fear of Eanswyth's interests suffering in the able hands which held their management. Only, the excessive caution manifested by the law's representatives would at times communicate to Eustace Milne a vague uneasiness. What if his cousin should be alive after all? What if he had escaped under circumstances which would involve perforce his absence during a considerable period? He might have gained the sea shore, for instance, and been picked up by a passing ship bound to some distant country, whose captain would certainly decline to diverge many days out of his course to oblige one unknown castaway. Such things had happened. Still, the idea was absurd, he told himself, for, even if it was so, sufficient time had elapsed for the missing man, in these days of telegraphs and swift mail steamers, to make known his whereabouts, even if not to return in person. He had not seen dim actually killed in his conflict with Hlangani—indeed, the fact of that strange duel having been fought with kerries, only seemed to point to the fact that no killing was intended. That he was only stunned and disabled when dragged away out of sight Eustace could swear, but why should that implacable savage make such a point of having the absolute disposal of his enemy, if it were not to execute the most deadly ferocious vengeance upon him which lay in his power? That the wretched man had been fastened down to be devoured alive by black ants, even as the pretended wizard had been treated, Eustace entertained hardly any doubt—would have entertained none, but that the witch-doctress's veiled hint had pointed to a fate, if possible, even more darkly horrible. No, after all this time, his unfortunate cousin could not possibly be alive. The actual mode of his death might forever remain a mystery, but that he was dead was as certain as anything in this world can be. Any suspicion to the contrary he resolved to dismiss effectually from his mind.

Eanswyth would often accompany her lover during his rides about the *veldt* looking after the stock. She would not go with him, however, when he was on sporting intent, she had tried it once or twice, but the bucks had a horrid knack of screaming in the most heart-rending fashion when sadly wounded and not killed outright, and Eustace's assurance that this was due to the influence of fear and not of pain, entirely failed to reconcile her to it. (A fact. The smaller species of antelope here referred to, however badly wounded, will not utter a sound until seized upon by man or dog, when it screams as described. The same holds good of the English hare.) But when on more peaceful errand bent, she was never so happy as when riding with him among the grand and romantic scenery of their mountain home. She was a first-rate horsewoman and equally at home in the saddle when her steed was picking his way along some dizzy mountain path on the side of a grass slope as steep as the roof of a house with a series of perpendicular *krantzes* below, or when pursuing some stony and rugged bush track where the springy *spekboem* boughs threatened to sweep her from her seat every few yards.

"We are partners now, you know, dearest," she would say gaily, when he would sometimes urge the fatigue and occasionally even the risk of these long and toilsome rides. "While that law business still hangs fire the partnership can't be dissolved, I suppose. Therefore I claim my right to do my share of the work."

It was winter now. The clear mountain air was keen and crisp, and although the nights were bitterly cold, the days were lovely. The sky was a deep, cloudless blue, and the sun poured his rays down into the valleys with a clear, genial warmth which just rendered perceptible the bracing exhilaration of the air. Thanks to the predominating *spekboem* and other evergreen bushes, the winter dress of Nature suffered but little diminution in verdure; and in grand contrast many a stately summit soared proudly aloft, capped with a white powdering of snow.

Those were days of elysium indeed, to those two, as they rode abroad among the fairest scenes of wild Nature; or, returning at eve, threaded the grassy bush-paths, while the crimson winged louris flashed from tree to tree, and the francolins and wild guinea-fowl, startled by the horses' hoofs, would scuttle across the path, echoing their grating note of alarm. And then the sun, sinking behind a lofty ridge, would fling his parting rays upon the smooth burnished faces of the great red cliffs until they glowed like molten fire.

Yes, those were indeed days to look back upon.

Chapter Thirty Nine.

From the Dead!

Eustace and the overseer were sitting on the *stoep* smoking a final pipe together before going to bed. It was getting on for midnight and, save these two, the household had long since retired.

Tempted by the beauty of the night they sat, well wrapped up, for it was winter. But the whole firmament was ablaze with stars, and the broad nebulous path of the Milky Way shone forth like the phosphoric trail in the wake of a steamer. The conversation between the two had turned upon the fate of Tom Carhayes.

"I suppose we shall soon know now what his end really was," the overseer was saying. "Kafirs are as close as death over matters of that kind while the war is actually going on. But they are sure to talk afterwards, and some of them are bound to know."

"Yes. And but for this administration business it might be just as well for us not to know," answered Eustace. "Depend upon it, whatever it is, it will be something more than ghastly, poor fellow. Tom made a great mistake in going to settle in Kafirland at all. He'd have done much better here."

"I suppose there isn't the faintest shadow of a chance that he may still be alive, Mr Milne?"

The remark was an unfortunate one. Cool-headed as he was, it awoke in Eustace a vague stirring of uneasiness—chiming in, as it did, with the misgivings which would sometimes pass through his own mind.

"Not a shadow of a chance, I should say," he replied, after a slight pause.

Bentley, too, began to realise that the remark was not a happy one—for of course he could not all this time have been blind to the state of affairs. He felt confused and relapsed into silence—puffing vigorously at his pipe.

The silence was broken—broken in a startling manner. A terrified scream fell upon their ears—not very loud, but breathing unmistakable tones of mortal fear. Both men sprang to their feet.

"Heavens!" cried the overseer. "That's Mrs Carhayes—"

But the other said not a word. In about a half a dozen steps he was through the sitting room and had gained the door which opened out of it. This was Eanswyth's bedroom, whence the terrified cry had proceeded.

"What is wrong, Eanswyth?" he cried, tapping at the door.

It opened immediately. She stood there wrapped in a long loose dressing gown, the wealth of her splendid hair falling in masses. But her face was white as death, and the large eyes were dilated with such a pitiable expression of fear and distress, as he certainly had never beheld there.

"What is it, my darling? What has frightened you so?" he said tenderly, moved to the core by this extraordinary manifestation of pitiable terror.

She gave a quick flurried look over her shoulder. Then clutching his hands—and he noticed that hers were trembling and as cold as ice—she gasped:

"Eustace—I have seen—him!"

"Who—in Heaven's name?"

"Tom."

"Darling, you must have dreamt it. You have been allowing your thoughts to run too much on the subject and—"

"No. It was no dream. I have not even been to bed yet," she interrupted, speaking hurriedly. "I was sitting there, at the table, reading one of my little books. I just happened to look up and—O Eustace"—with a violent shudder—"I saw *his* face staring in at the window just as plainly as I can see you now."

Eustace followed her cowering glance. The window, black and uncurtained, looked out upon the *veldt*. There were shutters, but they were hardly ever closed. His first thought, having dismissed the nightmare theory, was that some loafer was hanging about, and seeing the lighted window had climbed up to look in. He said as much.

"No. It was *him*," she interrupted decisively. "There was no mistaking him. If it were the last word I breathed I should still say so. What does it mean? Oh, what does it mean?" she repeated in tones of the utmost distress.

"Hush, hush, my dearest! Remember, Bentley will hear, and—"

"*There he is again!*"

The words broke forth in a shriek. Quickly Eustace glanced at the window. The squares of glass, black against the outer night, showed nothing in the shape of a human countenance. A large moth buzzed against them, and that was all.

Her terror was so genuine, as with blanched face and starting eyes she glared upon the black glass, that ever so slight a thrill of superstitious dread shot through him in spite of himself.

"Quick!" she gasped. "Quick! Go and look all round the house! I am not frightened to remain alone. Mr Bentley will stay with me. Go, quick!"

The overseer, who had judiciously kept in the background, now came forward.

"Certainly, Mrs Carhayes. Better come into this room and sit down for a bit. Why, you must have been mistaken," he went on, cheerily placing a chair at the sitting room fire, and kicking up the nearly dead logs. "Nobody could get up at your window. Why, its about fifteen feet from the ground and there's nothing lying about for them to step on. Not even a monkey could climb up there—though—wait. I did hear once of a case where a baboon, a wild one out of the *veldt*, climbed up on to the roof of a house and swung himself right into a room. I don't say I believe it, though. It's a little too much of a Dutchman's yarn to be readily swallowed."

Thus the good-natured fellow rambled on, intent on cheering her up and diverting her thoughts. The rooms occupied by himself and his family were at the other end of the house and opened outside on the *stoep*, hence the sound of her terrified shriek had not reached them.

Eustace, on investigation intent, had slipped round the outside of the house with the stealth and rapidity of a savage. But, as he had expected, there was no sign of the presence of any living thing. He put his ear to the ground and listened long and intently. Not a sound. No stealthy footfall broke the silence of the night.

But as he crouched there in the darkness, with every nerve, every faculty at the highest tension, a horrible thought came upon him. What if Carhayes had really escaped—was really alive? Why should he not avow himself openly—why come prowling around like a midnight assassin? And then the answer suggested itself. Might it not be that his mind, unhinged by the experiences of his captivity, was filled with the one idea—to exact a deadly vengeance upon the wife who had so soon forgotten him? Such things had been, and to this man, watching there in the darkness, the idea was horrible enough.

Stay! There was one way of placing the matter beyond all doubt. He remembered that the soil beneath Eanswyth's window was loose dust—a trifle scratched about by the fowls, but would give forth the print of a human foot with almost the distinctness of snow.

Quickly he moved to the spot. Striking a wax vesta, and then another, he peered eagerly at the ground. The atmosphere was quite still, and the matches flamed like a torch. His heart beat and his pulses quickened as he carefully examined the ground—then a feeling of intense relief came upon him. *There was no sign of a human footprint.*

No living thing could have stood under that window, much less climbed up to it, without leaving its traces. There were no traces; ergo, no living thing had been there, and he did not believe in ghosts. The whole affair had been a hallucination on the part of Eanswyth. This was bad, in that it seemed to point to a weak state of health or an overloaded mind. But it was nothing like so bad as the awful misfortune involved by the reality would have been—at any rate, to him.

He did not believe in ghosts, but the idea crossed his mind that so far as from allaying Eanswyth's fears, the utter impossibility of any living being having approached her window without leaving spoor in the sandy, impressionable soil, would have rather the opposite tendency. Once the idea got firmly rooted in her mind that the dead had appeared to her there was no foreseeing the limits of the gravity of the results. And she had been rather depressed of late. Very anxiously he re-entered the house to report the utter futility of his search.

"At all events we'll soon make it impossible for you to get another *schrek* in the same way, Mrs Carhayes," said the overseer cheerily. "We'll fasten the shutters up."

It was long before the distressed, scared look faded from her eyes. "Eustace," she said—Bentley having judiciously left them together for a while—"When *you* were—when I thought you dead—I wearied Heaven with prayers to allow me one glimpse of you again. I had no fear then, but now—O God! it is *his* spirit that I have seen."

He tried to soothe her, to reassure her, and in a measure succeeded. At last, to the surprise of himself and the overseer, she seemed to shake off her terror as suddenly as it had assailed her. She was very foolish, she declared. She would go to bed now, and not keep them up all night in that selfish manner. And she actually did—refusing all offers on the part of Eustace or the overseer to remain in the sitting room in order to be within call, or to patrol around the house for the rest of the night.

"No," she said, "I am ashamed of myself already. The shutters are fastened up and I shall keep plenty of light burning. I feel quite safe now."

It was late next morning when Eanswyth appeared. Thoroughly refreshed by a long, sound sleep, she had quite forgotten her fears. Only as darkness drew on again a restless uneasiness came over her, but again she seemed to throw it off with an effort. She seemed to have the faculty of pulling herself together by an effort of will—even as she had done that night beside the broken-down buggy, while listening for the approaching footsteps of their savage enemies in the darkness. To Eustace's relief, however, nothing occurred to revive her uneasiness.

But he himself, in his turn, was destined to receive a rude shock.

Chapter Forty.

A Letter from Hoste.

There was no postal delivery at Swaanepoel's Hoek, nor was there any regular day for sending for the mails. If anybody was driving or riding into Somerset East on business or pleasure, they would call at the post office and bring out whatever there was; or, if anything of greater or less importance was expected, a native servant would be despatched with a note to the postmaster.

Bentley had just returned from the township, bringing with him a batch of letters. Several fell to Eustace's share, all, more or less, of a business nature. All, save one—and before he opened this he recognised Hoste's handwriting:

> My Dear Milne (it began): This is going to be an important communication. So, before you go any further, you had better get into some sequestered corner by yourself to read it, for it's going to knock you out of time some, or I'm a Dutchman.

"That's a shrewd idea on the part of Hoste putting in that caution," he said to himself. "I should never have credited the chap with so much gumption."

He was alone in the shearing-house when the overseer had handed him his letters. His coat was off, and he was doing one or two odd carpentering jobs. The time was about midday. Nobody was likely to interrupt him here.

> Something has come to my knowledge (went on the letter) which you, of all men, ought to be the one to investigate. To come to the point, there is some reason to suppose that poor Tom Carhayes may still be alive.
>
> You remember that Kafir on whose behalf you interfered when Jackson and a lot of fellows were giving him beans? He is my informant. He began by inquiring for you, and when I told him you were far away, and not likely to be up here again, he seemed disappointed, and said he wanted to do you a good turn for standing his friend on that occasion. He said he now knew who you were, and thought he could tell you something you would like to know.
>
> Well, I told him he had better unburden himself to me, and if his information seemed likely to be of use, he might depend upon me passing it on to you. This, at first, he didn't seem to see—you know what a suspicious dog our black brother habitually is—and took himself off. But the secret seemed to weigh upon him, for, in a day or two, he turned

up again, and then, in the course of a good deal of "dark talking," he gave me to understand that Tom Carhayes was still alive; and, in fact, he knew where he was.

Milne, you may just bet your boots I felt knocked all out of time. I hadn't the least suspicion what the fellow was driving at, at first. Thought he was going to let out that he knew where old Kreli was hiding, or Hlangani, perhaps. So, you see, you must come up here at once, and look into the matter. I've arranged to send word to Xalasa—that's the fellow's name—to meet us at Anta's Kloof directly you arrive.

Don't lose any time. Start the moment you get this. Of course I've kept the thing as dark as pitch; but there's no knowing when an affair of this kind may not leak out and get into all the papers.

Kind regards to Mrs Carhayes—and keep this from her at present.

Yours ever, Percy F. Hoste.

Carefully Eustace read through every word of this communication; then, beginning again, he read it through a second time.

"This requires some thinking out," he said to himself. Then taking up the letter he went out in search of some retired spot where it would be absolutely impossible that he should be interrupted.

Wandering mechanically he found himself on the very spot where they had investigated the silver box together. That would do. No one would think of looking for him there.

He took out the letter and again studied every word of it carefully. There was no getting behind its contents: they were too plain in their fatal simplicity. And there was an inherent probability about the potentiality hinted at. He would certainly start at once to investigate the affair. Better to know the worst at any rate. And then how heartily he cursed the Kafir's obtrusive gratitude, wishing a thousand-fold that he had left that sable bird of ill-omen at the mercy of his chastisers. However, if there was any truth in the story, it was bound to have come to light sooner or later in any case—perhaps better now, before the mischief wrought was irreparable. But if it should turn out to be true—what then? Good-bye to this beautiful and idyllic dream in which they two had been living during all these months past. Good-bye to a life's happiness: to the bright golden vista they had been gazing into together. Why had he not closed with Hlangani's hideous proposal long ago? Was it too late even now?

The man suffered agonies as he sat there, realising his shattered hopes—the fair and priceless structure of his life's happiness levelled to the earth like a house of cards. Like Lucifer fallen from Paradise he felt ready for anything.

Great was Eanswyth's consternation and astonishment when he announced the necessity of making a start that afternoon.

"The time will soon pass," he said. "It is a horrible nuisance, darling, but there is no help for it. The thing is too important. The fact is, something has come to light—something which may settle that delayed administration business at once."

It might, indeed, but in a way very different to that which he intended to convey. But she was satisfied.

"Do not remain away from me a moment longer than you can help, Eustace, my life!" she had whispered to him during the last farewell, she having walked a few hundred yards with him in order to see the last of him. "Remember, I shall only exist—not live—during these next few days. This is the first time you have been away from me since—since that awful time."

Then had come the sweet, clinging, agonising tenderness of parting. Eanswyth, having watched him out of sight, returned slowly to the house, while he, starting upon his strange venture, was thinking in the bitterness of his soul how—when—they would meet again. His heart was heavy with a sense of coming evil, and as he rode along his thoughts would recur again and again to the apparition which had so terrified Eanswyth a few nights ago. Was it the product of a hallucination on her part after all, or was it the manifestation of some strange and dual phase of Nature, warning of the ill that was to come? He felt almost inclined to admit the latter.

Chapter Forty One.

Xalasa's Revelation.

"You ought to consider yourself uncommonly fortunate, Milne," said Hoste, as the two men drew near Anta's Kloof. "You are the only one of the lot of us not burnt out."

"That's a good deal thanks to Josane," replied Eustace, as the house came into sight. "He thought he could manage to save it. I didn't. But he was right."

"Ha-ha! I believe the old scamp has been enjoying himself all this time with the rebels. I dare say he has been helping to do the faggot trick."

"Quite likely."

Hoste eyed his companion with a curious glance. The latter had been rather laconic during their ride; otherwise he seemed to show no very great interest one way or another in the object of it. Yet there was reason for believing that if Xalasa's tale should prove true it would make every difference to the whole of Eustace Milne's future life.

The sun was just setting as they reached Anta's Kloof. The Kafir had stipulated that they should meet him at night. He did not want to incur potential pains and penalties at the hands of his compatriots as an "informer" if he could possibly help it. The house, as Hoste had said, was the only one in the whole neighbourhood which had escaped the torch, but that was all that could be said, for it was completely gutted. Everything portable had been carried off, if likely to prove of any use to the marauders, what was not likely so to prove being smashed or otherwise destroyed. Windows were broken and doors hung loose on their hinges; in fact, the place was a perfect wreck. Still it was something that the fabric would not need rebuilding.

Hardly had they off-saddled their horses, and, knee-haltering them close, turned them out to graze around the house, than the night fell.

"Xalasa should be here by now," remarked Hoste, rather anxiously. "Unless he has thought better of it. I always expected we should learn something more about poor Tom when the war was over. Kafirs will talk. Not that I ever expected to hear that he was alive, poor chap—if he is, that's to say. But what had been the actual method of his death: that was bound to leak out sooner or later."

Eustace made no reply. The remark irritated him, if only that his companion had made it, in one form or another, at least half a dozen times already. Then the sound of a light footstep was heard, and a tall, dark figure stood before them in the gloom, with a muttered salutation.

"Greeting, Xalasa!" said Eustace, handing the new arrival a large piece of Boer tobacco. "We will smoke while we talk. The taste of the fragrant plant is to conversation even as the oil unto the axles of a heavily laden waggon."

The Kafir promptly filled his pipe. The two white men did likewise.

"Have you been in the war, Xalasa?" went on Eustace, when the pipes were in full blast. "You need not be afraid of saying anything to us. We are not Government people."

"*Au*!" said the Gaika, with a quizzical grin upon his massive countenance. "I am a 'loyal,' Ixeshane."

"The chiefs of the Ama Ngqika, Sandili and the rest of them, have acted like children," replied Eustace, with apparent irrelevance. "They have allowed themselves to be dragged into war at the 'word' of Kreli, and against the advice of their real friends, and where are they now? In prison, with a lot of thieves and common criminals, threatened with the death of a dog!"

The Kafir uttered an emphatic murmur of assent. Hoste, who was excusably wondering what the deuce the recent bad behaviour, and eventual fate of Sandili and Co., had to do with that of Tom Carhayes, could hardly restrain his impatience. But Eustace knew what he was about. The Briton may, as he delights to boast, prefer plain and straightforward talking in matters of importance—or he may not. The savage, of whatever race or clime, unequivocally does not. He dearly loves what we should call beating around the bush. However important the subject under discussion, it must be led up to. To dash straight at the point is not his way. So after some further talk on the prospects and politics of the Gaika nation, and of the Amaxosa race in general—past, present, and to come—Eustace went on:

"You were not always a 'loyal,' Xalasa?"

"*Whau*!" cried the man, bringing his hand to his mouth, in expressive native fashion. "When the fire trumpet first sounded in the midnight sky, I answered its call. While the chiefs of the Ama Ngqika yet sat still, many of their children went forth to war at the 'word' of the Paramount Chief. Many of us crossed into the Gcaléka country and fought at the side of our brethren. Many of us did not return. *Hau*!"

"Then you became a 'loyal'?"

"*Ihuvumenté* (The Government) was very strong. We could not stand against it. Ha! *Amasoja—Amapolisi—bonké*. (Soldiers—police—all) I thought of all the men who had crossed the Kei with me. I thought of the few who had returned. Then I thought, 'Art thou a fool, Xalasa? Is thy father's son an ox that he should give himself to be slain to make strength for Sarili's fighting men?' *Hau*! I came home again and resolved to 'sit still.'"

"But your eyes and ears were open among the Ama-Gcaléka. They saw—they heard of my brother, Umlilwane?"

"Thy brother, Umlilwane, was alive at the time the white *Amagcagca* (Rabble) knocked me down and kicked me. He is alive still."

"How do you know he is alive still?" said Eustace, mastering his voice with an effort, for his pulses were beating like a hammer as he hung upon the other's reply. It came—cool, impassive, confident:

"The people talk."

"Where is he, Xalasa?"

"Listen, Ixeshane," said the Kafir, glancing around and sinking his voice to an awed whisper. "Where is he! *Au! Kwa 'Zinyoka.*"

"*Kwa 'Zinyoka!* 'The Home of the Serpents!'" Well he remembered the jeering, but ominous, words of the hideous witch-doctress at the time his unfortunate cousin was being dragged away insensible under the directions of his implacable foe, Hlangani. "*He will wake. But he will never be seen again.*" And now this man's testimony seemed to bear out her words.

"What is this 'Home of the Serpents,' Xalasa?" he said.

"*Au!*" returned the Kafir, after a thoughtful pause, and speaking in a low and apprehensive tone as a timid person in a haunted room might talk of ghosts. "It is a fearsome place. None who go there ever return—none—no, not one," he added, shaking his head. "But they say your magic is great, Ixeshane. It may be that you will find your brother alive. The war is nearly over now, but the war leaves every man poor. I have lost all I possessed. When you find your brother you will perhaps think Xalàsa is a poor man, and I have too many cattle in my kraal. I will send four or five cows to the man who told me my brother was alive."

In his heart of hearts Eustace thought how willingly he would send him a hundred for precisely the opposite intelligence.

"Where is 'The Home of the Serpents'?" he said.

"Where? Who knows? None save Ngcenika, who talks with the spirits. None save Hlangani, who rejoices in his revenge as he sees his enemy there, even the man who struck him, and drew the blood of the Great Chief's herald. Who knows? Not I. Those who go there never return," he added impressively, conveying the idea that in his particular instance "ignorance is bliss."

Eustace's first instinct was one of relief. If no one knew where the place was, clearly no one could tell. Then it struck him that this rather tended to complicate matters than to simplify them. There had been quite enough insinuated as to himself, and though guiltless as to his cousin's fate, yet once it got wind that the unfortunate man was probably alive somewhere, it would devolve upon himself to leave no stone unturned until that probability should become a certainty. Public opinion would demand that much, and he knew the world far too well to make the blunder of treating public opinion, in a matter of this kind, as a negligeable quantity.

"But if you don't know where the place is, Xalasa, how am I to find it?" he said at length. "I would give much to the man who would guide me to it. Think! Is there no man you know of who could do so?"

But the Kafir shook his head. "There is none!" he said. "None save Ngcenika. *Whau*, Ixeshane! Is not thy magic as powerful as hers? Will it not aid thee to find it? Now I must go. Where the 'Home of the Serpents' is, thy brother is there. That is all I can tell thee."

He spoke hurriedly now and in an altered tone—even as a man who has said too much and is not free from misgiving as to the consequences. He seemed anxious to depart, and seeing that nothing more was to be got out of him for the present, the two made no objection.

Hardly had he departed than Josane appeared. He had noted the arrival of Xalasa, though Xalasa was under the impression that he was many miles distant. He had waited until the *amakosi* (Literally "chiefs." In this connection "masters") had finished their *indaba* (Talk) and here he was. He was filled with delight at the sight of Ixeshane and his eyes felt good. His "father" and his "friend" had been away for many moons, but now he was back again and the night was lighter than the day. His "father" could see, too, how he had kept his trust, the old man went on. Where were the houses of all the other white *amakosi*! Heaps of ashes. The house of his "father" alone was standing—it alone the torch had passed by. As for the destruction which had taken place within it, that could not be prevented. The people "saw red." It had taxed the utmost effort of himself and Ncanduku to preserve the house. Reft of hyperbole, his narrative was plain enough. A marauding band had made a descent upon the place on the very night they had quitted it, and, although with difficulty dissuaded from burning it down, the savages had wrecked the furniture and looted the stores, as we have shown. This, however, was comparatively a small evil.

Hoste, wearied with all this talk, which moreover he understood but imperfectly, had waxed restive and strolled away. No sooner was he out of earshot than Josane, sinking his voice, remarked suddenly:

"Xalasa is a fool!"

Eustace merely assented. He saw that something was coming, and prepared to listen attentively.

"Do you want to find Umlilwane?" went on the old Kafir with ever so slight an expression on the "want."

"Of course I do," was the unhesitating reply. But for the space of half a minute the white man and the savage gazed fixedly into each other's faces in the starlight.

"*Au*! If I had known that!" muttered Josane in a disappointed tone. "If I had known that, I could have told you all that Xalasa has—*could have told you many moons ago.*"

"You knew it, then?"

"Yes."

"And is it true—that—that he is alive now?"

"Yes."

"But, Josane, how is it you kept your knowledge to yourself? He might have been rescued all this time. Now it may be too late."

"*Whau*, Ixeshane! Did *you* want him rescued?" said the old fellow shrewdly. "Did the *Inkosikazi* want him rescued?"

This was putting matters with uncomfortable plainness. Eustace reddened in the darkness.

"Whatever we 'wanted,' or did not want, is nothing," he answered. "This is a matter of life and death. He must be rescued."

"As you will," was the reply in a tone which implied that in the speaker's opinion the white man was a lunatic. And from his point of view such was really the case. The old savage was, in fact, following out a thoroughly virtuous line of conduct according to his lights. All this while, in order to benefit the man he liked, he had coolly and deliberately been sacrificing the man he—well, did not like.

"Where is 'The Home of the Serpents,' Josane? Do you know?"

"Yes. I know."

Eustace started.

"Can you guide me to it?" he said, speaking quickly.

"I can. But it is a frightful place. The bravest white man would take to his heels and run like a hunted buck before he had gone far inside. You have extraordinary nerve, Ixeshane—but—You will see."

This sounded promising. But the old man's tone was quiet and confident. He was not given to vapouring.

"How do you know where to find this place, Josane?" said Eustace, half incredulously in spite of himself. "Xalasa told us it was unknown to everybody—everybody but the witch-doctress?"

"Xalasa was right. I know where it is, because I have seen it. *I was condemned to it.*"

"By Ngcenika?"

"By Ngcenika. But my revenge is coming—my sure revenge is coming," muttered the old Gcaléka, crooning the words in a kind of ferocious refrain—like that of a war-song.

As this juncture they were rejoined by Hoste.

"Well, Milne," he said. "Had enough *indaba*? Because, if so, we may as well trek home again. Seems to me we've had a lot of trouble for nothing and been made mortal fools of down to the ground by that *schelm*, Xalasa's, cock-and-bull yarns."

"You're wrong this time," replied Eustace. "Just listen here a while and you'll see that we're thoroughly on the right scent."

At the end of half an hour the Kafir and the two white men arose. Their plans were laid. The following evening—at sundown—was the time fixed on as that for starting upon their perilous and somewhat dimly mysterious mission.

"You are sure three of us will be enough, Josane?" said Hoste.

"Quite enough. There are still bands of the Gcaléka fighting men in the forest country. If we go in a strong party they will discover us and we shall have to fight—*Au*! 'A fight is as the air we breathe,' you will say, *Amakosi*," parenthesised the old Kafir, whimsically—"But it will not help us to find 'The Home of the Serpents.' Still, there would be no harm in having one more in the party."

"Who can we get?" mused Hoste. "There's George Payne; but he's away down in the Colony—Grahamstown, I believe. It would take him days to get here and even then he might cry off. I have it; Shelton's the man, and I think he'll go, too. Depend upon it, Milne, Shelton's the very man. He's on his farm now—living in a Kafir hut, seeing after the rebuilding of his old house. We'll look him up this very night; we can get there in a couple of hours."

This was agreed to, and having arranged where Josane was to meet them the following evening, the two men saddled up and rode off into the darkness.

Chapter Forty Two.

The Search Party.

Midwinter as it was, the heat in the valley of the Bashi that morning was something to remember.

Not so much the heat as an extraordinary closeness and sense of oppression in the atmosphere. As the sun rose, mounting higher and higher into the clear blue of the heavens, it seemed that all his rays were concentrated and focussed down into this broad deep valley, whose sides were broken up into a grand panorama of soaring krantzes and wild rocky gorges, which latter, as also the great terraced slopes, were covered with dense forest, where the huge and spreading yellow-wood, all dangling with monkey trailers, alternated with the wild fig and the mimosa, the *spekboem* scrub and the *waacht-een-bietje* thorn, the spiky aloe and the plumed euphorbia, and where, in the cool dank shade, flourished many a rare orchid, beginning to show sign of blossoming, winter as it was.

But the four men riding there, making a path for themselves through this well-nigh virgin forest, had little thought to give to the beauties of Nature. Seriousness and anxiety was absent from none of those countenances. For to-day would see the object of their quest attained.

So far their expedition had been in no wise unattended by danger. Four men would be a mere mouthful if discovered by any of the scattered bands of the enemy, who still roamed the country in its wildest and most rugged parts. The ferocity of these savages, stimulated by a sullen but vengeful consciousness of defeat, would render them doubly formidable. Four men constituted a mere handful. So the party had travelled by circuitous ways, only advancing at night, and lying hidden during the daytime in the most retired and sequestered spots. Twice from such judicious hiding places had they espied considerable bodies of the enemy marching northward, and two or three times, patrols, or armed forces of their own countrymen. But these they were almost as careful to avoid as the savage Gcalékas. Four men advancing into the hostile country was an uncommon sight. They did not want their expedition talked about, even among their own countrymen, just yet. And now they were within two hours of the object of their search.

The dangers they had gone through, and those which were yet to come, were courted, be it remembered, not in search of treasure or riches, not even out of love of adventure. They were braved in order to rescue a friend and comrade from an unknown fate, whose mysteriousness was enhanced by vague hints at undefined horrors, on the part of the only man qualified to speak, viz., their guide.

For Josane had proved extraordinarily reticent as to details; and all attempts to draw him out during their journey had failed. As they drew near the dreaded spot this reticence had deepened to a remarkable degree. The old Gcaléka displayed an ominous taciturnity, a gloom even, which was in no degree calculated to raise the spirits of the three white men. Even Eustace failed to elicit from him any definite facts. He had been "smelt out" and condemned to "the Home of the Serpents" and had escaped while being taken into it, and to do this he had almost had to fly through the air. But the place would try their nerves to the uttermost; of that he warned them. Then he would subside again into silence, regardless of any further attempt to "draw" him.

There was one of the party whose motives, judged by ordinary human standards, were little short of heroic, and that one was Eustace Milne. He had nothing to gain by the present undertaking, nor had the others. But then they had nothing to lose by it except their lives, whereas he had not only that but everything that made life worth living into the bargain. Again and again he found himself cursing Xalasa's "gratitude," from the very depths of his soul. Yet never for a moment did he swerve in his resolve to save his unfortunate cousin if the thing were to be done, although there were times when he marvelled over himself as a strange and unaccountable paradox. A silence was upon them all, as they moved at a foot's pace through the dense and jungly tangle, mounting ever upwards. After an hour of this travelling they had reached a considerable height. Here in a sequestered glade Josane called a halt.

"We must leave the horses," he said. "It is impossible to take them where we are going. *Whau*!" he went on, looking upwards and snuffing the air like a stag. "There will be plenty of thunder by and by. We have no time to lose."

Taking with them a long twisted rawhide rope, of amazing strength, which might be necessary for climbing purposes, and a few smaller *reims*, together with a day's provisions, and every available cartridge, they started on foot, Josane leading the way. Each was armed with a double gun—one barrel rifled—and a revolver. The Gcaléka carried three small-bladed casting assegais, and a broad headed, close-quarter one, as well as a kerrie.

They had struck into a narrow gorge in the side of the hill. It was hard work making any headway at all. The dense bush, intertwined with creepers, met them in places in an unbroken wall, but Josane would hack away manfully with his broad-bladed assegai until he succeeded in forcing a way.

"It seems as if we were going to storm the devil's castle," said Shelton, sitting down to wipe his streaming brow. "It's hot enough anyway."

"Rather," assented Hoste. "Milne, old chap, how do you feel?"

"Headachy. There's a power of thunder sticking out—as Josane says—against when we get out."

"If we ever do get out."

"That's cheerful. Well, if we mean to get in, I suppose we'd better make a move? Eh, Josane!" The Kafir emphatically agreed. He had witnessed their dilatoriness not without concern. He appeared strangely eager to get the thing over—contrary to the habits of his kind, for savages, of whatever race, are never in a hurry. A line of rocky boulders in front, thickly grown with straight stemmed euphorbia, stiff and regular like the pipes of an organ, precluded any view of the sort of formation that lay beyond. Right across their path, if path it might be called, rose another impenetrable wall of thorns and creepers. In front of this Josane halted.

Chapter Forty Three.

"Kwa 'Zinyoka."

The brooding, oppressive stillness deepened. Not a breath of air stirred the sprays of the bush, which slept motionless as though carved in stone. Even the very bird voices were hushed. Far below, the sound of the river, flowing over its long stony reaches, came upwards in plaintive monotonous murmur.

All of a sudden Josane turned. He sent one keen searching glance straight in front of him, and another from side to side.

"The Home of the Serpents is a horrible place," he said. "I have warned you that it is so. It is not too late now. The *Amakosi* can yet turn back."

The awed solemnity of his tone could not fail to impress his hearers, especially two of them. The boding sense of oppression in the atmosphere, the utter wildness of the surroundings, the uneasy, mysterious nature of their quest, and the tall gaunt figure of the old Kafir standing in the semi-gloom beneath the funereal plumes of the straight stemmed euphorbia, like an oracle of misfortune—all this affected the imagination of two, at any rate, of these ordinarily hard-headed and practical men in a fashion they could scarcely have deemed possible. The third, however, was impervious to such influences. There was too much involved in the material side of the undertaking. No thought had he to spare apart from this; no scope was there for giving free rein to his imagination.

"I think I may say we none of us have the slightest idea of turning back!" he answered.

"Certainly not," assented the other two.

Josane looked fixedly at them for a moment. Then he said:

"It is good. Follow me—carefully, carefully. We do not want to leave a broad spoor."

The undergrowth among the straight stiff stems of the euphorbia looked dense and impenetrable as a wall. To the astonishment of the spectators, the old Kafir lay flat on his stomach, lifted the dense tangle just enough to admit the passage of his body, for all the world as though he were lifting a heavy curtain, and slipped through.

"Come," he whispered from the other side, for he had completely disappeared from view. "Come—as I did. But do not rend the bushes more than is absolutely necessary."

They followed, worming their way in the same fashion about a dozen yards. Then an ejaculation of amazement, not unmixed with alarm, broke from the lips of Shelton, who was leading. It found an echo on those of the other two. Their first instinct was to draw back.

They had emerged upon a narrow ledge, not of rock, or even earth; a narrow ledge of soft, yielding, quaking moss. And it overhung what had the appearance of a huge natural well.

It literally overhung. By peering cautiously outward they could see a smooth perpendicular wall of red rock falling sheer and straight to a depth of nearly two hundred feet. Three sides of the hollow—itself not that distance in width—were similarly constituted, the fourth being a precipitous, well-nigh perpendicular slope, with a sparse growth of stunted bushes jotting its rugged sides. A strange, gruesome looking hole, whose dismal depths showed not the smallest sign of life. Could this be the awesome, mysterious "Home of the Serpents?"

But Josane's next words disabused them on this point.

"Tarry not," he said. "Follow me. Do even as I do."

Right to the brink of this horrible abyss the bush grew in a dense jungly wall, and it was the roots of this, overgrown with an accumulation of moss and soil, that constituted the apology for a ledge along which they were expected to make their way. And there was a distance of at least sixty or seventy yards of this precarious footway, to miss which would mean a certain and terrible death.

It would have been something of an ordeal even had the foothold been firm. Now, however, as they made their way along this quivering, quaking, ladder-like pathway of projecting roots interleaved with treacherous moss, not one of the three was altogether free from a nervous and shaky sensation about the knees as he moved slowly forward, selecting the strongest-looking stems for hand-hold. Once a root whereon Hoste had put his foot gave way with a muffled crack, letting his leg through the fearful pathway up to the thigh. An involuntary cry escaped him as, grasping a stem above him, he drew it forth with a supreme effort, and his brown visage assumed a hue a good many shades paler, as through the hole thus made he contemplated a little cloud of leaves and sticks swirling away into the abyss.

"Great Heaven!" he ejaculated. "Are we never coming to the end of this ghastly place?"

"How would you like to cross it running at full speed, like a monkey, as I was forced to do? I told you I had to fly through the air," muttered Josane, who had overheard. "The horror of it has only just begun—just begun. *Hau!* Did I not say it was going to be a horrible place?"

But they were destined to reach the end of it without mishap, and right glad were they to find themselves crawling along a narrow ledge overhung by a great rock, still skirting the abyss, but at any rate there was hard ground under them; not a mere shaky network of more or less rotten roots.

"Is this the only way, Josane?" said Eustace at length, as they paused for a few minutes to recover breath, and, truth to say, to steady their nerves a trifle. Even he put the question with some diffidence, for as they drew nearer and nearer to the locality of their weird quest the old Gcaléka's manner had undergone a still further change. He had become morose and taciturn, gloomy and abstracted to a degree.

"It is not," he answered. "It is the only way I know. When I came here my eyes were shut; when I went away they were open. Then I approached it from above; now we have approached from below. The way by which I left, is the way you have seen."

"O Lord! I wouldn't travel the last infernal hundred yards again for a thousand pounds," muttered Hoste ruefully. "And now, I've got to do it again for nothing. I'd sooner run the gauntlet of the whole Gcaléka tribe, as we did before."

"We may have to do that as well," remarked Shelton. "But I think I never did see such an utterly dismal and God-forsaken corner in my life. Looks as if Old Nick had built it out of sheer devilment."

There was reason in what he said. The immense funnel-like hole seemed an extraordinary caprice of Nature. Nothing grew at the bottom but coarse herbage and a few stunted bushes. It seemed absolutely lacking in *raison d'être*. Occurring at the top of a mountain, it would at once have suggested an ancient crater. Occurring, as it did, in solid ground on the steep slope of a lofty river bank that theory seemed not to hold good. On all sides, save the narrow defile they had come through, it was shut in by lofty wooded heights breaking here and there into a red iron-stone cliff.

Their guide resumed his way, advancing in a listening attitude, and with intense caution. The ledge upon which they crept, now on all-fours, widened considerably. The projecting rock overhead jutted out further and further, till it overhung the abyss for a considerable distance. Beneath its shade they were already in semi-gloom. Crawling along, toilsomely, laboriously, one behind the other, each man with all his senses, all his faculties, on the alert, the fact that their guide had stopped came upon them as a surprise. Then, as they joined him, and crouched there side by side—each man's heart beat quicker, each man's face slightly changed colour. For the overhanging rock had heightened—the ledge had widened to an area of fifteen or twenty feet.

Flooring and rock-roof no longer met. At the bottom of this area, both yawned away from each other in a black horizontal rift.

Save through this rift there was no getting any further. Quickly each mind grasped the solution. The cave yawning in front of them was—

"Where does that hole lead to, Josane?" said Hoste.

"*Kwa 'zinyoka*," replied the Gcaléka, impressively.

Such creatures are we of the light and air, that it is safe to assert that not even the boldest among us can undertake the most cursory exploration into the bowels of the earth without a consciousness of ever so slight a sobering influence, a kind of misgiving begotten of the idea of darkness and weight— a feeling as though the cavern roof might crush down upon us, and bury us there throughout the aeons of eternity. It is not surprising, therefore, that our three friends—all men of tried courage—should sit down for a few minutes, and contemplate this yawning black hole in dubious silence.

It was no reflection on their courage, either. They had just dared and surmounted a peril trying and frightful enough to tax the strongest nerves— and now before them lay the entrance to an unknown *inferno*; a place bristling with grim and mysterious terrors such as even their stout-hearted guide—the only man who knew what they were—recoiled from braving again. They could hardly believe that the friend and fellow-countrymen, whom all these months they had reckoned among the slain, lay near them within that fearful place, alive, and perchance unharmed. It might be, however, that the cavern before them was but a tunnel, leading to some hidden and inaccessible retreat like the curious crater-like hollow they had just skirted.

"*Au*!" exclaimed Josane, with a dissatisfied shake of the head. "We cannot afford to *sleep* here. If we intend to go in we must do so at once."

There was reason in this. Their preparations were simple enough—and consisted in seeing that their weapons were in perfect readiness. Eustace, too, had lighted a strong bull's-eye lantern with a closing slide. Besides this, each man was plentifully supplied with candles, which, however, it was decided, should only be used if a quantity of light became absolutely necessary.

Be it remembered not one of the three white men had other than the vaguest idea of the nature of the horrors which this gruesome place might disclose. Whether through motives of superstition or from whatever cause, Josane had hitherto preserved a remarkable silence on the subject. Now he said, significantly:

"Hear my words, Amakosi. Tread one behind the other, *and look neither to the right nor to the left, nor above. But look where you place your steps, and look carefully.* Remember my words, for I know that of which I speak."

They compared their watches. It was just half-past one. They sent a last long look at the sky and the surrounding heights. As they did so there rolled forth upon the heavy air a long, low boom of distant thunder. Then they fell into their places and entered the cavern, the same unspoken thought in each man's mind—Would they ever behold the fair light of day again?

And the distant, muttering thunder peal, hoarse, heavy, sullen, breaking upon the sultry air, at the moment when they left the outer world, struck them as an omen—the menacing voice of outraged Nature booming the knell of those who had the temerity to seek to penetrate her innermost mysteries.

Chapter Forty Four.

Inferno.

For the first forty yards the roof of the cave was so low that they had to advance in a stooping posture. Then it heightened and the tunnel widened out simultaneously. Eustace led the way, his bull's-eye lantern strapped around him, throwing a wide disk of yellow light in front. Behind him, but keeping a hand on his shoulder in order to guide him, walked Josane; the other two following in single file.

A turn of the way had shut out the light from the entrance. Eustace closing the slide of the lantern for a moment, they were in black, pitchy darkness.

A perceptible current of air blew into the cavern. That looked as if there should be an outlet somewhere. Old Josane, while enjoining silence upon the rest of the party, had, from the moment they had entered, struck up a low, weird, crooning song, which sounded like an incantation. Soon a glimmer of light showed just in front.

"That is the other way in," muttered old Josane. "That is the way I came in. The other is the way I came out. *Hau*!"

An opening now became apparent—a steep, rock shaft, reaching away into the outer air. It seemed to take one or more turnings in its upward passage, for the sky was not visible, and the light only travelled down in a dim, chastened glimmer as though it was intercepted in its course. An examination of this extraordinary feature revealed the fact that it was a kind of natural staircase.

"This is the way I came in. Ha!" muttered Josane again, with a glare of resentment in his eyes as though recalling to mind some particularly ignominious treatment—as he narrowly scrutinised the slippery, rocky sides of the shaft.

"I suppose it'll be the best way for us to get out," said Hoste. "Anything rather than that devil of a scramble again."

"The time to talk of getting out is not yet," rejoined the Kafir drily. "We are not *in* yet."

They resumed their way. As they penetrated deeper, the cavern suddenly slanted abruptly upwards. This continued for some twenty or thirty yards, when again the floor became level, though ever with a slight upward bend. Great slabs of rock projected from the sides, but the width of the tunnel varied little, ranging between six and ten yards. The same held good of its height.

As they advanced they noticed that the current of air was no longer felt. An extraordinary foetid and overpowering atmosphere had taken its place. Similarly the floor and sides of the cavern, which before they reached the outlet had been moist and humid, now became dry and firm.

"Hand us your flask, Shelton," said Hoste. "Upon my soul I feel as if I was going to faint. Faugh!"

The odour was becoming more and more sickening with every step. Musky, rank, acreous—it might almost be felt. Each man required a pull at something invigorating, if only to neutralise the inhalation of so pestilential an atmosphere. Smoking was suggested, but this Josane firmly tabooed.

"It cannot be," he said. "It would be madness. Remember my words, *Amakosi. Look neither to the right nor to the left—only straight in front of you, where you set down your steps.*"

Then he resumed his strange wild chant, now sinking it to an awe-struck whisper hardly above his breath. It was a weird, uncanny sight, those four shadowy figures advancing through the thick black darkness, the fiery eye of the lantern darting forth its luminous column in front, while the deep-toned, long-drawn notes of the wild, heathenish *rune* died away in whispering echoes overhead.

"Oh! good Lord! Look at that!"

The cry broke from Shelton. All started, so great was the state of tension that their nerves were undergoing. Following his glance they promptly discovered what it was that had evoked it.

Lying upon a great slab of rock, about on a level with their chests, was an enormous puff-adder. The bloated proportions of the hideous reptile were disposed in a sinuous coil—shadowy, repulsive to the last degree, in the light of the lantern. A shudder ran through every one of the three white men.

"Quick, Josane. Hand me one of your kerries," said Shelton. "I can get a whack at him now."

But the Kafir, peremptorily, almost angrily refused.

"Why did you not listen to my words?" he said. "Look neither to the right nor to the left, was what I told you. Then you would have seen nothing. Now let us move on."

But Shelton and Hoste stood, irresolutely staring at the horrid reptile as though half fascinated. It—as if resenting the intrusion—began to unwind its sluggish folds, and raising its head, emitted a low, warning hiss, at the same time blowing itself out with a sound as of a pair of bellows collapsing, after the fashion which has gained for this most repulsive of all serpents its distinctive name.

"You must not kill it," repeated the Kafir, in a tone almost of command. "This is 'The Home of the Serpents,' remember. Did I not warn you?"

They saw that he was deadly in earnest. Here in this horrible den, right in the heart of the earth, the dark-skinned, superstitious savage seemed the one to command. It was perhaps remarkable that no thought of disobeying him entered the mind of any one of the three white men; still more so, that no resentment entered in either. They resumed their way without a murmur; not, however, without some furtive glances behind, as though dreading an attack on the part of the deadly reptile they were leaving in their rear. More than once they thought to detect the sound of that slow, crawling glide—to discern an indistinct and sinuous shadow moving in the subdued light.

"This is 'The Home of the Serpents'!" chanted Josane, taking up once more his weird refrain.

"This is The Home of the Serpents, the abode of the Spirit-dead. O *Inyoka 'Nkúlu* (Great Serpent) do us no hurt! O Snake of Snakes, harm us not!

"The shades of thy home are blacker than blackest night.

"We tread the dark shades of thy home in search of the white man's friend.

"Give us back the white man's friend, so may we depart in peace—

"In peace from The Home of the Serpents, the abode of the Spirit-dead.

"Into light from the awe-dealing gloom, where the shades of our fathers creep.

"So may we return to the daylight in safety with him whom we seek.

> "Harm us not,
> O Snake of snakes!
> Do us no hurt,
> O *Inyoka 'Nkúlu!*"

The drawn out notes of this lugubrious refrain were uttered with a strange, low, concentrative emphasis which was indescribably thrilling. Eustace, the only one of the party who thoroughly grasped its burden, felt curiously affected by it. The species of devil worship implied in the heathenish invocation communicated its influence to himself. His spirits, up till now depressed and burdened as with a weight of brooding evil, seemed to rise to an extraordinary pitch of exaltation, as though rejoicing at the prospect of prompt admission into strange mysteries. Far otherwise, however, were the other two affected by the surroundings. Indeed, it is by no means certain that had their own inclinations been the sole guide in the matter, they would there and then have turned round and beat a hasty and ignominious retreat, leaving Tom Carhayes and his potential fate to the investigation of some more enterprising party.

The atmosphere grew more foetid and pestilential. Suddenly the cavern widened out. Great slabs of rock jutted horizontally from the sides, sometimes so nearly meeting that there was only just room to pass in single file between. Then a low cry of horror escaped the three white men. They stopped short, as though they had encountered a row of fixed bayonets, and some, at any rate, of the party were conscious of the very hair on their heads standing erect.

For, lying about upon the rock slabs were numbers of shadowy, sinuous shapes, similar to the one they had just disturbed. Some were lying apart, some were coiled up together in a heaving, revolting mass. As the light of the lantern flashed upon them, they began to move. The hideous coils began to separate, gliding apart, head erect, and hissing till the whole area of the grisly cavern seemed alive with writhing, hissing serpents. Turn the light which way they would, there were the same great wriggling coils, the same frightful heads. Many, hitherto unseen, were pouring their loathsome, gliding shapes down the rocks overhead, and the dull, dragging heavy sound, as the horrible reptiles crawled over the hard and stony surface, mingled with that of strident hissing. What a sight to come upon in the heart of the earth!

It is safe to assert that no object in Nature is held in more utter and universal detestation by man than the serpent. And here were these men penned up within an underground cave in the very heart of the earth, with scores, if not hundreds, of these frightful and most deadly reptiles—some too, of abnormal size—around them; all on the move, and so near that it was as much as they could do to avoid actual contact. Small wonder that their flesh should creep and that every drop of blood should seem to curdle within their veins. It was a position to recur to a man in his dreams until his dying day.

"Oh, I can't stand any more of this," said Hoste, who was walking last. "Hang it. Anything above ground, you know—but this—! Faugh! We've got no show at all. Ugh-h!"

Something cold had come in contact with his hand. He started violently. But it was only the clammy surface of a projecting rock.

And now the whole of the gloomy chamber resounded with shrill and angry hissing, as the disturbed reptiles glided hither and thither—was alive with waving necks and distended jaws, glimpsed shadowy on the confines of the disk of light which shot into the remote corners of the frightful den.

Curiously enough, not one of the serpents seemed to be lying in the pathway itself. All were on the ledges of rock which bordered it.

"Keep silence and follow close on my steps," said Josane shortly. Then he raised his voice and threw a marvellously strange, soft melodiousness into the weird song, which he had never ceased to chant. Eustace, who was the first to recover to some extent his self-possession, and who took in the state of affairs, now joined in with a low, clear, whistling accompaniment. The effect was extraordinary. The writhing contortions of the reptiles ceased with a suddenness little short of magical. With heads raised and a slight waving motion of the neck they listened, apparently entranced. It was a wonderful sight, terrible in its weird ghastliness—that swarm of deadly serpents held thus spell-bound by the eerie barbaric music. It really looked as though there was more than met the eye in that heathenish adjuration as they walked unharmed through the deadly reptiles to the refrain of the long-drawn, lugubrious chant.

> "Harm us not,
> O Snake of Snakes!
> Do us no hurt,
> O *Inyoka 'Nkúlu*!"

Thus they passed through that fearful chamber, sometimes within a couple
of yards of two or three serpents lying on a level with their faces.
Once it was all that even Eustace, the self-
possessed, could do to keep
himself from ducking violently as the head of a huge puff-adder
noiselessly shot up horribly close to his ear, and a very marked quaver
came into his whistling notes.

As the cavern narrowed to its former tunnel-
like dimensions the serpents
grew perceptibly scarcer. One or two would be seen to wriggle away, here
and there; then no more were met with. The sickening closeness of the
air still continued, and now this stood amply accounted for. It was due
to the foetid exhalations produced by this mass of noisom

e reptiles congregated within a confined space far removed from the outer air.

"Faugh!" ejaculated Hoste. "Thank Heaven these awful brutes seem to have grown scarce again. Shall we have to go back through them, Josane?"

"It is not yet time to talk of going back," was the grim reply. Then he had hardly resumed his magic song before he broke it off abruptly. At the same time the others started, and their faces blanched in the semi-darkness.

For, out of the black gloom in front of them, not very far in front either, there burst forth such a frightful diabolical howl as ever curdled the heart's blood of an appalled listener.

Chapter Forty Five.

A Fearful Discovery.

They stood there, turned to stone. They stood there, strong men as they were, their flesh creeping with horror. The awful sound was succeeded by a moment of silence, then it burst forth again and again, the grim subterraneous walls echoing back its horrible import in ear-splitting reverberation. It sounded hardly human in its mingled intonation of frenzied ferocity and blind despair. It might have been the shriek of a lost soul, struggling in the grasp of fiends on the brink of the nethermost pit.

"Advance now, cautiously, *amakosi*," said Josane. "Look where you are stepping or you may fall far. Keep your candles ready to light. The Home of the Serpents is a horrible place. There is no end to its terrors. Be prepared to tread carefully."

His warning was by no means superfluous. The ground ended abruptly across their path. Suddenly, shooting up, as it were, beneath their very feet, pealed forth again that frightful, blood-curdling yell.

It was awful. Starting backward a pace or two, the perspiration pouring from their foreheads, they stood and listened. On the Kafir no such impression had the incident effected. He understood the position in all its grim significance.

"Look down," he said, meaningly. "Look down, *amakosi*."

They did so. Before them yawned an irregular circular hole or pit, about thirty feet deep by the same in diameter. The sides were smooth and perpendicular; indeed, slightly overhanging from the side on which they stood. Opposite, the glistening surface of the rock rose into a dome. But with this hole the cavern abruptly ended, the main part of it, that is, for a narrow cleft or "gallery" branched off abruptly at right angles. From this pit arose such a horrible effluvium that the explorers recoiled in disgust.

"Look down. Look down," repeated Josane.

The luminous disk from the lantern swept round the pit. Upon its nearly level floor crawled the loathsome, wriggling shapes of several great serpents. Human skulls strewn about, grinned hideously upwards, and the whole floor of this ghastly hell-pit seemed literally carpeted with a crackling layer of pulverised bones. But the most awful sight of all was yet to come.

Gathered in a heap, like a huge squatting toad, crouched a human figure. Human? Could it be? Ah! it had been once. Nearly naked, save for a few squalid rags black with filth, this fearful object, framed within the brilliantly defined circle of the bull's-eye, looked anything but human. The head and face were one mass of hair, and the long, bushy, tangled beard screening almost the whole body in its crouching attitude imparted to the creature the appearance of a head alone, supported on two hairy, ape-like arms, half man, half tarantula. The eyes were glaring and blinking in the light with mingled frenzy and terror, and the mouth was never still for a moment. What a sight the grizzly denizen of that appalling hell-pit—crouching there, mopping and mowing among the gliding, noisome reptiles, among the indescribable filth and the grinning human skulls! No wonder that the spectators stood spellbound, powerless, with a nerveless, unconquerable repulsion.

Suddenly the creature opened its mouth wide and emitted that fearful demoniacal howl which had frozen their blood but a few moments back. Then leaping to its feet, it made a series of desperate springs in its efforts to get at them. Indeed it was surprising the height to which these springs carried it, each failure being signalled by that blood-curdling yell. Once it fell back upon a serpent. The reptile, with a shrill hiss, struck the offending leg. But upon the demoniac those deadly fangs seemed to produce no impression whatever. Realising the futility of attempting to reach them, the creature sank back into a corner, gathering itself together, and working its features in wild convulsions. Then followed a silence—a silence in its way almost as horrible as the frightful shrieks which had previously broken it.

The spectators looked at each other with ashy faces. Heavens! could this fearful thing ever have been a man—a man with intellect and a soul—a man stamped with the image of his maker?

"He is the last, *Amakosi*," said the grave voice of Josane. "He is the last, but not the first. There have been others before him," designating the skulls which lay scattered about. "Soon he will be even as they—as I should have been had I not escaped by a quick stroke of luck."

"Great Heaven, Josane! Who is he?" burst from the horror-stricken lips of Shelton and Hoste simultaneously. Eustace said nothing, for at that moment as he gazed down upon the mouldering skulls, there came back to him vividly the witch-doctress's words, "They who look upon 'The Home of the Serpents' are seen no more in life." Well did he understand them now.

"The man whom you seek," was the grave reply. "He whom the people call Umlilwane."

An ejaculation of horror again greeted the Kafir's words. This awful travesty, this wreck of humanity, that this should be Tom Carhayes! It was scarcely credible. What a fate! Better had he met his death, even amid torture, at the time they had supposed, than be spared for such an end as this.

Then amid the deep silence and consternation of pity which this lugubrious and lamentable discovery evoked, there followed an intense, a burning desire for vengeance upon the perpetrators of this outrage; and this feeling found its first vent in words. Josane shook his head.

"It might be done," he muttered. "It might be done. Are you prepared to spend several days in here, *Amakosi?*"

This was introducing a new feature into the affair—the fact being that each of the three white men was labouring under a consuming desire to find himself outside the horrible hole once more—again beneath the broad light of day. It was in very dubious tones, therefore, that Shelton solicited an explanation.

"Even a maniac must eat and drink," answered Josane. "Those who keep Umlilwane here do not wish him to die—"

"You mean that some one comes here periodically to bring him food?"

"*Ewa.*"

"But it may not be the persons who put him here; only some one sent by them," they objected.

"This place is not known to all the Gcaléka nation," said Josane. "There are but two persons known to me who would dare to come within a distance of it. Those are Ngcenika, the witch-doctress, and Hlangani, who is half a witch-doctor himself."

"By lying in wait for them we might capture or shoot one or both of them when they come to bring the poor devil his food, eh, Josane?" said Shelton. "When are they likely to come?"

"It may not be for days. But there is another side to that plan. What if they should have discovered that we are in here and decide to lie in wait for us?"

"Oh, by Jove! That certainly is a reverse side to the medal," cried Hoste, with a long whistle of dismay. And indeed the idea of two such formidable enemies as the redoubted Gcaléka warrior and the ferocious witch-doctress lurking in such wise as to hold them entirely at their mercy was not a pleasant one. There was hardly a yard of the way where one determined adversary, cunningly ambushed, would not hold their lives in his hand. No. Any scheme for exacting reprisals had better keep until they were once more in the light of day. The sooner they rescued their unfortunate friend and got quit of the place the better.

And even here they had their work fully cut out for them. How were they to get at the wretched maniac? The idea of descending into that horrible pit was not an alluring one; and, apart from this, what sort of reception would they meet with from its occupant? That the latter regarded them in anything but a friendly light was manifest. How, then, were they ever to convey to the unfortunate creature that their object was the reverse of hostile? Tom Carhayes was well-known to be a man of great physical power. Tom Carr hayes—a gibbering, mouthing lunatic—a furious demoniac—no wonder they shrank from approaching him.

"Silence! Darken the light!"

The words, quick, low, peremptory—proceeded from Josane. In an instant Eustace obeyed. The slide of the lantern was turned.

"I listen—I hear," went on the Kafir in the same quick whisper. "There are steps approaching."

Every ear was strained to the uttermost. Standing in the pitchy blackness and on the brink of that awful pit, no one dared move so much as a foot.

And now a faint and far-away sound came floating through the darkness; a strange sound, as of the soft bass of voices from the distant spirit-world wailing weirdly along the ghostly walls of the tunnel. It seemed, too, that ever so faint a light was melting the gloom in the distance. The effect was indescribable in its awesomeness. The listeners held their very breath.

"Up here," whispered Josane, referring to the shaft already mentioned. "No! show no light—not a glimmer. Hold on to each other's shoulder—you, Ixeshane, hold on to mine—Quick—*Hamba-ké.*" (Go on.)

This precaution, dictated by the double motive of keeping together in the darkness, and also to avoid any one of the party accidentally falling into the pit—being observed, the Kafir led the way some little distance within the shaft.

"Heavens!" whispered Hoste. "What about the snakes? Supposing we tread on one?"

In the excitement of the moment this consideration had been quite overlooked. Now it struck dismay into the minds of the three white men. To walk along in pitch darkness in a narrow tunnel which you know to be infested with deadly serpents, with more than an even chance of treading upon one of the noisome reptiles at every step, is a position which assuredly needs a powerful deal of excitement to carry it through.

"*Au*! Flash one beam of light in front, Ixeshane," whispered the guide. "Not behind—for your life, not behind!"

Eustace complied, carefully shading the sides of the light with the flaps of his coat. It revealed that the cave here widened slightly, but made a curve. It further revealed no sign of the most dreaded enemy of the human race.

Here, then, it was decided to lie in wait. The lights carried by those approaching would hardly reach them here, and they could lurk almost concealed, sheltered by the formation of the tunnel.

The flash from Eustace's lantern had been but momentary. And now, as they crouched in the inky gloom, the sense of expectation became painful in its intensity. Nearer and nearer floated the wailing chant, and soon the lurking listeners were able to recognise it as identical with the wild, heathenish *rune* intoned by their guide—the weird, mysterious invocation of the Serpent.

> "Harm us not,
> O Snake of snakes!
> Do us no hurt
> O *Inyeka 'Nkúlu!*"

The sonorous, open vowels rolled forth in long-drawn cadence, chanted by two voices—both blending in wonderful harmony. Then a cloud of nebulous light filled up the entrance to their present hiding place, hovering above the fearful hell-pit where the maniac was imprisoned, throwing the brink into distinct relief.

The watchers held their very breath. The song had ceased. Suddenly there was a flash of light in their eyes, as from a lantern.

Two dark figures were standing on the brink of the hole. Each carried a lantern, one of those strong, tin-rimmed concerns used by transport-riders for hanging in their waggon-tents. There was no lack of light now.

"Ho, Umlilwane!" cried a deep, bass voice, which rumbled in hoarse echoes beneath the domed roof, while the speaker held his lantern out over the pit. "Ho, Umlilwane! It is the dog's feeding time again. We have brought the dog his bones. Ho, ho!"

The wretched maniac who, until now, had kept silence, here broke forth again into his diabolical howls. By the sound the watchers could tell that he was exhausting himself in a series of bull-dog springs similar to those prompted by his frenzy on first discovering themselves. At each of these futile outbursts the two mocking fiends shouted and roared with laughter. But they little knew how near they were laughing for the last time. Three rifles were covering them at a distance of fifty yards—three rifles in the hands of men who were dead shots, and whose hearts were bursting with silent fury. Josane, seeing this, took occasion to whisper under cover of the lunatic's frenzied howls:

"The time is not yet. The witch-doctress is for me—for me. I will lure her in here, and when I give the word—but not before—shoot Hlangani. The witch-doctress is for me."

The identity of the two figures was distinct in the light. The hideous sorceress, though reft of most of the horrid accessories and adornments of her order, yet looked cruel and repulsive as a very fiend—fitting figure to harmonise with the Styx-like gloom of the scene. The huge form of the warrior loomed truly gigantic in the sickly lantern light. "Ho, Umlilwane, thou dog of dogs!" went on the latter. "Art thou growing tired of thy cool retreat? Are not the serpents good companions? *Hau!* Thou wert a fool to part so readily with thy mind. After so many moons of converse with the serpents, thou shouldst have been a mighty soothsayer—a mighty diviner—by now. How long did it take thee to lose thy mind? But a single day? But a day and a night? That was quick! Ho, ho!" And the great taunting laugh was echoed by the shriller cackle of the female fiend.

"Thou wert a mighty man with thy fists, a mighty man with thy gun, O Umlilwane!" went on the savage, his mocking tones now sinking to those of devilish hatred. "But now thou art no longer a man—no longer a man. *Au*! What were my words to thee? 'Thou hadst better have cut off thy right hand before shedding the blood of Hlangani *for it is better to lose a hand than one's mind.*' What thinkest thou now of Hlangani's revenge? Hi!"

How plain now to one of the listeners were those sombre words, over whose meaning he had so anxiously pondered. This, then, was the fearful vengeance promised by the Gcaléka warrior. And for many months his wretched victim had lain here a raving maniac—had lain here in a darkness as of the very pit of hell—had lain among noisome serpents—among crawling horrors untold—small wonder his reason had given way after a single night of such, as his tormentor had just declared. Small wonder that he had indeed lost his mind!

A fiendish yell burst from the maniac. Suddenly a great serpent was thrown upward from the pit. Petrified with horror, the watchers saw its thick, writhing form fly through the air and light on the witch-doctress's shoulder. With a shrill laugh the hag merely seized the wriggling, squirming reptile, which, with crest waving, was hissing like a fury, and hurled it back into the pit again. What sort of devil's influence was protecting these people, that they could handle the most deadly reptiles with absolute impunity? Were they, indeed, under some demoniac spell? To one, however, among the white spectators, the real solution of the mystery may have suggested itself.

"Here are thy bones, dog," resumed the great barbarian, throwing what looked like a half-filled sack into the hole. "Here is thy drink," and he lowered a large calabash at the end of a string. "Eat, drink, and keep up thy strength. Perhaps one day I may turn thee loose again. Who knows! Then when thy people see thee coming they will cry: 'Here comes Hlangani's Revenge.' And they will fly from thee in terror, as from the approach of a fell disease."

The watchers looked at each other. These last words, coupled with the act of throwing down the food, seemed to point to the speedy conclusion of the visit. They could hear the miserable victim mumbling and crunching what sounded like literally bones, and growling like a dog. But Hlangani went on.

"Wouldst thou not rather have gone to feed the black ants, or have died the death of the red-hot stones, Umlilwane? Thou wouldst be at rest now. And now thou hast only just begun to live—alone in the darkness—alone with the serpents—a man whose mind is gone. Thou wilt never see the light of day again. *Whau*! The sun is shining like gold outside. And thy wife, Umlilwane—thy beautiful wife—tall and graceful, like the stem of the budding *umbona* (Maize)—dost thou never think of her? Ha! There is another who does—another who does. I have seen him—I have seen them both—him and thy beautiful wife—"

Eustace had nudged Josane in such wise as to make that individual understand that the curtain must be rung down on this scene—and that at once. Simultaneously the "yap" of a puppy dog burst forth almost beneath his feet. Its effect upon the pair at the pit's brink was electric.

"*Yau*!" cried Ngcenika, turning toward the sound. "The little dog has followed me in after all. Ah, the little brute. I will make him taste the stick!"

"Or throw him down to Umlilwane," laughed her companion. "He will do for him to play with, two dogs together. *Mawo*!"

Again the "yap" was heard, now several times in rapid succession. So perfect was the imitation that the watchers themselves were for a moment taken in.

"*Iza, inja! Injane, izapa*!" ("Come, dog! Little dog—come here!") cried the witch-doctress coaxingly, advancing into the lateral gallery, holding her lantern in front of her. Josane, with his mouth to the ground was emitting a perfect chorus of yaps.

"Now," he whispered, under cover of the echoes produced, as the width of the gallery left a clear chance at Hlangani, without endangering the witch-doctress. "Remember—the female beast, Ngcenika, is for me. Shoot Hlangani—*Now*!"

Scarce had the word left his mouth than the shots crashed forth simultaneously.

Chapter Forty Six.

The End of the Witch-Doctress.

To convey anything like an adequate idea of what followed is well-nigh impossible. The stunning, deafening roar of the volley in that narrow space was as though the very earth had exploded from its foundations. Through it came the shivering crash of glass, as Hlangani's lantern fell into the pit, but whether its owner followed it or not could not be determined through the overpowering din. Still holding the lantern, the hideous witch-doctress was seen through the sulphurous smoke, standing there as one turned to stone—then like lightning, a dark, lithe body sprang through the spectators and with a growl like that of a wild beast leaped upon the bewildered Ngcenika. There was the gleam of an assegai in the air—then darkness and the shatter of glass. The lantern fell from the sorceress' hand.

"Turn on the light, Milne; quick!" cried the other two.

"I'm trying to, but the infernal thing won't work. The slide's jammed—Oh!"

For he was swept off his feet. Two heavy bodies rolled over him—striving, cursing, struggling, stabbing—then half stumbled, half rolled away into the gloom beyond.

The others bethought them of their candles, which, up till now, had been kept unused. Quickly two of them were produced and lighted.

The din of the scuffle seemed to be receding further and further; nor in the faint and flickering impression cast upon the cavernous gloom by the light of the candles could anything be seen of the combatants. But that the scuffle was a hard and fierce one was evident from the sounds.

Just then Eustace succeeded in opening the lantern slide, and now they were able to advance boldly in the strong disk of light. The latter revealed the object of their search.

Rolling over and over each other were two dark bodies, one now uppermost, now the other. Both seemed equally matched; even if in point of sheer physical strength the advantage did not lie slightly with the witch-doctress, for Josane, though wiry and active, was a good deal older than he looked. Each firmly gripped the other's right wrist, for the purpose of preventing the use of the broad-bladed, murderous assegai with which the right hand of each was armed. Victory would lie with whoever could hold out the longest.

As soon as the light fell upon the two struggling bodies, the witch-doctress threw all her energies into afresh and violent effort. She seemed to divine that the new arrivals would refrain from shooting at her for fear of injuring Josane. So she redoubled her struggles and kicked and bit and tore like one possessed.

"Keep her in that position a moment, Josane," sung out Hoste. "I'll put a hunk of lead through the devil's carcase. There—so!"

But it was not to be. With a supreme effort she wrenched her wrist free from her opponent's grasp, and turning with the rapidity of a cat, leaped out of sight in the darkness. But a moment later she stumbled over a boulder and sprawled headlong. Before she could rise her pursuer was upon her and had stabbed her twice through the body with his assegai.

"Ha! Spawn of a Fingo dog!" cried Josane, his voice assuming a fierce, throaty growl in the delirious satiety of his vengeance. "I am Josane—whom thou wouldst have thrown to the serpents, as thou didst this white man—ha! whom thou wouldst have given alive to feed the black ants, as thou didst Vudana, my kinsman. Ha! I am Josane, who was eaten up at thy accursed bidding. Ha! But I lived for revenge and it has come. Ha! How does this feel?—and this?—and this?"

With each ejaculation "ha!" he had plunged his assegai into the writhing body of the prostrate witch-doctress. To the white men his aspect was that of a fiend—standing there in the cavernous gloom, his eyes rolling in frenzy—literally digging with his spear into the body of his vanquished enemy, out of which the red blood was squirting in a dozen great jets. Not until the corpse had entirely ceased to move did he cease his furious stabs.

"The hell-hag is dead!" he cried, as he at length turned to leave. "The hell-hag is dead," he repeated, turning the words into a fierce chant of exultation. "The hell-hag bleeds, and my revenge is sweet. Ha! Revenge is brighter than the sun in the heavens, for it is red, blood red. Ha! Mine enemy is dead!"

By this time they had returned to the brink of the pit. But there was no sign of Hlangani. Something like dismay was on every face. The fragments of his shattered lantern lay strewn about at the bottom of the hole, but of the savage himself there was no sign. It was marvellous. All three men were first-rate shots. It was impossible that any one of them could have missed him at that distance, let alone all three. How could he have got away with three bullets in his body?

Cautiously they hunted everywhere with increasing anxiety, but nothing occurred to reward their search. The latter led them almost back to the great rock-chamber where the serpents swarmed. Still no sign of Hlangani.

This was serious in the extreme. They would have their hands full enough with the wretched maniac, even if they succeeded in bringing him away at all; and the idea that the fierce Gcaléka, desperately wounded perhaps, might be lying in wait, in some awkward place, ready to fall upon them with all the reckless, despairing ferocity of a cornered leopard, was anything but encouraging. Or, what if he had escaped altogether, and were to bring back a swarm of his countrymen to cut off their retreat.

"I tell you what it is," said Hoste. "The sooner we get this poor chap out, and clear out ourselves, the better."

This was true enough; but how to act upon it was another thing.

Several candles were lighted and stuck about on the rocks, making the black, gloomy cavern a trifle less sepulchral. Then they advanced to the pit's brink. The lunatic, crouched on the ground gnawing a bone, stared stupidly at them.

"Don't you know me, Tom?" said Eustace, speaking quietly. "We are come to get you away from here, old chap. You know me? Come now!"

But the poor wretch gave no sign of intelligence, as he went on munching his revolting food. Several times they tried him, each in different ways, but always without success. It was pitiable.

"We shall have to get him out by force," said Shelton. "But how the deuce we are going to do it beats me."

"We might lasso him with a *reim*, and haul him up that way," suggested Hoste.

"I had thought of that," said Eustace. "First of all, though, I'm going to have another try at the *suaviter in modo*. He may recognise me—nearer."

"Nearer? What? How? You are never going down there!" cried Shelton.

"That's just what I am going to do. Where's that long *reim*, Josane?"

This was the long, stout rawhide rope they had brought with them in case it might be wanted for climbing purposes. Quickly Eustace had made a running noose in it.

"I hope you're in good hard form, Milne," said Shelton gravely. "The poor chap may try and tear you to pieces. I wouldn't risk it, if I were you."

"And the snakes?" put in Hoste. "What about the snakes?"

"I shall have to chance them," returned Eustace, having a shrewd suspicion that the reptiles had been rendered harmless by the extraction of their fangs, and were, in fact, kept there by the witch-doctress in order to lend additional horror to this *inferno*, whither she consigned her victims. Even then the act of descending into that noisome pit, with the almost certainty of a hand-to-hand struggle with a raging lunatic of enormous strength, was an ordeal calculated to daunt the stoutest of hearts. Certain it is that neither of the other two would have cared to undertake it. More than ever, then, did they endeavour to dissuade him.

"This is my idea," he said. "I must try and get him round against this side of the hole. Then, while I hold his attention, Josane must drop his blanket over his head. Then I'll fling the noose round him, and you must all man the *reim*, and haul him up like a sack. Only it must be done sharp. Directly I sing out '*Trek*,' you must haul away for dear life."

"But how about yourself, old chap?"

"Never mind about me. I can wait down there until you're ready for me. But when you have got him up here you must tie him up as tight as a log, and sharp, too. Now, Josane, is your blanket ready?"

The old Kafir, who had been knotting a small stone into each corner so that the thing should fall quickly, answered in the affirmative. In a second the *reim* was dropped over the side, and Eustace, sliding down, stood at the bottom of the pit.

The indescribably fearful effluvium fairly choked him. He felt dizzy and faint. The lunatic, still crouching at the other side, made no aggressive movement, merely staring with lack-lustre eyes at the new arrival. Keeping his eye upon him, Eustace took advantage of this welcome truce to feel for his flask and counteract his fast overpowering nausea with a timely pull.

"Tom," he said, in a most persuasive tone, approaching the wretched being. "Tom—you know me, don't you?"

Then an awful change came into the maniac's countenance. His eyes glared through the tangle of his matted hair; the great bushy beard began to bristle and quiver with rage. He rose to his feet and, opening his mouth, emitted that same horrible howl. Those above held their breath.

Well for Eustace was it that he never quailed. Standing there in the middle of the pit—at the mercy of this furious lunatic—he moved not a muscle. But his eyes held those of the demoniac with a piercing and steady gaze.

The crisis was past. Whimpering like a child, the wretched creature sank to the ground, again covering his face with his hands.

This was good enough as a first triumph, but the maniac had to be coaxed round to the other side of the hole. Eustace dared not remove his glance, even for the fraction of a second. His foot struck against something, which yielded suddenly and started away hissing. His pulses stood still with horror, yet he knew better than to remove his eyes from his unhappy kinsman.

"Come, Tom," he said coaxingly, advancing a couple of steps. "Get up, man, and go and sit over there."

With an affrighted cry, the other edged away round the wall of his prison, bringing himself much nearer the point where it was intended he should be brought. He cowered, with face averted, moaning like an animal in pain. Not to overdo the thing, Eustace waited a moment, then advanced a step or two nearer. It had the desired effect. The madman shuffled away as before. He must be in the right place now. Still Eustace dared not look up.

"He's all right now, if you're ready," whispered a voice from above.

"Ready!" was the quick reply.

Something dropped. The madman's head and shoulders disappeared under the voluminous folds of old Josane's red blanket. Quick as lightning Eustace had sprung to his side and whipped the running noose round him.

"*Trek!*" he cried, with an energy sufficient to start a dozen spans of oxen.

The body of Tom Carhayes swung into the air. Kicking, struggling, howling, he disappeared over the brink above. Eustace, alone at the bottom of the pit, could hear the sounds of a furious scuffle—sounds, too, which seemed to be receding as though into distance. What did it all mean? They seemed a long time securing the maniac.

Then, as he looked around this horrible dungeon, at the crawling shapes of the serpents gliding hither and thither, hissing with rage over their late disturbance, as he breathed the unspeakably noisome atmosphere, he realised his own utter helplessness. What if anything untoward should occur to prevent his comrades from rescuing him? Life was full of surprises. They might be attacked by a party of Kafirs, brought back there by the missing Hlangani, for instance. What if he had merely exchanged places with his unfortunate kinsman and were to be left there in the darkness and horror? How long would he be able to keep his reason? Hardly longer than the other, he feared. And the perspiration streamed from every pore, as he began to realise what the miserable maniac had undergone.

A silence had succeeded to the tumult above. What did it mean? Every second seemed an hour. Then, with a start of unspeakable relief, he heard Hoste's voice above.

"Ready to come up, old chap?"

"Very much so. Why have you taken so long?" he asked anxiously.

"We had to tie up poor Tom twice, you know; first with the big *reim*, then with others. Then we had to undo the big *reim* again. Here it is," chucking it over.

Eustace slipped the noose under his armpits, and, having given the word to haul away, a very few moments saw him among them all again. The madman was securely bound and even gagged, only his feet being loosened sufficiently to enable him to take short steps.

So they started on their return track, longing with a greater longing than words can tell, to breathe the open air, to behold the light of day again.

To their astonishment the poor lunatic became quite tractable. As long as Eustace talked to him, he was quiet enough and walked among the rest as directed. One more repellent ordeal had to be gone through—the serpents' den, to wit. This they had now almost reached.

Suddenly a warning cry went up from Josane, who recoiled a step.

"*Au! Kangéla!*" ("Look there!")

A face was peering at them from over a rock slab a few feet overhead. A black face, with glazing eyes and half-parted lips, and such a scowl of hate upon the distorted features, in the darkness, as was perfectly devilish. Quickly every weapon was aimed at the head and as quickly lowered. For they realised that it was the head of a dead man.

"Why, it's Hlangani! Let's see where we pinked him," said Shelton, climbing up to the ledge, followed by Hoste. "By Jove! he's plugged himself where we plugged him," he went on. "That accounts for his leaving no blood spoor."

He had. There were two great holes in the dead man's ribs, where the bullets had entered. Both wounds were mortal. But, with the desperate endurance of his race, the stricken warrior had rent off fragments of his blanket and *had deliberately plugged the gaping orifices.* Then, crawling away, the fierce savage had sought out a position where he might lurk in ambush, and had found it, too. Here he lay, a broad assegai still grasped in his hand, waiting to strike one fell and fatal blow at his slayers ere death should come upon him. But death had overtaken him too quickly; and luckily, indeed, for the objects of his enmity that it had.

"Why, how's this?" cried Shelton in amazement. "I could have sworn I hit him, and yet there are only two bullet holes!"

"So could I," said Hoste emphatically. "Sure there are only two?"

"Dead certain," replied the other, after a second investigation.

"I think I can solve the mystery," cut in Eustace quietly. "You both hit, all right. The fact is, I never fired."

"Never fired!" they echoed. "And why the deuce not?"

"Well, you see, this very Hlangani saved my life. I might have been put down there with poor Tom, but for him. Whatever he had done I couldn't bring myself to 'draw' on a fellow who had done that much for me."

There was something in that, yet Eustace thought he detected a curious look pass between his two friends. But it mattered nothing.

Leaving the body of the dead Gcaléka, the two climbed down from the ledge again. Further surprise was in store for them. Josane had disappeared.

"He'll be back directly," said Eustace. "He said he had forgotten something."

Whether it was that the sight of the dead warrior's body had inspired in him one of those unreasoning and unaccountable outbreaks of savagery to which all barbarian natures are more or less suddenly liable, or whether he had misgivings on his own account as to the completeness of his vengeance, is uncertain. But rapidly muttering: "*Au*! Ixeshane! I have not drunk enough blood. Wait here until I return," he had seized his assegai and disappeared in the direction of the pit again. Those under his guidance had no alternative but to await his return, with what patience they might.

Meanwhile Josane was speeding along the gloomy tunnel, eagerly, fiercely, like a retriever on the track of a wounded partridge. His head was bent forward and his hand still grasped the broad assegai, clotted with the blood of the witch-doctress. Humming a low, ferocious song of vengeance, he gained the brink of the now empty pit. Seizing one of the lighted candles, which still burned—no one having thought it worth while to put them out—he turned his steps into the lateral gallery. A fiendish chuckle escaped him. He stopped short, threw the light in front of him, then held it over his head and looked again. Again he chuckled.

"*Au*!" he cried, "there is more revenge, more blood. I thirst for more blood. Ha! The witch is not dead yet. Where art thou, Ngcenika, spawn of a she-Fingo dog? Where art thou, that my broad *umkonto* may drink again of thy foul blood? Lo!"

The last ejaculation escaped him in a quick gasp. Just outside the circle of light he beheld a shadowy object, which seemed to move. It was the form of the wretched witch-doctress. He gathered himself together like a tiger on the spring.

"Ho! Ngcenika," he cried, in a tone of exultation mingled with suppressed fury. "Thou art not dead yet—toad—carrion bird!"

He was standing over the inanimate form, his assegai uplifted in his right hand, in his left the dim and sputtering candle. He made a feint to plunge it into her body, then as rapidly withdrew it.

"Ha! I have a better plan. Thou shalt take Umlilwane's place."

He stuck his candle on a projecting slab of rock, then bending down he laid hold of the witch-doctress by the feet and began to drag her along the ground. She was massive in her proportions, and he did not make rapid headway; the more so that the wretched creature began to struggle, though feebly, for she had lost an enormous quantity of blood, and indeed but for the endurance of her race, which dies as hard as it lives, life would have been extinct in her long ago. It was a horrible scene. The almost nude body of the hag was one mass of blood, which, coagulated over a dozen ghastly wounds, now began to well forth afresh; the muscular, half-bent form of the grim old warrior, glistening with perspiration, as with the blaze of unsatiated revenge burning in his eyes he dragged her along that grisly cavern floor. Tugging, hauling, perspiring, growling, he at length reached the brow of the pit with his ghastly freight. Then pausing a moment, with a devilish grin on his face, to contemplate the object of his deadly rancour, he pushed the body over. A dull thud and a smothered groan told that it had reached the bottom.

"*Hau*! hell cat—toad's spawn!" he cried. "How do you feel down there? Where is the great witch-doctress of the Gcaléka nation now? Where is Sarili's great councillor of the Spirit-world now? With those whom her wizard arts destroyed. Men, brave fighting men all, were they—what are they now? Bones, skulls, among which the serpents crawl in and out," and as if to emphasise his words, a hissing went forth from the reptiles disturbed by this new invasion of their prison house. "Ha, ha, ha!" he laughed. "Wise witch-doctress, thou canst 'smell out' their spirits once more in the darkness before thou diest. Thou art a great magician, but the magic of the white men—the magic of Ixeshane—is greater than thine, and it has delivered thee into my hand.

"Hlangani, the valiant—the fighting chief of the Ama Gcaléka—the herald of Sarili—is dead. *Hau*!" Then raising his voice to a high taunting pitch, he cried, "where is Maqwela, the warrior who struck the Amanglezi in three wars? His skull is beside thee—talk to it. Where is Mpunhla, erstwhile my friend? He, too, was condemned to 'The Home of the Serpents' by thee. He, too, is beside thee. Where is Vudana, my kinsman? The black ants have picked his bones. This, too, was thy work, and I, Josane, would be even as they, but that I have been reserved to deal out vengeance to their slayer! And now when Sarili—when the *amapakati* of the house of Gcaléka call for their wise witch-doctress, they will call long and loud but will get no answer, for 'The Home of the Serpents' yields not up its secrets. Fare thee well, Ngcenika; rest peacefully. My vengeance is complete. *Hlala-gahle*!"

The weird flickering light of the dying candles danced on the figure of the savage standing there on the brink of that horrible hell-pit, gibing at his once terrible but now vanquished foe. Verily there was an appropriateness, a real poetic justice in the fate which had overwhelmed this female fiend. Many a man had she doomed to this awful, this unspeakably horrible fate, through the dictates of revenge, of intrigue, or of sheer devilish, gratuitous savagery. They had languished and died—some in raving mania—here in black darkness and amid horrors unspeakable. Now the same fate had overtaken herself.

Josane paused. The groans of his victim were becoming fainter and fainter.

"*Hau*! It is music to my ears," he muttered. Then, turning, he deliberately blew out all the lights save the one that he carried, and once more humming his fierce improvised song of vengeance, he sped away through the gloom to rejoin his white companions, leaving this horrible pit of Tophet to the grisly occupancy of its hissing, crawling serpents and its new but fast dying human denizen.

Chapter Forty Seven.

Into Space.

"Heavens! What a glorious thing is the light of day!" exclaimed Hoste, looking around as if he never expected to behold that blessing again, instead of having just been restored to it.

"Let's hope that philosophical reflection will console us throughout our impending ducking," rejoined Eustace drily. "We are going to get it in half an hour at the outside."

Great storm clouds were rolling up beyond the Bashi Valley. The same brooding stillness, now greatly intensified, hung in the air; broken every now and again by fitful red flashes and the dull, heavy boom of thunder. The far off murmur of the river rose up between its imprisoning *krantzes* and steep forest-clad slopes to the place where their halt was made.

They had emerged safely to the upper air with their unfortunate and oft-times troublesome charge. Recognising the impracticability of conveying the latter along the perilous causeway which had taxed their own powers so severely, they had elected to try the other way out, to wit, the vertical shaft, beneath which they had passed shortly after first entering the cavern, and, after a toilsome climb, by no means free from danger, burdened as they were with the unhappy lunatic, had regained the light of day in safety.

But their difficulties and dangers were by no means at an end. For the first, they were a long way above the spot where they had left their horses. To regain this would take several hours. It was frightfully rugged and tangled country, and they had but an hour of daylight left. Moreover a tremendous thunderstorm was working up, and one that, judging by the heavy aspect of the clouds, and the brooding sense of oppression in the atmosphere, threatened to last the best part of the night. For the second, they had every reason to believe that these wild and broken fastnesses of bush and rock held the lurking remnants of the Gcaléka bands who were still under arms, and should these discover the presence of intruders, the position of the four men, dismounted, scantily supplied with food, and hampered with their worse than useless charge, would be serious indeed.

The latter they still deemed it necessary to keep carefully secured. His transition to the upper air had effected a curious change in him. He was no longer violent. He seemed dazed, utterly subdued. He would blink and shut his eyes, as if the light hurt them. Then he would open them again and stare about him with a gaze of the most utter bewilderment. A curious feature in his demeanour was that the world at large seemed to excite his interest rather than its living inhabitants. In these, as represented by his rescuers, he seemed to evince no interest at all. His gaze would wander past them, as though unaware of their presence, to the broad rugged river-valley, with its soaring *krantzes* and savage forest-clad depths, as if he had awakened in a new world. And indeed he had. Think of it! Seven or eight months spent in utter darkness; seven or eight months without one glimmer of the blessed light of Heaven; seven or eight months in the very bowels of the earth, in starvation and filth, among living horrors which had turned his brain; the only glint of light, the only sound of the human voice vouchsafed to him being on those occasions when his barbarous tormentors came to taunt him and bring him his miserable food! Small wonder that the free air, the light, and the spreading glories of Nature, had a dazing, subduing effect on the poor lunatic.

His own safety necessitated the continuance of his bonds—that of his rescuers, that he should be kept securely gagged. It would not do, out of mistaken kindness, to run any risks; to put it in the poor fellow's power to break forth into one of his paroxysms of horrible howls, under circumstances when their lives might depend upon secrecy and silence. It would be time enough to attempt the restoration of the poor clouded brain, when they should have conveyed him safe home again. It was a curious thing that necessity should oblige his rescuers to bring him back bound as though a prisoner.

Their camp—rather their halting place, for caution would preclude the possibility of building a fire—had been decided upon in a small bushy hollow, a kind of eyrie which would enable them to keep a wide look out upon the river-valley for many miles, while affording them a snug and tolerably secure place of concealment. In front a lofty *krantz* fell sheer to a depth of at least two hundred feet. Behind, their retreat was shut in by a line of bush-grown rocks. It was going to be a wet and comfortless night. The storm was drawing nearer and nearer, and they would soon be soaked to the skin, their waterproof wraps having been left with the horses. Food, too, was none too plentiful—indeed, beyond some biscuit and a scrap or two of cold meat, they had none. But these were mere trivial incidents to such practised campaigners. They had succeeded in their quest—they had rescued a friend and comrade from a fate ten thousand-fold more hideous than the most fearful form of death; moreover, as Hoste had remarked, the light of day alone, even when seen through streaming showers, was glorious when compared with the utter gloom of that awful cave and the heaving, hissing, revolting masses of its serpent denizens. On the whole they felt anything but down-hearted.

"I tell you what it is, Hoste," said Shelton, seizing the moment when Eustace happened to be beyond earshot. "There have been a good many nasty things said and hinted about Milne of late; but I should just like to see any one of the fellows who have said them do what he did. Heavens! The cool nerve he showed in deliberately going down into that horrible hole with the chances about even between being strangled by poor Tom there, or bitten by a puff-adder, was one of the finest things I ever saw in my life. It's quite enough to give the lie to all these infernal reports, and I'll take care that it does, too."

"Rather. But between you and me and Josane there, who can't understand us," answered Hoste, lowering his voice instinctively, "it's my private opinion that poor Milne has no particular call to shout 'Hurrah' over the upshot of our expedition. Eh? Sort of Enoch Arden business, don't you know. Likely to prove inconvenient for all parties."

"So? All the more to his credit, then, that he moved heaven and earth to bring it about. By Jove! I believe I'd have thought a long while before going down there myself."

"Rather. But I can't help being deuced sorry for him."

If need hardly be said that Hoste had indeed put the whole case into a nutshell as far as Eustace was concerned. Even then, lying there on the brink of the cliff above-mentioned, and whither he had withdrawn on the pretence of keeping a look out, but really in order to be alone, he was indulging in the full bitterness of his feelings. All had come to an end. The cup had been dashed from his lips. The blissful glow of more than earthly happiness in which he had moved for the past few months, had turned to blight and ruin and blackness, even as the cloudless sunlight of the morning had disappeared into the leaden terrors of the oncoming storm. Would that from it a bolt might fall which should strike him dead!

Even in the full agony of his bitterness he could not wish that the awful fate of his cousin had ever remained a mystery, could not regret the part he had borne in rescuing him from that fate. It might be that the minutes he himself had spent, helpless at the bottom of the noisome pit, had brought home to his mind such a vivid realisation of its horrors as those surveying it from the brink could never attain. Anyway, while musing upon his own blighted life, his dream of love and possession suddenly and cruelly quenched, he could not wish the poor wretch back in such a living hell again.

Yet for what had he been rescued? Of what value was the life of a raving, gibbering maniac to himself or the world in general? And this was the thing to which Eanswyth was now bound. A warm, beautiful, living body chained to a loathsome, festering corpse; and his had been the hand which had forged the links, his the hand which had turned the key in the padlock. He could not even lay to his soul the flattering unction that the unfortunate man would eventually succumb to the after results of his horrible sufferings. Lunatics, barring accidents, are proverbially long-lived, and Tom Carhayes had the strength and constitution of an elephant. He would be far more likely to injure other people than himself.

Meanwhile, those left in camp were resting appreciatively after their labours, and conversing.

"*Amakosi*," said Josane, with a queer smile. "Do you think you could find 'The Home of the Serpents' again?"

"Why, of course," was the unhesitating reply. The old Kafir grinned.

"Do you mean to say you don't believe we could?" said Hoste, in amazement.

"Yes, *amakosi*. I do not believe you could," was the unhesitating rejoinder.

"What—when we have only just come out of it?"

The old Gcaléka grinned harder than ever.

"I do not believe you could light on the exact way in from either side," he repeated.

"Well, by Jove! I believe he's right," said Hoste dubiously, as he went over in his mind the inexplicable way in which both entrances were concealed, and that by the hand of Nature.

"Right about what?" said another voice, whose owner rejoined the circle at that moment.

"Why, what do you think Josane is trying to cram us with, Milne? He swears we couldn't find the entrance of, that infernal hole again."

"Well, I don't believe we could," said Eustace quietly. "But that's no great disadvantage, for I suppose none of us will ever be smitten with the remotest inclination to try."

"Not I, for one," assented Hoste. "I wouldn't go through those awful, beastly heaps of snakes again—faugh!—not for a thousand pounds. Hallo! It's coming!"

A roll of thunder—longer, louder, nearer—caused them to look upward. The whole heavens were shrouded in masses of black, angry clouds, sweeping slowly onward.

Then, as their glances sought the earth again, a quick whistle of amazement escaped Shelton. It found a ready echo in a startled ejaculation from the others.

"Where is he?"

For the place occupied by the unfortunate lunatic knew him no more. He had disappeared.

For a second they stared blankly into each others' faces, then all four moved forward instinctively.

He had been sitting idly, vacantly, perfectly quietly staring into space. In the height of their conversation they had given little heed to his presence. Well, he could not go far, for his legs were so secured as to preclude him making steps of ordinary length.

The place was bushy, but not very thickly so. Spreading out they entered the scrub by the only side on which he could have disappeared.

"There he is!" cried Hoste suddenly, when they had gone about fifty yards.

Slinking along in a crouching attitude, slipping from bush to bush, they spied the poor fellow. That was all right. There would be no difficulty now.

No difficulty? Was there not? As soon as he saw that he was discovered he began to run—to run like a buck. And then, to their consternation, they perceived that his legs were free. By some means or other he had contrived, with a lunatic's stealthy cunning, to cut the *reim* which had secured them. They could see the severed ends flapping as he ran.

"Well, we've got to catch him, poor chap, so here goes," said Hoste, starting with all his might in pursuit.

But the maniac wormed in and out of the bushes with marvellous rapidity. Shelton had tripped and come a headlong cropper, and Hoste was becoming blown, but they seemed to get no nearer. Suddenly the bush came to an end. Beyond lay a gradual acclivity, open and grassy, ending abruptly in air.

"Heavens!" cried Eustace in a tone of horror. "The *krantz!*"

His tones found an echo in those of his companions. The precipice in front was a continuation of the lofty perpendicular cliff which fell away from the front of their halting place. Any one who should go over that giddy brink would leave no sort of shadow of uncertainty as to his fate. They stopped in their pursuit.

"Tom!" cried Eustace persuasively, "Come back, old chap. It's going to rain like fits in a minute. You'll be much snugger at the camp."

The lunatic, now half-way across the open, stopped at the voice and stood listening. Then he ran forward again, but at a decreased pace. Heavens! He was only twenty yards from the brink. His pursuers were more than twice that distance behind. Any move forward would inevitably have the effect of driving him over.

"What *are* we to do?" gasped Hoste, exhausted by the mingled exertion and excitement.

"We had better leave him alone, and watch him from where he can't see us," was Eustace's reply.

The poor fellow had now gained the very brink. Then he turned, but his pursuers had deftly concealed themselves behind a small bush which opportunely grew in the midst of the open. His hands were still tied fast, and the gag was in his mouth. If only they could have reached him.

He stood for a moment, balanced on the edge of the abyss, looking *into it*. Then he turned again. There was a horrible leer of triumphant insanity upon the distorted face as his gaze failed to discover the presence of anybody likely to prove hostile.

The thunder rolled out heavily from overhead, and the figure of the maniac stood in bold relief against the leaden sky, photographed in black relief against the red flashes of lightning which played with well-nigh unintermittent incandescence athwart the storm cloud beyond. There he stood, his features working horribly, the tangled masses of his beard and hair floating in the fitful gusts which came whistling up from the dizzy height. Never, to their dying day, would the spectators forget the sight. Yet they could do nothing.

With a choking cackle, like an attempt at a laugh, the maniac turned again to the awful height. The spectators held their breaths and their blood ran cold. Then they saw him gather his legs beneath him and spring far out into space.

Petrified with horror, they rushed to the brink and peered over. The smooth rock face fell without a break down to the tree-tops at a dizzy depth beneath. These were still quivering faintly as though recently disturbed. But at that moment heaven's artillery roared in one vast deafening, crackling roll. The air was ablaze with vivid blue flame, and driven before the tornado blast, sheet upon sheet of deluging rain crashed down upon them, beating them to the earth by the very weight and fury of its volume.

Chapter Forty Eight.

Envoi.

Ring we the curtain down—for our tale is ended and we have no desire to point a moral thereto. Years have gone by, and new homesteads have risen upon the ashes of the old ones; and flocks and herds are once more grazing in security upon those grassy plains, those pleasant plains, so sunny, so peaceful, so smiling.

And how the broken and decimated tribes were settled on new locations, and how the ringleaders and prominent fighting men of those who owned British allegiance were sentenced to long terms of imprisonment, and how the Gaika location was parcelled out into farms, and as such leased by the Department of Crown Lands to white settlers; and how in consideration of certain acts of forbearance and humanity exercised during the period of hostilities and resulting in the saving of several European lives, the sentences of imprisonment passed upon Nteya and Ncanduku were remitted—mainly through the exertions of Eustace Milne—and the two sub-chiefs were allowed to rejoin the banished remnant of their tribe in its new location beyond the Kei—are not all these things matters of history?

And how the sad relics of poor Tom Carhayes, his fate now under no sort of doubt, were gathered together beneath the great *krantz* in the Bashi valley on the morning after his insane and fatal leap, and conveyed to the settlement for burial, and how Eustace Milne, punctilious to a hair in his dealings with his barbarous neighbours, had paid over the stipulated ransom, even to the very last hoof, to the relatives of Hlangani, even though the contingency of that warrior's demise was in no wise provided for in the original agreement—these things, too, are they not graven in the memories of all concerned?

But if, to some, the war has brought ruin and death and bereavement, it has entailed vastly different results upon two other persons at any rate; and those, needless to say, the two with whom our story has been mainly concerned. For their good fortune has been great—greater, we fear, than they had any right to expect. They are flourishing exceedingly, and now, after years of union, it still seems to them that they have only just begun to enter upon that glowing vista of lifelong happiness, down which they had gazed so wistfully in the old, troubled, and well-nigh hopeless time. But after sorrow and heaviness cometh joy—sometimes. And it has come to these two, by a weird irony of Fate, has come through the agency of a wild and sanguinary drama—through the consistent ferocity of a vindictive barbarian and the logical outcome thereof—even Hlangani's Revenge.

Milton Keynes UK
Ingram Content Group UK Ltd.
UKHW032232011124
450424UK00008B/910